KEEP UP YOUR

Biblical Greek

IN TWO MINUTES A DAY

THE TWO MINUTES A DAY
BIBLICAL LANGUAGE SERIES
INCLUDES:

Keep Up Your Biblical Greek in Two Minutes a Day
Volume 1
365 Selections for Easy Review

Keep Up Your Biblical Greek in Two Minutes a Day
Volume 2
365 More Selections for Easy Review

Keep Up Your Biblical Hebrew in Two Minutes a Day
Volume 1
365 Selections for Easy Review

Keep Up Your Biblical Hebrew in Two Minutes a Day
Volume 2
365 More Selections for Easy Review

Keep Up Your Biblical Aramaic in Two Minutes a Day
365 Selections for Easy Review

VOL **1**

─── **KEEP UP YOUR** ───

Biblical Greek

IN TWO MINUTES A DAY

365 SELECTIONS FOR EASY REVIEW

Compiled and edited by
Jonathan G. Kline

HENDRICKSON
PUBLISHERS

Keep Up Your Biblical Greek in Two Minutes a Day, Volume 1

© 2017 by Hendrickson Publishers
an imprint of Hendrickson Publishing Group
Hendrickson Publishers, LLC
P. O. Box 3473
Peabody, Massachusetts 01961-3473
www.hendricksonpublishers.com

ISBN 978-1-68307-056-6

Book cover and jacket design by Maria Poulopoulos

Printed in China

Third Printing — March 2024

Library of Congress Cataloging-in-Publication Data

Names: Kline, Jonathan G., compiler.
Title: Keep up your Biblical Greek in two minutes a day : 365 selections for easy review / compiled and edited by Jonathan G. Kline.
Description: Peabody, Massachusetts : Hendrickson Publishers, 2017- | Includes bibliographical references and index.
Identifiers: LCCN 2017045338 | ISBN 9781683070566 (alk. paper)
Subjects: LCSH: Greek language, Biblical--Textbooks.
Classification: LCC PA695 .K57 2017 | DDC 487/.4--dc23
  LC record available at https://lccn.loc.gov/2017045338

CONTENTS

Preface

Keep Up Your Biblical Greek in Two Minutes a Day has been specially designed to help you build on your previous study of Greek by reading a small amount of the New Testament in its original language every day in an easy, manageable, and spiritually enriching way. This book does not do away with the need to consult traditional textbooks and to review paradigms and the fundamentals of Greek grammar, which are essential tasks for developing an enduring ability to read and understand Greek well. Rather, this book complements such grammatical study by enabling you to build a robust vocabulary base and by encouraging you to work with the biblical text and review morphology and syntax in a largely inductive manner.

In order to help you reconnect with Greek in a direct and efficient way, this book contains no grammatical jargon or extraneous material—only verses from the New Testament, in Greek and English, carefully selected and presented (along with brief vocabulary entries) in a manner intended to facilitate rapid and enjoyable learning. The book is designed to be used on a daily basis (ideally), or in any case with some measure of consistency. The page for each day includes the following:

- one new vocabulary word, with transliteration and meanings, and two review words from earlier in the book

- the English text of a New Testament verse, with these three Greek words embedded in it, as they appear in the verse

- the Greek text of the verse, in full and then divided into phrases or clauses, with the corresponding English phrases or clauses next to them

To encourage you to spend a little time with Greek on a regular basis, each page is labeled with a day number (from 1 to 365), a date (from January 1 to December 31), and a week number (from Week 1 to Week 52). The book is thus designed so that you can work through it in a calendar year (whether starting on January 1 or any other date), though of course you need not use it according to this scheme. What is important, in any event, is not perfection or following a rigid schedule, but regular practice. There is no reason to feel bad if you miss a day or two, for example; the next time you have a chance to use the book, you can simply pick up where you left off, or skip to the page for the current date.

As the title *Keep Up Your Biblical Greek in Two Minutes a Day* indicates, spending at least two minutes with each day's page is recommended. Yet glancing at the page for a given day for even ten or fifteen seconds can still provide real benefits; and in any case this is better than not opening the book at all. Here are some suggestions for different ways you might wish to use this book, depending on how much time you have on a particular day:

10 seconds to 1 minute. *Activity:* Read the daily Bible verse in English, noticing the Greek words in parentheses. *Benefit:* You have read a Bible verse in English and have been quickly reminded of what a few Greek words mean and perhaps of an aspect or two of Greek grammar. *Alternate activity:* Look at the Greek word for the day and read its definitions. *Benefit:* You have been reminded of the basic range of meaning of a Greek word that occurs with a relatively high frequency in the New Testament.

2 to 5 minutes. *Activity:* Read the daily Bible verse in English, noticing the Greek words in parentheses. Next, look at the Greek word for the day and its meanings. Finally, read the Greek text as best you can, perhaps only in the phrase/clause section on the lower half of the page, simply ignoring what you don't understand (even if this is all or most of the words). *Benefit:* You have read a Bible verse in English and (as much as you are able) in Greek. You have been reminded of what at least a few, and perhaps many, Greek words mean, and perhaps also of certain principles of Greek morphology and syntax.

10 to 20 minutes. *Activity:* Every day of a given week, look at all seven pages for the present week, spending whatever amount of time you desire on each page (perhaps skimming some pages and spending more time on others). *Benefit:* After the week is over, you will likely have developed a deep familiarity with the week's biblical texts and a lasting knowledge of the week's vocabulary words. You will also have deepened your familiarity with various principles of Greek morphology and syntax.

As these suggestions indicate, although this book has been designed to provide substantial benefits if you use it for only two minutes a day, mulling over (and, as need be, puzzling through) its contents for longer periods of time can help you even further along the journey toward achieving a lasting mastery of Greek.

Another interesting and helpful way to use this book—one that is especially suited for more advanced users—is to review vocabulary by means of a "chain" method. For example, pick a day in the book, perhaps at random and preferably toward the end (say, Day 354), and read the page. Then, pick one of the two review words for the day (e.g., διώκω), go to the page on which that word is the new word for the day (Day 333), and read that page. Next, pick one of the review words on this new page (e.g., μᾶλλον), go to the page on which it is the new word for the day (Day 211), and read that page. You can repeat this process as many times as you want, until you reach (or get as close as possible to) the beginning of the book.

If the verse for a particular day is one that you would like to internalize or try to memorize in Greek, feel free to temporarily suspend your regular reading of a new page each day and instead spend several days, or perhaps even a week, reading the same page every day. By doing so, you may notice new things about the grammar or syntax of the verse, and at least some, if not all, of the verse will likely remain in your mind and heart for a long time to come. If you take the time to meditate on a verse in this way, you may also wish to look up the verse in a technical commentary or two to see what scholars have said about it; or you may choose to look up the verse in the index of an intermediate or advanced Greek grammar in order to learn about the morphology of the words the verse contains or about its syntax. Meditating on or memorizing even two or three Greek verses in this way over the course of a year can go a long way toward helping you internalize and become proficient in the language.

As the foregoing discussion indicates, the benefits you derive from using this book will obviously depend on how much time you spend with it and how often, the specific ways you choose to use it, your current level of Greek proficiency, and your ability to learn inductively. Nevertheless, I have done my best to design the book so that it can help you make substantial and enduring gains in learning even if you are able to use it for only short periods of time at most sittings and even if your Greek is at a rudimentary level when you begin.

The Vocabulary

Keep Up Your Biblical Greek in Two Minutes a Day presents, one day at a time and in order of descending frequency, the 365 most frequently occurring words in the New Testament—that is, all the words that occur 42 times or more, plus about half of those that occur 41 times. This amounts to about 20 percent more vocabulary than one typically learns in a first-year Greek class. If you master these 365 words, you will know the lexical form lying behind most of the Greek words that *The Greek New Testament: A Reader's Edition* assumes knowledge of (i.e., the words that that volume does not gloss in its apparatus). Another encouraging—and somewhat startling—fact is that although the 365 lexemes (dictionary forms) presented in this book account for only 2 percent of the total number of unique lexemes that occur in the New Testament, *more than 80 percent of the actual words found in the New Testament* are forms of the 365 words found in this book. Learning the details of morphology is essential, of course, for identifying which words in the biblical text are forms of which lexical forms presented in this book; but mastering the core vocabulary found in this book is an important first step for gaining proficiency in reading the New Testament in Greek.

I created the initial list of 365 core review words for this book by comparing the main frequency list of vocabulary found in Warren C. Trenchard's *Complete Vocabulary Guide to the Greek New Testament* (Zondervan) and a similar list generated using the computer program BibleWorks. I checked the frequency data from these sources against those found in an unpublished database created by Mark House and Maurice Robinson for Hendrickson Publishers and then made my own decisions regarding which words should be included in this book's list and their frequencies. In general, though not invariably, the frequency I provide for each day's vocabulary word (found to the right of the gray box containing the word's gloss(es) and followed by an "x") is based on the number of times the word occurs in the Westcott-Hort edition of the Greek New Testament (on which see further below).

For readers who are in the beginning stages of their knowledge of Greek grammar and who are accustomed to using Strong's concordance in their study of the vocabulary of the New Testament, I have also included the Strong's number for each daily vocabulary word. These numbers are prefixed with an "S" and are found below the frequency numbers.

In order to facilitate rapid review—and as a reflection of the fact that *Keep Up Your Biblical Greek in Two Minutes a Day* is intended primarily as a resource for review and skill building, not as a tool for scientific research—I have almost invariably presented lexical forms in as pared down a form as possible. For example, I have generally not provided the genitive forms of nouns or the feminine or neuter forms of adjectives. On occasion, however, I have made an exception to such rules and have included more than one lexical form—for example, for lexemes that do not have straightforward inflections (such as the pronoun ἐγώ, "I," for which I have included the plural form ἡμεῖς; and the number εἷς, "one," for which I have included its feminine and neuter forms, μία and ἕν, which cannot be intuited easily through a knowledge of the normal rules that govern noun inflection).

The Glosses

I generated the initial list of glosses for each day's vocabulary word by abridging the entries in Hendrickson's *Compact Greek-English Lexicon of the New Testament*, a 2008 revision by Mark House of an earlier pocket dictionary created by Alexander Souter. In a good number of cases I further modified an entry after consulting a standard modern lexicon of the Greek New Testament or, occasionally, by looking in detail at the contexts in which a word occurs.

As with the lexical forms, I have intentionally kept the glosses basic and brief so that you can quickly grasp a word's essential or most common meaning(s). The glosses are not exhaustive. For more comprehensive and nuanced glosses or definitions, please consult a standard Greek lexicon or vocabulary guide.

Likewise, and again to facilitate rapid and easy review, I have kept grammatical information in the glosses to an absolute minimum. For example, I have not indicated which meanings of a preposition accompany which noun cases, and I have almost never indicated which of a verb's meanings are attested in which voice (the active, middle, or passive). The only exception I made to this latter rule is in the case of the verb ἄρχω (Day 201), whose meanings in the middle ("to begin") and active ("to rule") are so distinct that I thought noting the voices would be helpful.

Finally, and contrary to standard practice, I have glossed all verbs as infinitives rather than as first-person singulars (even though, of course, the lexical form presented is the first-person singular present form). My hope is that this will allow you to quickly focus on the verb's meanings.

The Verses

In this book I have attempted to present an interesting and inspiring variety of verses from the New Testament, in terms of both content and grammar. The process by which I chose the verses was an organic and creative one that was guided by grammatical, theological, aesthetic, and—above all—pedagogical concerns. I have included verses from every book of the New Testament and of varying lengths and difficulties. The verses contain content that is inspiring, comforting, challenging, and thought provoking. This allows you, if you wish, to use the book as a kind of daily devotional. Whether you think of the book in this way or not, my goal in creating it has been not only to help you improve your knowledge of Greek for its own sake, but also—and more importantly—to help you engage closely with, meditate on, wrestle with, be challenged by, and find solace and hope in the words of the New Testament writers.

The Phrases and Clauses

In breaking up each day's verse into phrases and/or clauses, I have done my best to help you see the correspondence between brief elements in the day's Greek text and English translation. Naturally, however, a one-to-one correspondence does not always exist (and in a technical sense never completely exists) between a Greek word, phrase, or clause and its English translation. For this reason, you may occasionally find the way that I have matched up parts of the Greek and English verses to be slightly forced. It goes without saying that the correspondences shown are not meant to be completely scientific or precise in every case; rather, they are a pedagogical tool intended to help you work through each day's verse little by little and in a short amount of time, in order to arrive at a basic understanding of the grammar and syntax of the Greek.

Correlatively, in an attempt to be sensitive to the unique content of each day's verse and to help you understand it as well as possible, I have sometimes divided syntactically or grammatically identical structures found in different verses in different ways. Such inconsistencies are intentional and, again, are always the result of my trying to present the parts of a given day's verse in the way that I thought would be most helpful, as well as in a way that makes the most sense in light of the specific English translation used for the day in question. By breaking up the verses in different ways, in fact, I hope to have made the point that there is no rigid or single system that one ought to use for analyzing a Greek sentence's grammar in order to achieve understanding.

The Words in Bold Type

On each day's page (except on the first two days, when there are not two review words), there are three Greek words embedded in the English verse, with the English equivalents marked in bold type. In keeping with the minimalist approach I have used for the lexical forms and glosses, I have kept the number of English words in bold type to a minimum, especially for non-verbs, since this formatting is intended primarily to remind you of a word's basic meaning, not (as a rule) to convey syntactic information communicated by the word in question. Thus, for example, if a Greek noun appears in the dative (e.g., πίστει, "by faith," in Heb 11:29, quoted on Day 62), I have put only the word that reflects the noun's basic meaning ("faith") in bold type. Similarly, if the best way to render a participle in a certain instance is by means of a phrase beginning with an English word such as "while" or "because" (e.g., προσευχομένου, "while he was praying," in Luke 3:21, quoted on Day 221), I have not put such conjunctions in bold type; rather, I have placed in bold only what I judged to be the more basic information conveyed by the participle ("he was praying"). As this example indicates, for participles—and also for finite verbal forms—I have normally placed in bold the relevant English pronoun (if one is present) and any information conveying tense or aspect. When a Greek personal pronoun accompanies a finite verbal form, I have not put the English pronoun in bold type—in order to draw your attention to the presence of the Greek pronoun.

Such details as the foregoing, which may occasionally result in apparent inconsistencies in formatting, reflect the fact, again, that a one-to-one correspondence does not exist between Greek and English (or, of course, between any two languages). I have done my best to be as consistent as possible in how

I have formatted the text, and I was always guided by what I thought would be most helpful to you, the reader. As with the way I have broken up the text into phrases and clauses, the bold type is not meant to reflect a "scientific" analysis of the Greek text but simply to help you quickly understand what the words mean.

Sources Used

The Greek text quoted in this book is taken from the edition of the New Testament prepared by B. F. Westcott and F. J. A. Hort, which is in the public domain. The differences between the Westcott-Hort edition and more modern scholarly ones such as the Nestle-Aland and UBS editions are generally of little significance for those who are not professional practitioners of textual criticism, and this is especially true of the small number of such differences found in the verses quoted in *Keep Up Your Greek in Two Minutes a Day*. Here are two illustrations, to give you a sense of their minor nature: (1) in Matt 19:29 (the verse for Day 51 of this book), Westcott-Hort contains the reading "many times as much," whereas the Nestle-Aland editions read "a hundred times as much"; (2) in 1 Cor 1:4 (the verse for Day 30 of the successor volume to this book, *Keep Up Your Greek in Two Minutes a Day: Volume 2*), Westcott-Hort has "I thank God," and the Nestle-Aland editions have "I thank my God."

In their original work, Westcott and Hort marked substitutions, additions to, and omissions from their text found in New Testament manuscripts by means of various sigla. In order to help you read an unencumbered text, in this book I have retained only their siglum for omissions (i.e., square brackets). The substitutions and additions Westcott and Hort marked can be found in the apparatus of Hendrickson's 2007 edition of their text, published under the title *The Greek New Testament*. (For the interested reader, this apparatus also notes all the differences between the Westcott-Hort text and one of the recent Nestle-Aland editions, as well as the variant readings attested in a scholarly reconstruction of the Byzantine text tradition.)

The following English translations are used in this book: NRSV, ESV, NASB, NIV, HCSB, CSB, and MLB. I chose these seven translations because most of them are widely used, and I wanted to help provide a sense of different ways in which Greek can be rendered in English. Another reason I chose these particular translations is because most of them—especially the NASB, ESV, and NRSV—tend to be rather "literal" renderings; one indication of this is that their syntax often corresponds closely to that of the Greek, making it relatively easy to show which parts of the English text parallel which parts of the Greek text (a key feature of this book). The other translations used here—the NIV, HCSB, CSB, and MLB—are often relatively literal but, in contrast to the NASB, ESV, and NRSV, they usually lie further toward the "dynamic equivalence" end of the translation spectrum. I hope that by seeing how each of these translations deals with a sampling of verses, you will grow in your familiarity with and appreciation of the translation philosophies that underlie them.

In addition to embedding three Greek words in each day's English translation, I have made a number of minor modifications to the punctuation and formatting of the translations for the sake of clarity and consistency of presentation. The most common changes include the following: the change of a comma or semicolon at the end of a verse to a period; the insertion of an opening or closing quotation mark when a quotation is carried on from the previous verse or carries on into the next verse; and the capitalization of a lowercase letter at the beginning of a verse. When a verse constitutes a complete quotation, I have removed the quotation marks at the beginning and end of the verse. I have also removed the italics from words in the NASB that mark English words that do not explicitly correspond to a word in the Greek.

For the most part, I have cited entire verses. Occasionally, however, in order to make all the text fit on the page for the day, it was necessary to omit material. Material omitted from the middle of a verse is always marked with ellipses, but material omitted from the beginning or end of a verse is generally not marked. Occasionally I have used ellipses at the end of a verse not to indicate omitted material but to signal that the text that has been quoted constitutes an incomplete sentence.

In a few instances, I have inserted one or more words in brackets in the English Bible translation to indicate a word (or more than one) that is present in the Greek but not reflected in the translation. On a greater number of occasions, I have inserted a more literal rendering in brackets, prefixing it with "lit."

Because both the English and Greek verses quoted in this book are presented in isolation, I encourage you, as often as you are able, to look at them in their original contexts in order to gain a better understanding of their meaning and how they function in the passages from which they have been excerpted.

* * * * *

I offer this book with empathy and in friendship to everyone who has spent countless hours studying Greek but who has experienced difficulty, principally on account of a lack of time, in keeping up with the language. May you receive encouragement, challenge, hope, joy, and peace from the time you spend with the biblical texts on these pages.

—Jonathan G. Kline, PhD

Where is **the (ὁ)** newborn king of **the (τῶν)** Jews? For we saw His star [lit., **the (τὸν)** star of him] in **the (τῇ)** east and we have come to worship Him. (MLB)

ὁ, ἡ, τό	the	19761x
ho, hē, to		S3588

Ποῦ ἐστὶν **ὁ** τεχθεὶς βασιλεὺς **τῶν** Ἰουδαίων; εἴδομεν γὰρ αὐτοῦ **τὸν** ἀστέρα ἐν **τῇ** ἀνατολῇ καὶ ἤλθομεν προσκυνῆσαι αὐτῷ.

Where is	Ποῦ ἐστὶν
the newborn	**ὁ** τεχθεὶς
king of **the** Jews?	βασιλεὺς **τῶν** Ἰουδαίων;
For we saw	εἴδομεν γὰρ
His star [lit., **the** star of him]	αὐτοῦ **τὸν** ἀστέρα
in **the** east	ἐν **τῇ** ἀνατολῇ
and we have come	καὶ ἤλθομεν
to worship Him	προσκυνῆσαι αὐτῷ

But Jesus [lit., **the (ὁ)** Jesus], taking him by **the (τῆς)** hand, raised him **and (καὶ)** he stood up. (MLB)

καί	and, even, also	9098x
kai		S2532

ὁ, ἡ, τό ➤ DAY 1

ὁ δὲ Ἰησοῦς κρατήσας **τῆς** χειρὸς αὐτοῦ ἤγειρεν αὐτόν, **καὶ** ἀνέστη.

But Jesus [lit., **the** Jesus]	**ὁ** δὲ Ἰησοῦς
taking him by **the** hand	κρατήσας **τῆς** χειρὸς αὐτοῦ
raised him	ἤγειρεν αὐτόν
and he stood up	**καὶ** ἀνέστη

As **the (τοῦ)** people were in suspense **and (καὶ)** were all wondering in their hearts [lit., in **the (ταῖς)** hearts of **them (αὐτῶν)**] about John [lit., **the (τοῦ)** John], whether **he (αὐτὸς)** might perhaps be **the (ὁ)** Christ, . . . (MLB)

| **αὐτός, αὐτή, αὐτό** | he, she, it, self | 5563x |
| *autos, autē, auto* | | S846 |

| **ὁ, ἡ, τό** ➤ DAY 1 | | **καί** ➤ DAY 2 |

Προσδοκῶντος δὲ **τοῦ** λαοῦ **καὶ** διαλογιζομένων πάντων ἐν **ταῖς** καρδίαις **αὐτῶν** περὶ **τοῦ** Ἰωάνου, μήποτε **αὐτὸς** εἴη ὁ χριστός,

As **the** people were in suspense	Προσδοκῶντος δὲ **τοῦ** λαοῦ
and were all wondering	**καὶ** διαλογιζομένων πάντων
in their hearts [lit., in **the** hearts of **them**]	ἐν **ταῖς** καρδίαις **αὐτῶν**
about John [lit., **the** John]	περὶ **τοῦ** Ἰωάνου
whether . . . perhaps	μήποτε
he might . . . be	**αὐτὸς** εἴη
the Christ	ὁ χριστός

Now Peter was sitting outside in the courtyard. **And (καὶ)** a servant girl came up to **him (αὐτῷ)** and said, "**You (σὺ) also (Καὶ)** were with Jesus the Galilean." (ESV)

σύ, (pl) ὑμεῖς	you	2891x
su, (pl) *humeis*		S4771

    καί ➤ DAY 2   **αὐτός, αὐτή, αὐτό** ➤ DAY 3

Ὁ δὲ Πέτρος ἐκάθητο ἔξω ἐν τῇ αὐλῇ· **καὶ** προσῆλθεν **αὐτῷ** μία παιδίσκη λέγουσα **Καὶ σὺ** ἦσθα μετὰ Ἰησοῦ τοῦ Γαλιλαίου·

Now Peter	Ὁ δὲ Πέτρος
was sitting outside	ἐκάθητο ἔξω
in the courtyard	ἐν τῇ αὐλῇ
And a servant girl	**καὶ** . . . μία παιδίσκη
came up to **him**	προσῆλθεν **αὐτῷ**
and said	λέγουσα
You also	**Καὶ σὺ**
were with	ἦσθα μετὰ
Jesus the Galilean	Ἰησοῦ τοῦ Γαλιλαίου

He (αὐτὸς) asked **them (αὐτούς)**, "But (δὲ) you (Ὑμεῖς), who do you say I am?" Peter answered **Him (αὐτῷ)**, "**You (Σὺ)** are the Christ." (MLB)

δέ	but, and, on the other hand	2786x
de		S1161

αὐτός, αὐτή, αὐτό ➤ DAY 3   **σύ, (pl) ὑμεῖς** ➤ DAY 4

καὶ **αὐτὸς** ἐπηρώτα **αὐτούς** Ὑμεῖς **δὲ** τίνα με λέγετε εἶναι; ἀποκριθεὶς ὁ Πέτρος λέγει **αὐτῷ** Σὺ εἶ ὁ χριστός.

He asked **them**	καὶ **αὐτὸς** ἐπηρώτα **αὐτούς**
But you	Ὑμεῖς **δὲ**
who do you say I am?	τίνα με λέγετε εἶναι;
Peter answered **Him**	ἀποκριθεὶς ὁ Πέτρος λέγει **αὐτῷ**
You are the Christ	**Σὺ** εἶ ὁ χριστός

But (δὲ) you (σὺ), be sober **in (ἐν)** all things, endure hardship, do the work of an evangelist, fulfill **your (σου)** ministry. (NASB)

ἐν	in, into, during, at, with	2741x
en		S1722

σύ, (pl) ὑμεῖς ➤ DAY 4   δέ ➤ DAY 5

σὺ δὲ νῆφε ἐν πᾶσιν, κακοπάθησον, ἔργον ποίησον εὐαγγελιστοῦ, τὴν διακονίαν **σου** πληροφόρησον.

But you	σὺ δὲ
be sober **in** all things	νῆφε **ἐν** πᾶσιν
endure hardship	κακοπάθησον
do	ποίησον
the work of an evangelist	ἔργον . . . εὐαγγελιστοῦ
fulfill	πληροφόρησον
your ministry	τὴν διακονίαν **σου**

But (δὲ) if I do what I have no desire to do, then I am no longer doing it **myself (ἐγὼ)**, but rather sin that makes itself at home **in (ἐν)** me. (MLB)

ἐγώ, (pl) ἡμεῖς	I, me; (pl) we	2653x
egō, (pl) *hēmeis*		S1473

δέ ➤ DAY 5   **ἐν** ➤ DAY 6

εἰ **δὲ** ὃ οὐ θέλω τοῦτο ποιῶ, οὐκέτι **ἐγὼ** κατεργάζομαι αὐτὸ ἀλλὰ ἡ οἰκοῦσα **ἐν** ἐμοὶ ἁμαρτία.

But if I do what I have no desire to do	εἰ **δὲ** ὃ οὐ θέλω τοῦτο ποιῶ
then I am no longer doing it **myself**	οὐκέτι **ἐγὼ** κατεργάζομαι αὐτὸ
but rather sin that makes itself at home **in** me	ἀλλὰ ἡ οἰκοῦσα **ἐν** ἐμοὶ ἁμαρτία

Not that I am speaking of being in need, for **I (ἐγὼ)** have learned **in (ἐν)** whatever situation **I am (εἰμὶ) to be (εἶναι)** content. (ESV)

εἰμί	to be, exist	2444x
eimi		S1510

ἐν ▷ DAY 6   **ἐγώ,** (pl) **ἡμεῖς** ▷ DAY 7

οὐχ ὅτι καθ᾽ ὑστέρησιν λέγω, **ἐγὼ** γὰρ ἔμαθον **ἐν** οἷς **εἰμὶ** αὐτάρκης **εἶναι·**

Not that	οὐχ ὅτι
I am speaking	λέγω
of being in need	καθ᾽ ὑστέρησιν
for **I** have learned	**ἐγὼ** γὰρ ἔμαθον
in whatever situation **I am**	**ἐν** οἷς **εἰμὶ**
to be content	αὐτάρκης **εἶναι**

Jesus **said (εἶπεν)** to them, "Truly, truly, **I say (λέγω)** to you, before Abraham was born, **I (ἐγὼ) am (εἰμί)**." (NASB)

λέγω	to say, speak	2228x
legō		S3004

ἐγώ, (pl) ἡμεῖς ➢ DAY 7   εἰμί ➢ DAY 8

εἶπεν αὐτοῖς Ἰησοῦς Ἀμὴν ἀμὴν **λέγω** ὑμῖν, πρὶν Ἀβραὰμ γενέσθαι **ἐγὼ εἰμί**.

Jesus **said** to them	**εἶπεν** αὐτοῖς Ἰησοῦς
Truly, truly	Ἀμὴν ἀμὴν
I say to you	**λέγω** ὑμῖν
before Abraham was born	πρὶν Ἀβραὰμ γενέσθαι
I am	**ἐγὼ εἰμί**

And when he had given thanks, he broke it and **said (εἶπεν)**, "This **is (ἐστιν)** my body, which is for you; do this **in (εἰς)** remembrance of me." (NIV)

εἰς	into, in, for, until	1765x
eis		S1519

εἰμί ➢ DAY 8   **λέγω** ➢ DAY 9

καὶ εὐχαριστήσας ἔκλασεν καὶ **εἶπεν** Τοῦτό μού **ἐστιν** τὸ σῶμα τὸ ὑπὲρ ὑμῶν· τοῦτο ποιεῖτε **εἰς** τὴν ἐμὴν ἀνάμνησιν.

And when he had given thanks	καὶ εὐχαριστήσας
he broke it	ἔκλασεν
and **said**	καὶ **εἶπεν**
This **is** my body	Τοῦτό μού **ἐστιν** τὸ σῶμα
which is for you	τὸ ὑπὲρ ὑμῶν
do this	τοῦτο ποιεῖτε
in remembrance of me	**εἰς** τὴν ἐμὴν ἀνάμνησιν

I do not say (οὐ λέγω) this to condemn you, for I said before that you are in our hearts, [**in order (εἰς)**] to die together and to live together. (NRSV)

οὐ, οὐκ, οὐχ	no, not	1622x
ou, ouk, ouch		S3756

λέγω ➤ DAY 9   **εἰς** ➤ DAY 10

πρὸς κατάκρισιν **οὐ λέγω**, προείρηκα γὰρ ὅτι ἐν ταῖς καρδίαις ἡμῶν ἐστὲ **εἰς** τὸ συναποθανεῖν καὶ συνζῆν.

I do not say this	**οὐ λέγω**
to condemn you	πρὸς κατάκρισιν
for I said before	προείρηκα γὰρ
that you are	ὅτι . . . ἐστὲ
in our hearts	ἐν ταῖς καρδίαις ἡμῶν
[**in order**] to die together	**εἰς** τὸ συναποθανεῖν
and to live together	καὶ συνζῆν

Truly I tell you, **anyone who (ὅς)** will not receive the kingdom of God like a little child will **never (οὐ μὴ)** enter [**into (εἰς)**] it. (NIV)

ὅς, ἥ, ὅ	who, which	1401x
hos, hē, ho		S3739

εἰς ➤ DAY 10   **οὐ, οὐκ, οὐχ** ➤ DAY 11

ἀμὴν λέγω ὑμῖν, **ὃς** ἂν μὴ δέξηται τὴν βασιλείαν τοῦ θεοῦ ὡς παιδίον, **οὐ** μὴ εἰσέλθῃ **εἰς** αὐτήν.

Truly	ἀμὴν
I tell you	λέγω ὑμῖν
anyone who will not receive	**ὃς** ἂν μὴ δέξηται
the kingdom of God	τὴν βασιλείαν τοῦ θεοῦ
like a little child	ὡς παιδίον
will **never** enter [**into**] it	**οὐ** μὴ εἰσέλθῃ **εἰς** αὐτήν

For you have had five husbands and **the one (ὅν)** you are now living with is **not (οὐκ)** your husband; in saying **this (τοῦτο)** you told the truth. (MLB)

οὗτος, αὕτη, τοῦτο	this, he, her, it	1385x
houtos, hautē, touto		S3778

οὐ, οὐκ, οὐχ ➤ DAY 11	**ὅς, ἥ, ὅ** ➤ DAY 12

πέντε γὰρ ἄνδρας ἔσχες, καὶ νῦν **ὅν** ἔχεις **οὐκ** ἔστιν σου ἀνήρ· **τοῦτο** ἀληθὲς εἴρηκας.

For you have had	γὰρ . . . ἔσχες
five husbands	πέντε . . . ἄνδρας
and **the one** you are now living with	καὶ νῦν **ὅν** ἔχεις
is **not**	**οὐκ** ἔστιν
your husband	σου ἀνήρ
in saying **this** you told the truth	**τοῦτο** ἀληθὲς εἴρηκας

And the scribes and the Pharisees began to question, saying,
"Who is **this (οὗτος) who (ὃς)** speaks blasphemies? Who can
forgive sins but **God (θεός)** alone?" (ESV)

θεός	God, god	1312x
theos		S2316

ὅς, ἥ, ὅ ➤ DAY 12   οὗτος, αὕτη, τοῦτο ➤ DAY 13

καὶ ἤρξαντο διαλογίζεσθαι οἱ γραμματεῖς καὶ οἱ Φαρισαῖοι
λέγοντες Τίς ἐστιν **οὗτος ὃς** λαλεῖ βλασφημίας; τίς δύναται
ἁμαρτίας ἀφεῖναι εἰ μὴ μόνος ὁ **θεός**;

And the scribes and the Pharisees	καὶ . . . οἱ γραμματεῖς καὶ οἱ Φαρισαῖοι
began to question, saying	ἤρξαντο διαλογίζεσθαι . . . λέγοντες
Who is **this**	Τίς ἐστιν **οὗτος**
who speaks blasphemies?	**ὃς** λαλεῖ βλασφημίας;
Who can forgive sins	τίς δύναται ἁμαρτίας ἀφεῖναι
but **God** alone?	εἰ μὴ μόνος ὁ **θεός**;

And we know **that (ὅτι)** the Son of **God (θεοῦ)** has come and has given us insight to know the true One. And we are in union with the true One, with His Son Jesus Christ. **He (οὗτός)** is the true **God (θεὸς)** and life eternal. (MLB)

| ὅτι | because, for, that; (introduces direct speech) | 1304x |
| *hoti* | | S3754 |

| **οὗτος, αὕτη, τοῦτο** ➤ DAY 13 | **θεός** ➤ DAY 14 |

οἴδαμεν δὲ **ὅτι** ὁ υἱὸς τοῦ **θεοῦ** ἥκει, καὶ δέδωκεν ἡμῖν διάνοιαν ἵνα γινώσκομεν τὸν ἀληθινόν· καί ἐσμεν ἐν τῷ ἀληθινῷ, ἐν τῷ υἱῷ αὐτοῦ Ἰησοῦ Χριστῷ. **οὗτός** ἐστιν ὁ ἀληθινὸς **θεὸς** καὶ ζωὴ αἰώνιος.

And we know **that** the Son of **God** has come	οἴδαμεν δὲ **ὅτι** ὁ υἱὸς τοῦ **θεοῦ** ἥκει
and has given us insight to know the true One	καὶ δέδωκεν ἡμῖν διάνοιαν ἵνα γινώσκομεν τὸν ἀληθινόν
And we are in union with the true One	καί ἐσμεν ἐν τῷ ἀληθινῷ
with His Son Jesus Christ	ἐν τῷ υἱῷ αὐτοῦ Ἰησοῦ Χριστῷ
He is the true **God** and life eternal	**οὗτός** ἐστιν ὁ ἀληθινὸς **θεὸς** καὶ ζωὴ αἰώνιος

Without a shadow of doubt, then, let **the whole (πᾶς)** house of Israel know **that (ὅτι) God (θεός)** made Him both Lord and Christ—this Jesus whom you crucified. (MLB)

πᾶς	all, the whole, every (kind of), everything	1240x
pas		S3956

θεός ▻ DAY 14   **ὅτι** ▻ DAY 15

ἀσφαλῶς οὖν γινωσκέτω **πᾶς** οἶκος Ἰσραὴλ **ὅτι** καὶ κύριον αὐτὸν καὶ χριστὸν ἐποίησεν ὁ **θεός**, τοῦτον τὸν Ἰησοῦν ὃν ὑμεῖς ἐσταυρώσατε.

Without a shadow of doubt, then	ἀσφαλῶς οὖν
let **the whole** house of Israel know	γινωσκέτω **πᾶς** οἶκος Ἰσραὴλ
that God made Him	**ὅτι** . . . αὐτὸν . . . ἐποίησεν ὁ **θεός**
both Lord and Christ	καὶ κύριον . . . καὶ χριστὸν
this Jesus	τοῦτον τὸν Ἰησοῦν
whom you crucified	ὃν ὑμεῖς ἐσταυρώσατε

Truly I tell you [**that (ὅτι)**], this generation will **certainly not** (οὐ **μὴ**) pass away until **all (πάντα)** these things have happened. (NIV)

μή	not, lest, perhaps	1058x
mē		S3361

ὅτι ➤ DAY 15   **πᾶς** ➤ DAY 16

ἀμὴν λέγω ὑμῖν **ὅτι** οὐ **μὴ** παρέλθῃ ἡ γενεὰ αὕτη μέχρις οὗ ταῦτα **πάντα** γένηται.

Truly I tell you [**that**]	ἀμὴν λέγω ὑμῖν **ὅτι**
this generation	ἡ γενεὰ αὕτη
will **certainly not** pass away	οὐ **μὴ** παρέλθῃ
until	μέχρις οὗ
all these things	ταῦτα **πάντα**
have happened	γένηται

For (γὰρ) God so loved the world that he gave his only Son, so that **everyone (πᾶς)** who believes in him may **not (μὴ)** perish but may have eternal life. (NRSV)

| **γάρ** | for | 1039x |
| *gar* | | S1063 |

πᾶς ➤ DAY 16   **μή** ➤ DAY 17

Οὕτως **γὰρ** ἠγάπησεν ὁ θεὸς τὸν κόσμον ὥστε τὸν υἱὸν τὸν μονογενῆ ἔδωκεν, ἵνα **πᾶς** ὁ πιστεύων εἰς αὐτὸν **μὴ** ἀπόληται ἀλλὰ ἔχῃ ζωὴν αἰώνιον.

For God so loved the world	Οὕτως **γὰρ** ἠγάπησεν ὁ θεὸς τὸν κόσμον
that he gave	ὥστε . . . ἔδωκεν
his only Son	τὸν υἱὸν τὸν μονογενῆ
so that **everyone** who believes	ἵνα **πᾶς** ὁ πιστεύων
in him	εἰς αὐτὸν
may **not** perish	**μὴ** ἀπόληται
but may have	ἀλλὰ ἔχῃ
eternal life	ζωὴν αἰώνιον

For (γὰρ) it would be better for them **never (μὴ)** to have known the way of righteousness than, after knowing it, to turn back **from (ἐκ)** the holy commandment that was imparted to them. (MLB)

ἐκ	from, out of	913x
ek		S1537

μή ➤ DAY 17	**γάρ** ➤ DAY 18	

κρεῖττον **γὰρ** ἦν αὐτοῖς **μὴ** ἐπεγνωκέναι τὴν ὁδὸν τῆς δικαιοσύνης ἢ ἐπιγνοῦσιν ὑποστρέψαι **ἐκ** τῆς παραδοθείσης αὐτοῖς ἁγίας ἐντολῆς·

For it would be better for them	κρεῖττον **γὰρ** ἦν αὐτοῖς
never to have known	**μὴ** ἐπεγνωκέναι
the way of righteousness	τὴν ὁδὸν τῆς δικαιοσύνης
than, after knowing it	ἢ ἐπιγνοῦσιν
to turn back	ὑποστρέψαι
from the holy commandment	**ἐκ** τῆς . . . ἁγίας ἐντολῆς
that was imparted to them	παραδοθείσης αὐτοῖς

When this man heard that **Jesus (Ἰησοῦς)** had come **from (ἐκ)** Judea into Galilee, he went to him and pleaded with him to come down and heal his son, **since (γὰρ)** he was about to die. (CSB)

Ἰησοῦς	Jesus, Joshua	913x
Iēsous		S2424

γάρ	➤ DAY 18	ἐκ	➤ DAY 19

οὗτος ἀκούσας ὅτι **Ἰησοῦς** ἥκει **ἐκ** τῆς Ἰουδαίας εἰς τὴν Γαλιλαίαν ἀπῆλθεν πρὸς αὐτὸν καὶ ἠρώτα ἵνα καταβῇ καὶ ἰάσηται αὐτοῦ τὸν υἱόν, ἤμελλεν **γὰρ** ἀποθνήσκειν.

When this man heard that	οὗτος ἀκούσας ὅτι
Jesus had come	**Ἰησοῦς** ἥκει
from Judea	**ἐκ** τῆς Ἰουδαίας
into Galilee	εἰς τὴν Γαλιλαίαν
he went to him	ἀπῆλθεν πρὸς αὐτὸν
and pleaded with him	καὶ ἠρώτα
to come down	ἵνα καταβῇ
and heal his son	καὶ ἰάσηται αὐτοῦ τὸν υἱόν
since he was about to die	ἤμελλεν **γὰρ** ἀποθνήσκειν

Then they picked up stones to hurl **at (ἐπ')** Him; but **Jesus (Ἰησοῦς)** concealed Himself and passed **out of (ἐκ)** the temple. (MLB)

ἐπί	on, upon, at, in, near, over, about, concerning,	885x
epi	on account of, in the presence of	S1909

ἐκ ➤ DAY 19   **Ἰησοῦς** ➤ DAY 20

ἦραν οὖν λίθους ἵνα βάλωσιν **ἐπ'** αὐτόν· **Ἰησοῦς** δὲ ἐκρύβη καὶ ἐξῆλθεν **ἐκ** τοῦ ἱεροῦ.

Then they picked up stones	ἦραν οὖν λίθους
to hurl **at** Him	ἵνα βάλωσιν **ἐπ'** αὐτόν
but **Jesus** concealed Himself	**Ἰησοῦς** δὲ ἐκρύβη
and passed **out of** the temple	καὶ ἐξῆλθεν **ἐκ** τοῦ ἱεροῦ

So they said, "Believe **on (ἐπὶ)** the **Lord (κύριον) Jesus (Ἰησοῦν)**, and you will be saved—you and your household." (HCSB)

κύριος	lord, Lord, owner, master, sir	718x
kurios		S2962

Ἰησοῦς ➤ DAY 20   ἐπί ➤ DAY 21

οἱ δὲ εἶπαν Πίστευσον **ἐπὶ** τὸν **κύριον Ἰησοῦν**, καὶ σωθήσῃ σὺ καὶ ὁ οἶκός σου.

So they said	οἱ δὲ εἶπαν
Believe	Πίστευσον
on the **Lord Jesus**	**ἐπὶ** τὸν **κύριον Ἰησοῦν**
and you will be saved	καὶ σωθήσῃ
you	σὺ
and your household	καὶ ὁ οἶκός σου

On (ἐπὶ) his robe and **on (ἐπὶ)** his thigh **he has (ἔχει)** a name inscribed, "King of kings and **Lord (κύριος)** of **lords (κυρίων)**." (NRSV)

| ἔχω | to have, hold, possess, receive, acquire | 705x |
| *echō* | | S2192 |

ἐπί ➤ DAY 21   **κύριος** ➤ DAY 22

καὶ **ἔχει ἐπὶ** τὸ ἱμάτιον καὶ **ἐπὶ** τὸν μηρὸν αὐτοῦ ὄνομα γεγραμμένον Βασιλεὺς βασιλέων καὶ **κύριος κυρίων**.

On his robe and **on** his thigh	**ἐπὶ** τὸ ἱμάτιον καὶ **ἐπὶ** τὸν μηρὸν αὐτοῦ
he has a name inscribed	καὶ **ἔχει** . . . ὄνομα γεγραμμένον
King of kings	Βασιλεὺς βασιλέων
and **Lord** of **lords**	καὶ **κύριος κυρίων**

Simon Peter answered Him, "**Lord (Κύριε)**, **to (πρὸς)** whom shall we go? **You have (ἔχεις)** the words of eternal life." (MLB)

πρός	near, for, at, to, toward, close to, in the interests of, according to	695x
pros		S4314

κύριος ➤ DAY 22　　　　　**ἔχω** ➤ DAY 23

ἀπεκρίθη αὐτῷ Σίμων Πέτρος **Κύριε**, **πρὸς** τίνα ἀπελευσόμεθα; ῥήματα ζωῆς αἰωνίου **ἔχεις**,

Simon Peter	Σίμων Πέτρος
answered Him	ἀπεκρίθη αὐτῷ
Lord	**Κύριε**
to whom	**πρὸς** τίνα
shall we go?	ἀπελευσόμεθα;
You have	**ἔχεις**
the words of eternal life	ῥήματα ζωῆς αἰωνίου

Yet you do not want to come **to (πρός)** Me **in order to (ἵνα) have (ἔχητε)** life. (MLB)

| ἵνα | that, so that, in order that | 669x |
| *hina* | | S2443 |

ἔχω ➤ DAY 23   πρός ➤ DAY 24

καὶ οὐ θέλετε ἐλθεῖν **πρός** με **ἵνα** ζωὴν **ἔχητε**.

Yet you do not want	καὶ οὐ θέλετε
to come **to** Me	ἐλθεῖν **πρός** με
in order to have life	**ἵνα** ζωὴν **ἔχητε**

For perhaps he was **for** this **reason (διά)** separated from you **for (πρὸς)** a while, **that (ἵνα)** you would have him back forever. (NASB)

διά	through, throughout, on account of, because of,	668x
dia	by reason of, for the sake of	S1223

πρός ➤ DAY 24   **ἵνα** ➤ DAY 25

τάχα γὰρ **διὰ** τοῦτο ἐχωρίσθη **πρὸς** ὥραν **ἵνα** αἰώνιον αὐτὸν ἀπέχῃς,

For perhaps	τάχα γὰρ
he was . . . separated from you	ἐχωρίσθη
for this **reason**	**διὰ** τοῦτο
for a while	**πρὸς** ὥραν
that you would have him back	**ἵνα** . . . αὐτὸν ἀπέχῃς
forever	αἰώνιον

I do all things **for the sake of (διὰ)** the gospel, **so that (ἵνα) I may become (γένωμαι)** a fellow partaker of it. (NASB)

γίνομαι	to be born, come into being, become, come	664x
ginomai	about, happen	S1096

ἵνα ➢ DAY 25   διά ➢ DAY 26

πάντα δὲ ποιῶ **διὰ** τὸ εὐαγγέλιον, **ἵνα** συνκοινωνὸς αὐτοῦ **γένωμαι**.

I do all things	πάντα δὲ ποιῶ
for the sake of the gospel	**διὰ** τὸ εὐαγγέλιον
so that I may become	**ἵνα** . . . **γένωμαι**
a fellow partaker of it	συνκοινωνὸς αὐτοῦ

And after **there had been (γενομένης)** much debate, Peter stood up and said to them, "Brothers, you know that in [lit., **from (ἀφ᾽)**] the early days God made a choice among you, that **by (διὰ)** my mouth the Gentiles should hear the word of the gospel and believe." (ESV)

ἀπό	from, away from	650x
apo		S575

　　διά ➤ DAY 26　　　　**γίνομαι** ➤ DAY 27

Πολλῆς δὲ ζητήσεως **γενομένης** ἀναστὰς Πέτρος εἶπεν πρὸς αὐτούς Ἄνδρες ἀδελφοί, ὑμεῖς ἐπίστασθε ὅτι **ἀφ᾽** ἡμερῶν ἀρχαίων ἐν ὑμῖν ἐξελέξατο ὁ θεὸς **διὰ** τοῦ στόματός μου ἀκοῦσαι τὰ ἔθνη τὸν λόγον τοῦ εὐαγγελίου καὶ πιστεῦσαι,

And after **there had been** much debate	Πολλῆς δὲ ζητήσεως **γενομένης**
Peter stood up and said to them	ἀναστὰς Πέτρος εἶπεν πρὸς αὐτούς
Brothers	Ἄνδρες ἀδελφοί
you know that in [lit., **from**] the early days	ὑμεῖς ἐπίστασθε ὅτι **ἀφ᾽** ἡμερῶν ἀρχαίων
God made a choice among you	ἐν ὑμῖν ἐξελέξατο ὁ θεὸς
that **by** my mouth the Gentiles should hear the word of the gospel and believe	**διὰ** τοῦ στόματός μου ἀκοῦσαι τὰ ἔθνη τὸν λόγον τοῦ εὐαγγελίου καὶ πιστεῦσαι

Father, if you are willing, take this cup **from (ἀπ᾿)** me; yet not my will, **but (ἀλλὰ)** yours **be done (γινέσθω)**. (NIV)

| ἀλλά | but, except | 638x |
| *alla* | | S235 |

γίνομαι ➤ DAY 27   **ἀπό** ➤ DAY 28

Πάτερ, εἰ βούλει παρένεγκε τοῦτο τὸ ποτήριον **ἀπ᾿** ἐμοῦ· πλὴν μὴ τὸ θέλημά μου **ἀλλὰ** τὸ σὸν **γινέσθω**.

Father	Πάτερ
if you are willing	εἰ βούλει
take	παρένεγκε
this cup	τοῦτο τὸ ποτήριον
from me	**ἀπ᾿** ἐμοῦ
yet not my will	πλὴν μὴ τὸ θέλημά μου
but yours	**ἀλλὰ** τὸ σὸν
be done	**γινέσθω**

He longed to be filled **with (ἀπὸ)** what fell **from (ἀπὸ)** the rich man's table, **but (ἀλλά)** instead the dogs **would come (ἐρχόμενοι)** and lick his sores. (CSB)

ἔρχομαι	to go, come	631x
*er*chomai		S2064

ἀπό ➤ DAY 28　　　　ἀλλά ➤ DAY 29

καὶ ἐπιθυμῶν χορτασθῆναι **ἀπὸ** τῶν πιπτόντων **ἀπὸ** τῆς τραπέζης τοῦ πλουσίου· **ἀλλὰ** καὶ οἱ κύνες **ἐρχόμενοι** ἐπέλειχον τὰ ἕλκη αὐτοῦ.

He longed	καὶ ἐπιθυμῶν
to be filled	χορτασθῆναι
with what fell	**ἀπὸ** τῶν πιπτόντων
from the rich man's table	**ἀπὸ** τῆς τραπέζης τοῦ πλουσίου
but instead	**ἀλλὰ** καὶ
the dogs **would come**	οἱ κύνες **ἐρχόμενοι**
and lick	ἐπέλειχον
his sores	τὰ ἕλκη αὐτοῦ

I tell you, **however (ἀλλὰ)**, that Elijah **has come (ἐλήλυθεν)** and
they have treated (ἐποίησαν) him as they pleased, just as it has
been written of him. (MLB)

| ποιέω | to do, make, produce, construct, cause | 562x |
| *poieō* | | S4160 |

ἀλλά ➤ DAY 29   **ἔρχομαι** ➤ DAY 30

ἀλλὰ λέγω ὑμῖν ὅτι καὶ Ἡλείας **ἐλήλυθεν**, καὶ **ἐποίησαν** αὐτῷ
ὅσα ἤθελον, καθὼς γέγραπται ἐπ' αὐτόν.

I tell you . . . that	λέγω ὑμῖν ὅτι
however	**ἀλλὰ**
Elijah **has come**	καὶ Ἡλείας **ἐλήλυθεν**
and **they have treated** him	καὶ **ἐποίησαν** αὐτῷ
as they pleased	ὅσα ἤθελον
just as it has been written	καθὼς γέγραπται
of him	ἐπ' αὐτόν

When therefore the owner of the vineyard **arrives (ἔλθῃ), what (τί) will he do (ποιήσει)** to those tenant farmers? (MLB)

τίς, τί	who? what? which?	560x
tis, ti		S5101

     ἔρχομαι ➢ DAY 30   **ποιέω** ➢ DAY 31

ὅταν οὖν **ἔλθῃ** ὁ κύριος τοῦ ἀμπελῶνος, **τί ποιήσει** τοῖς γεωργοῖς ἐκείνοις;

When therefore	ὅταν οὖν
the owner of the vineyard	ὁ κύριος τοῦ ἀμπελῶνος
arrives	**ἔλθῃ**
what will he do	**τί ποιήσει**
to those tenant farmers?	τοῖς γεωργοῖς ἐκείνοις;

so that we may say boldly, "The Lord is my Helper, I will not fear.
What (τί) can man do (ποιήσει . . . ἄνθρωπος) to me?" (MLB)

ἄνθρωπος	human being	547x
anthrōpos		S444

ποιέω ➤ DAY 31   **τίς, τί** ➤ DAY 32

ὥστε θαρροῦντας ἡμᾶς λέγειν Κύριος ἐμοὶ βοηθός, οὐ
φοβηθήσομαι· **τί ποιήσει** μοι **ἄνθρωπος;**

so that we may say	ὥστε . . . ἡμᾶς λέγειν
boldly	θαρροῦντας
The Lord	Κύριος
is my Helper	ἐμοὶ βοηθός
I will not fear	οὐ φοβηθήσομαι
What can man do	**τί ποιήσει . . . ἄνθρωπος;**
to me?	μοι

The crowd answered Him, "We have learned from the Law that
the **Christ (χριστὸς)** remains forever, and how can You say that
the Son of **Man (ἀνθρώπου)** must be lifted up? **Who (τίς)** is this
Son of **Man (ἀνθρώπου)**?" (MLB)

Χριστός	Christ, the Anointed, the Messiah	531x
Christos		S5547

τίς, τί ➤ DAY 32		**ἄνθρωπος** ➤ DAY 33	

ἀπεκρίθη οὖν αὐτῷ ὁ ὄχλος Ἡμεῖς ἠκούσαμεν ἐκ τοῦ νόμου ὅτι ὁ
χριστὸς μένει εἰς τὸν αἰῶνα, καὶ πῶς λέγεις σὺ ὅτι δεῖ ὑψωθῆναι
τὸν υἱὸν τοῦ **ἀνθρώπου**; **τίς** ἐστιν οὗτος ὁ υἱὸς τοῦ **ἀνθρώπου**;

The crowd answered Him	ἀπεκρίθη οὖν αὐτῷ ὁ ὄχλος
We have learned from the Law that	Ἡμεῖς ἠκούσαμεν ἐκ τοῦ νόμου ὅτι
the **Christ** remains forever	ὁ **χριστὸς** μένει εἰς τὸν αἰῶνα
and how can You say that	καὶ πῶς λέγεις σὺ ὅτι
the Son of **Man**	τὸν υἱὸν τοῦ **ἀνθρώπου**;
must be lifted up?	δεῖ ὑψωθῆναι
Who is this Son of **Man**?	**τίς** ἐστιν οὗτος ὁ υἱὸς τοῦ **ἀνθρώπου**;

Beware of **anyone (τις)** carrying you captive through philosophy and empty deceitfulness along lines of **human (ἀνθρώπων)** tradition and the world's elementary principles and not according to **Christ (Χριστόν)**. (MLB)

τὶς, τὶ	someone, anyone, something	517x
tis, ti		S5100

ἄνθρωπος ➤ DAY 33   **Χριστός** ➤ DAY 34

Βλέπετε μή **τις** ὑμᾶς ἔσται ὁ συλαγωγῶν διὰ τῆς φιλοσοφίας καὶ κενῆς ἀπάτης κατὰ τὴν παράδοσιν τῶν **ἀνθρώπων**, κατὰ τὰ στοιχεῖα τοῦ κόσμου καὶ οὐ κατὰ **Χριστόν·**

Beware of **anyone** carrying you captive	Βλέπετε μή **τις** ὑμᾶς ἔσται ὁ συλαγωγῶν
through philosophy	διὰ τῆς φιλοσοφίας
and empty deceitfulness	καὶ κενῆς ἀπάτης
along lines of **human** tradition	κατὰ τὴν παράδοσιν τῶν **ἀνθρώπων**
and the world's elementary principles	κατὰ τὰ στοιχεῖα τοῦ κόσμου
and not according to **Christ**	καὶ οὐ κατὰ **Χριστόν**

. . . whoever [lit., if **anyone (τις)**] speaks, **as (ὡς)** one who speaks oracles of God; whoever [lit., if **anyone (τις)**] serves, **as (ὡς)** one who serves by the strength that God supplies—in order that in everything God may be glorified through Jesus **Christ (Χριστοῦ)**.

(ESV)

ὡς	about, how, as, so as to	505x
hōs		S5613

Χριστός ➤ DAY 34   **τὶς, τὶ** ➤ DAY 35

εἴ **τις** λαλεῖ, **ὡς** λόγια θεοῦ· εἴ **τις** διακονεῖ, **ὡς** ἐξ ἰσχύος ἧς χορηγεῖ ὁ θεός· ἵνα ἐν πᾶσιν δοξάζηται ὁ θεὸς διὰ Ἰησοῦ **Χριστοῦ**,

whoever [lit., if **anyone**] speaks	εἴ **τις** λαλεῖ
as one who speaks oracles of God	**ὡς** λόγια θεοῦ
whoever [lit., if **anyone**] serves	εἴ **τις** διακονεῖ
as one who serves	**ὡς**
by the strength that God supplies	ἐξ ἰσχύος ἧς χορηγεῖ ὁ θεός
in order that in everything	ἵνα ἐν πᾶσιν
God may be glorified through Jesus **Christ**	δοξάζηται ὁ θεὸς διὰ Ἰησοῦ **Χριστοῦ**

As (ὡς) we have said before, so now I say again: **If (εἴ) anyone (τις)** is preaching to you a gospel contrary to the one you received, let him be accursed. (ESV)

εἰ	if, indeed, assuredly	502x
ei		S1487

τὶς, τὶ ➤ DAY 35   ὡς ➤ DAY 36

ὡς προειρήκαμεν, καὶ ἄρτι πάλιν λέγω, **εἴ τις** ὑμᾶς εὐαγγελίζεται παρ᾽ ὃ παρελάβετε, ἀνάθεμα ἔστω.

As we have said before	ὡς προειρήκαμεν
so now	καὶ ἄρτι
I say again	πάλιν λέγω
If anyone	**εἴ τις**
is preaching to you a gospel	ὑμᾶς εὐαγγελίζεται
contrary to	παρ᾽
the one you received	ὃ παρελάβετε
let him be	ἔστω
accursed	ἀνάθεμα

So (οὖν) if (εἰ) you consider me a partner, welcome him **as (ὡς)** you would me. (CSB)

οὖν	then, therefore	494x
oun		S3767

ὡς ➤ DAY 36   εἰ ➤ DAY 37

εἰ οὖν με ἔχεις κοινωνόν, προσλαβοῦ αὐτὸν **ὡς** ἐμέ.

So if	εἰ οὖν
you consider me	με ἔχεις
a partner	κοινωνόν
welcome him	προσλαβοῦ αὐτὸν
as you would me	**ὡς** ἐμέ

If (εἰ), then (οὖν), He were still on earth, He would not be a priest at all; for here they offer the gifts **as prescribed by (κατὰ)** the Law. (MLB)

κατά	against, down from, throughout, by, among, according to	471x
kata		S2596

εἰ ➤ DAY 37   οὖν ➤ DAY 38

εἰ μὲν **οὖν** ἦν ἐπὶ γῆς, οὐδ' ἂν ἦν ἱερεύς, ὄντων τῶν προσφερόντων **κατὰ** νόμον τὰ δῶρα·

If, then	**εἰ** . . . **οὖν**
He were still	μὲν . . . ἦν
on earth	ἐπὶ γῆς
He would not be a priest at all	οὐδ' ἂν ἦν ἱερεύς
for here they offer the gifts	ὄντων τῶν προσφερόντων . . . τὰ δῶρα
as prescribed by the Law	**κατὰ** νόμον

But **since (εἰ)** it is a matter of questions about words and names and your **own (καθ᾽)** law, **see to (ὄψεσθε)** it yourselves; I do not wish to be a judge of these matters. (NRSV)

ὁράω	to see, experience	470x
horaō		S3708

εἰ ▷ DAY 37   κατά ▷ DAY 39

εἰ δὲ ζητήματά ἐστιν περὶ λόγου καὶ ὀνομάτων καὶ νόμου τοῦ **καθ᾽** ὑμᾶς, **ὄψεσθε** αὐτοί· κριτὴς ἐγὼ τούτων οὐ βούλομαι εἶναι.

But **since** it is	**εἰ** δὲ . . . ἐστιν
a matter of questions	ζητήματά
about words	περὶ λόγου
and names	καὶ ὀνομάτων
and your **own** law	καὶ νόμου τοῦ **καθ᾽** ὑμᾶς
see to it	**ὄψεσθε**
yourselves	αὐτοί
I do not wish	ἐγὼ . . . οὐ βούλομαι
to be a judge	κριτὴς . . . εἶναι
of these matters	τούτων

Suddenly, as they looked around, **they** no longer **saw (εἶδον)** anyone **with (μεθ')** them except [lit., **if (εἰ)** not] Jesus only. (MLB)

| **μετά** | with, beyond, after, behind | 469x |
| *meta* | | S3326 |

εἰ ➤ DAY 37   **ὁράω** ➤ DAY 40

καὶ ἐξάπινα περιβλεψάμενοι οὐκέτι οὐδένα **εἶδον μεθ'** ἑαυτῶν **εἰ** μὴ τὸν Ἰησοῦν μόνον.

Suddenly	καὶ ἐξάπινα
as they looked around	περιβλεψάμενοι
they no longer **saw**	οὐκέτι . . . **εἶδον**
anyone	οὐδένα
with them	**μεθ'** ἑαυτῶν
except [lit., **if** not]	**εἰ** μὴ
Jesus only	τὸν Ἰησοῦν μόνον

What **we have seen (ἑωράκαμεν)** and **heard (ἀκηκόαμεν)** we proclaim to you also, so that you too may have fellowship **with (μεθ᾽)** us; and indeed our fellowship is **with (μετὰ)** the Father, and **with (μετὰ)** His Son Jesus Christ. (NASB)

ἀκούω	to hear, listen	428x
akouō		S191

ὁράω	➤	DAY 40	μετά	➤	DAY 41

ὃ **ἑωράκαμεν** καὶ **ἀκηκόαμεν** ἀπαγγέλλομεν καὶ ὑμῖν, ἵνα καὶ ὑμεῖς κοινωνίαν ἔχητε **μεθ᾽** ἡμῶν· καὶ ἡ κοινωνία δὲ ἡ ἡμετέρα **μετὰ** τοῦ πατρὸς καὶ **μετὰ** τοῦ υἱοῦ αὐτοῦ Ἰησοῦ Χριστοῦ·

What **we have seen**	ὃ **ἑωράκαμεν**
and **heard**	καὶ **ἀκηκόαμεν**
we proclaim to you also	ἀπαγγέλλομεν καὶ ὑμῖν
so that you too may have	ἵνα καὶ ὑμεῖς . . . ἔχητε
fellowship **with** us	κοινωνίαν . . . **μεθ᾽** ἡμῶν
and indeed our fellowship	καὶ ἡ κοινωνία δὲ ἡ ἡμετέρα
is **with** the Father	**μετὰ** τοῦ πατρὸς
and **with** His Son	καὶ **μετὰ** τοῦ υἱοῦ αὐτοῦ
Jesus Christ	Ἰησοῦ Χριστοῦ

Therefore (οὖν) take care how **you listen (ἀκούετε)**. For whoever has, more **will be given (δοθήσεται)** to him; and whoever does not have, even what he thinks he has will be taken away from him. (CSB)

δίδωμι	to give, offer, put, place	416x
didōmi		S1325

οὖν ➤ DAY 38   ἀκούω ➤ DAY 42

Βλέπετε **οὖν** πῶς **ἀκούετε**· ὃς ἂν γὰρ ἔχῃ, **δοθήσεται** αὐτῷ, καὶ ὃς ἂν μὴ ἔχῃ, καὶ ὃ δοκεῖ ἔχειν ἀρθήσεται ἀπ᾽ αὐτοῦ.

Therefore	**οὖν**
take care	Βλέπετε
how **you listen**	πῶς **ἀκούετε**
For whoever has	ὃς ἂν γὰρ ἔχῃ
more **will be given** to him	**δοθήσεται** αὐτῷ
and whoever does not have	καὶ ὃς ἂν μὴ ἔχῃ
even what he thinks he has	καὶ ὃ δοκεῖ ἔχειν
will be taken away from him	ἀρθήσεται ἀπ᾽ αὐτοῦ

And I shall ask the **Father (πατέρα)** and **He will give (δώσει)** you another Helper to stay **with (μεθ')** you forever. (MLB)

πατήρ	father, Father, ancestor	414x
patēr		S3962

μετά ➤ DAY 41　　　　**δίδωμι** ➤ DAY 43

κἀγὼ ἐρωτήσω τὸν **πατέρα** καὶ ἄλλον παράκλητον **δώσει** ὑμῖν ἵνα ἦ **μεθ'** ὑμῶν εἰς τὸν αἰῶνα,

And I shall ask	κἀγὼ ἐρωτήσω
the **Father**	τὸν **πατέρα**
and **He will give** you	καὶ . . . **δώσει** ὑμῖν
another Helper	ἄλλον παράκλητον
to stay	ἵνα ἦ
with you	**μεθ'** ὑμῶν
forever	εἰς τὸν αἰῶνα

In hope he believed against hope, that he should become the
father (πατέρα) of **many (πολλῶν)** nations, **as (κατὰ)** he had
been told, "So shall your offspring be." (ESV)

πολύς	much, many	409x
polus		S4183

κατά ➤ DAY 39   **πατήρ** ➤ DAY 44

ὃς παρ᾽ ἐλπίδα ἐπ᾽ ἐλπίδι ἐπίστευσεν εἰς τὸ γενέσθαι αὐτὸν
πατέρα πολλῶν ἐθνῶν **κατὰ** τὸ εἰρημένον Οὕτως ἔσται τὸ
σπέρμα σου·

In hope	παρ᾽ ἐλπίδα
he believed	ὃς . . . ἐπίστευσεν
against hope	ἐπ᾽ ἐλπίδι
that he should become	εἰς τὸ γενέσθαι αὐτὸν
the **father**	**πατέρα**
of **many** nations	**πολλῶν** ἐθνῶν
as he had been told	**κατὰ** τὸ εἰρημένον
So shall . . . be	Οὕτως ἔσται
your offspring	τὸ σπέρμα σου

Be glad in that **day (ἡμέρᾳ)** and leap for joy, for behold, your reward is **great (πολὺς)** in heaven. For in the same way their **fathers (πατέρες)** used to treat the prophets. (NASB)

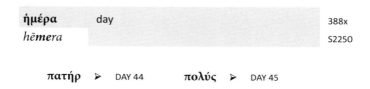

| ἡμέρα | day | 388x |
| hēmera | | S2250 |

πατήρ ➤ DAY 44   **πολύς** ➤ DAY 45

χάρητε ἐν ἐκείνῃ τῇ **ἡμέρᾳ** καὶ σκιρτήσατε, ἰδοὺ γὰρ ὁ μισθὸς ὑμῶν **πολὺς** ἐν τῷ οὐρανῷ· κατὰ τὰ αὐτὰ γὰρ ἐποίουν τοῖς προφήταις οἱ **πατέρες** αὐτῶν.

Be glad	χάρητε
in that **day**	ἐν ἐκείνῃ τῇ **ἡμέρᾳ**
and leap for joy	καὶ σκιρτήσατε
for behold	ἰδοὺ γὰρ
your reward	ὁ μισθὸς ὑμῶν
is **great** in heaven	**πολὺς** ἐν τῷ οὐρανῷ
For in the same way	κατὰ τὰ αὐτὰ γὰρ
their **fathers**	οἱ **πατέρες** αὐτῶν
used to treat the prophets	ἐποίουν τοῖς προφήταις

For **many (πολλὰς) days (ἡμέρας)** she kept this up; then Paul was annoyed and, turning to the **spirit (πνεύματι)**, said, "I order you in the name of Jesus Christ to come out of her." And that moment it left her. (MLB)

πνεῦμα	wind, breath, spirit	379x
pneuma		S4151

πολύς ➤ DAY 45 ἡμέρα ➤ DAY 46

τοῦτο δὲ ἐποίει ἐπὶ **πολλὰς ἡμέρας**. διαπονηθεὶς δὲ Παῦλος καὶ ἐπιστρέψας τῷ **πνεύματι** εἶπεν Παραγγέλλω σοι ἐν ὀνόματι Ἰησοῦ Χριστοῦ ἐξελθεῖν ἀπ᾽ αὐτῆς· καὶ ἐξῆλθεν αὐτῇ τῇ ὥρᾳ.

For **many days**	ἐπὶ **πολλὰς ἡμέρας**
she kept this up	τοῦτο δὲ ἐποίει
then Paul was annoyed	διαπονηθεὶς δὲ Παῦλος
and, turning to the **spirit**, said	καὶ ἐπιστρέψας τῷ **πνεύματι** εἶπεν
I order you	Παραγγέλλω σοι
in the name of Jesus Christ	ἐν ὀνόματι Ἰησοῦ Χριστοῦ
to come out of her	ἐξελθεῖν ἀπ᾽ αὐτῆς
And that moment	καὶ . . . αὐτῇ τῇ ὥρᾳ
it left her	ἐξῆλθεν

It will be in the last **days (ἡμέραις)**, says God, that I shall pour out My **Spirit (πνεύματός)** upon all flesh. Your **sons (υἱοὶ)** and your daughters will prophesy . . . (MLB)

| **υἱός** | son | 375x |
| *huios* | | S5207 |

ἡμέρα ➤ DAY 46   **πνεῦμα** ➤ DAY 47

Καὶ ἔσται ἐν ταῖς ἐσχάταις **ἡμέραις**, λέγει ὁ θεός, ἐκχεῶ ἀπὸ τοῦ **πνεύματός** μου ἐπὶ πᾶσαν σάρκα, καὶ προφητεύσουσιν οἱ **υἱοὶ** ὑμῶν καὶ αἱ θυγατέρες ὑμῶν,

It will be	Καὶ ἔσται
in the last **days**	ἐν ταῖς ἐσχάταις **ἡμέραις**
says God	λέγει ὁ θεός
that I shall pour out	ἐκχεῶ
My **Spirit**	ἀπὸ τοῦ **πνεύματός** μου
upon all flesh	ἐπὶ πᾶσαν σάρκα
Your **sons**	καὶ . . . οἱ **υἱοὶ** ὑμῶν
and your daughters	καὶ αἱ θυγατέρες ὑμῶν
will prophesy	προφητεύσουσιν

And **one (εἷς)** of the crowd answered Him, "Teacher, I brought You my **son (υἱόν)**, possessed with a **spirit (πνεῦμα)** which makes him mute." (NASB)

εἷς, μία, ἕν	one	345x
*heis, **mia**, hen*		S1520

πνεῦμα ➤ DAY 47   **υἱός** ➤ DAY 48

καὶ ἀπεκρίθη αὐτῷ **εἷς** ἐκ τοῦ ὄχλου Διδάσκαλε, ἤνεγκα τὸν **υἱόν** μου πρὸς σέ, ἔχοντα **πνεῦμα** ἄλαλον·

And **one** of the crowd	καὶ . . . **εἷς** ἐκ τοῦ ὄχλου
answered Him	ἀπεκρίθη αὐτῷ
Teacher	Διδάσκαλε
I brought You	ἤνεγκα . . . πρὸς σέ
my **son**	τὸν **υἱόν** μου
possessed with a **spirit**	ἔχοντα **πνεῦμα**
which makes him mute	ἄλαλον

For truly I tell you, until heaven and earth pass away, not **one (ἓν)** letter, not [lit., **or (ἤ)**] **one (μία)** stroke of a letter, will pass from the law until all **is accomplished (γένηται)**. (NRSV)

ἤ	or, than	343x
ē		S2228

γίνομαι ➢ DAY 27   **εἷς, μία, ἕν** ➢ DAY 49

ἀμὴν γὰρ λέγω ὑμῖν, ἕως ἂν παρέλθῃ ὁ οὐρανὸς καὶ ἡ γῆ, ἰῶτα **ἓν ἢ μία** κερέα οὐ μὴ παρέλθῃ ἀπὸ τοῦ νόμου ἕως [ἂν] πάντα **γένηται.**

For truly I tell you	ἀμὴν γὰρ λέγω ὑμῖν
until	ἕως ἂν
heaven and earth	ὁ οὐρανὸς καὶ ἡ γῆ
pass away	παρέλθῃ
not **one** letter, not [lit., **or**] **one** stroke of a letter, will pass	ἰῶτα **ἓν ἢ μία** κερέα οὐ μὴ παρέλθῃ
from the law	ἀπὸ τοῦ νόμου
until	ἕως [ἂν]
all	πάντα
is accomplished	**γένηται**

And **everyone (πᾶς)** who has left houses **or (ἢ) brothers (ἀδελφοὺς) or (ἢ)** sisters **or (ἢ)** father **or (ἢ)** mother **or (ἢ)** children **or (ἢ)** farms for My name's sake, will receive many times as much, and will inherit eternal life. (NASB)

ἀδελφός	brother	342x
adelphos		S80

πᾶς ➤ DAY 16   **ἢ** ➤ DAY 50

καὶ **πᾶς** ὅστις ἀφῆκεν οἰκίας **ἢ ἀδελφοὺς ἢ** ἀδελφὰς **ἢ** πατέρα **ἢ** μητέρα **ἢ** τέκνα **ἢ** ἀγροὺς ἕνεκεν τοῦ ἐμοῦ ὀνόματος, πολλαπλασίονα λήμψεται καὶ ζωὴν αἰώνιον κληρονομήσει.

And **everyone** who	καὶ **πᾶς** ὅστις
has left houses	ἀφῆκεν οἰκίας
or brothers or sisters	**ἢ ἀδελφοὺς ἢ** ἀδελφὰς
or father **or** mother	**ἢ** πατέρα **ἢ** μητέρα
or children **or** farms	**ἢ** τέκνα **ἢ** ἀγροὺς
for My name's sake	ἕνεκεν τοῦ ἐμοῦ ὀνόματος
will receive	λήμψεται
many times as much	πολλαπλασίονα
and will inherit	καὶ . . . κληρονομήσει
eternal life	ζωὴν αἰώνιον

If (ἐὰν) a **brother (ἀδελφὸς)** or **(ἤ)** sister is poorly clothed and lacking in daily food, . . . (ESV)

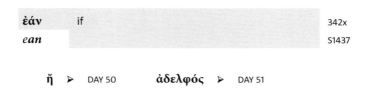

| ἐάν | if | 342x |
| ean | | S1437 |

ἤ   ➤   DAY 50   ἀδελφός   ➤   DAY 51

ἐὰν ἀδελφὸς ἤ ἀδελφὴ γυμνοὶ ὑπάρχωσιν καὶ λειπόμενοι τῆς ἐφημέρου τροφῆς,

If	ἐὰν
a **brother**	ἀδελφὸς
or sister	ἤ ἀδελφὴ
is	ὑπάρχωσιν
poorly clothed	γυμνοὶ
and lacking	καὶ λειπόμενοι
in daily food	τῆς ἐφημέρου τροφῆς

If (Ἐάν) anyone sees his **brother (ἀδελφὸν)** committing a sin that does not bring death, he should ask, and God will give life to him—to those who commit sin that doesn't bring death. There is sin that brings death. I am not saying he should pray **about (περὶ)** that. (HCSB)

περί	about, concerning, with regard to, on account	333x
peri	of, for, over, around	S4012

ἀδελφός   ➤   DAY 51   **ἐάν**   ➤   DAY 52

Ἐάν τις ἴδῃ τὸν **ἀδελφὸν** αὐτοῦ ἁμαρτάνοντα ἁμαρτίαν μὴ πρὸς θάνατον, αἰτήσει, καὶ δώσει αὐτῷ ζωήν, τοῖς ἁμαρτάνουσιν μὴ πρὸς θάνατον. ἔστιν ἁμαρτία πρὸς θάνατον· οὐ **περὶ** ἐκείνης λέγω ἵνα ἐρωτήσῃ.

If anyone sees his **brother**	Ἐάν τις ἴδῃ τὸν **ἀδελφὸν** αὐτοῦ
committing a sin that does not bring death	ἁμαρτάνοντα ἁμαρτίαν μὴ πρὸς θάνατον
he should ask, and God will give life to him	αἰτήσει, καὶ δώσει αὐτῷ ζωήν
to those who commit sin that doesn't bring death	τοῖς ἁμαρτάνουσιν μὴ πρὸς θάνατον
There is sin that brings death	ἔστιν ἁμαρτία πρὸς θάνατον
I am not saying he should pray **about** that	οὐ **περὶ** ἐκείνης λέγω ἵνα ἐρωτήσῃ

But **word (λόγος) about (περὶ)** Him spread even more, and large crowds gathered **to listen (ἀκούειν)** and to be healed of their diseases. (MLB)

λόγος	word, utterance, speech, discourse, saying	330x
logos		S3056

ἀκούω ➤ DAY 42   περί ➤ DAY 53

διήρχετο δὲ μᾶλλον ὁ **λόγος περὶ** αὐτοῦ, καὶ συνήρχοντο ὄχλοι πολλοὶ **ἀκούειν** καὶ θεραπεύεσθαι ἀπὸ τῶν ἀσθενειῶν αὐτῶν·

But **word about** Him	δὲ . . . ὁ **λόγος περὶ** αὐτοῦ
spread even more	διήρχετο . . . μᾶλλον
and large crowds	καὶ . . . ὄχλοι πολλοὶ
gathered	συνήρχοντο
to listen	**ἀκούειν**
and to be healed	καὶ θεραπεύεσθαι
of their diseases	ἀπὸ τῶν ἀσθενειῶν αὐτῶν

Accordingly, every one of us will give **account (λόγον) of (περὶ)** **himself (ἑαυτοῦ)** to God. (MLB)

ἑαυτοῦ	self, himself, herself, itself	315x
heautou		S1438

περί ➤ DAY 53   **λόγος** ➤ DAY 54

ἄρα [οὖν] ἕκαστος ἡμῶν **περὶ ἑαυτοῦ λόγον** δώσει [τῷ θεῷ].

Accordingly	ἄρα [οὖν]
every one	ἕκαστος
of us	ἡμῶν
will give **account**	**λόγον** δώσει
of himself	**περὶ ἑαυτοῦ**
to God	[τῷ θεῷ]

Jesus, **knowing (εἰδὼς)** in **himself (ἑαυτῷ)** that his disciples were complaining **about (περὶ)** this, asked them, "Does this offend you?" (CSB)

οἶδα	to know, remember	314x
oida		S3609a

περί ➤ DAY 53   **ἑαυτοῦ** ➤ DAY 55

εἰδὼς δὲ ὁ Ἰησοῦς ἐν **ἑαυτῷ** ὅτι γογγύζουσιν **περὶ** τούτου οἱ μαθηταὶ αὐτοῦ εἶπεν αὐτοῖς Τοῦτο ὑμᾶς σκανδαλίζει;

Jesus, **knowing**	**εἰδὼς** δὲ ὁ Ἰησοῦς
in **himself**	ἐν **ἑαυτῷ**
that	ὅτι
his disciples	οἱ μαθηταὶ αὐτοῦ
were complaining	γογγύζουσιν
about this	**περὶ** τούτου
asked them	εἶπεν αὐτοῖς
Does this offend you?	Τοῦτο ὑμᾶς σκανδαλίζει;

But **we do** not **know (οἴδαμεν)** how he now sees, neither **do** we
know (οἴδαμεν) who opened his eyes. Ask him; he is of age; he
will speak (λαλήσει) for **himself (ἑαυτοῦ)**. (MLB)

| **λαλέω** | to say, speak | 292x |
| *laleō* | | S2980 |

ἑαυτοῦ ➤ DAY 55   **οἶδα** ➤ DAY 56

πῶς δὲ νῦν βλέπει οὐκ **οἴδαμεν**, ἤ τίς ἤνοιξεν αὐτοῦ τοὺς
ὀφθαλμοὺς ἡμεῖς οὐκ **οἴδαμεν**· αὐτὸν ἐρωτήσατε, ἡλικίαν ἔχει,
αὐτὸς περὶ **ἑαυτοῦ λαλήσει**.

But . . . how he now sees	πῶς δὲ νῦν βλέπει
we do not **know**	οὐκ **οἴδαμεν**
neither **do** we **know**	ἤ . . . ἡμεῖς οὐκ **οἴδαμεν**
who opened	τίς ἤνοιξεν
his eyes	αὐτοῦ τοὺς ὀφθαλμοὺς
Ask him	αὐτὸν ἐρωτήσατε
he is of age	ἡλικίαν ἔχει
he **will speak**	αὐτὸς . . . **λαλήσει**
for **himself**	περὶ **ἑαυτοῦ**

Jesus **spoke (ἐλάλησεν)** these things; and lifting up His eyes to **heaven (οὐρανὸν)**, He said, "Father, the hour has come; glorify Your **Son (υἱόν)**, that the **Son (υἱὸς)** may glorify You." (NASB)

οὐρανός	sky, heaven	273x
ouranos		S3772

υἱός ➤	DAY 48	**λαλέω** ➤	DAY 57

Ταῦτα **ἐλάλησεν** Ἰησοῦς, καὶ ἐπάρας τοὺς ὀφθαλμοὺς αὐτοῦ εἰς τὸν **οὐρανὸν** εἶπεν Πάτερ, ἐλήλυθεν ἡ ὥρα· δόξασόν σου τὸν **υἱόν**, ἵνα ὁ **υἱὸς** δοξάσῃ σέ,

Jesus **spoke**	**ἐλάλησεν** Ἰησοῦς
these things	Ταῦτα
and lifting up His eyes	καὶ ἐπάρας τοὺς ὀφθαλμοὺς αὐτοῦ
to **heaven**	εἰς τὸν **οὐρανὸν**
He said	εἶπεν
Father	Πάτερ
the hour has come	ἐλήλυθεν ἡ ὥρα
glorify Your **Son**	δόξασόν σου τὸν **υἱόν**
that the **Son**	ἵνα ὁ **υἱὸς**
may glorify You	δοξάσῃ σέ

At that time the **disciples (μαθηταὶ)** came to Jesus and asked,
"**Who (Τίς)**, then, is the greatest in the kingdom of **heaven
(οὐρανῶν)**?" (NIV)

μαθητής	disciple, learner	262x
mathētēs		S3101

τίς, τί ➤ DAY 32   **οὐρανός** ➤ DAY 58

Ἐν ἐκείνῃ τῇ ὥρᾳ προσῆλθον οἱ **μαθηταὶ** τῷ Ἰησοῦ λέγοντες **Τίς**
ἄρα μείζων ἐστὶν ἐν τῇ βασιλείᾳ τῶν **οὐρανῶν;**

At that time	Ἐν ἐκείνῃ τῇ ὥρᾳ
the **disciples** came	προσῆλθον οἱ **μαθηταὶ**
to Jesus	τῷ Ἰησοῦ
and asked	λέγοντες
Who, then	**Τίς** ἄρα
is the greatest	μείζων ἐστὶν
in the kingdom	ἐν τῇ βασιλείᾳ
of **heaven**?	τῶν **οὐρανῶν;**

Then **He took (λαβὼν)** the five loaves and the two fish, and looking up to **heaven (οὐρανὸν)**, He blessed them, and broke them, and kept giving them to the **disciples (μαθηταῖς)** to set before the people. (NASB)

λαμβάνω	to take, receive, get	257x
lambanō		S2983

οὐρανός ➤ DAY 58   **μαθητής** ➤ DAY 59

λαβὼν δὲ τοὺς πέντε ἄρτους καὶ τοὺς δύο ἰχθύας ἀναβλέψας εἰς τὸν **οὐρανὸν** εὐλόγησεν αὐτοὺς καὶ κατέκλασεν καὶ ἐδίδου τοῖς **μαθηταῖς** παραθεῖναι τῷ ὄχλῳ.

Then **He took**	**λαβὼν** δὲ
the five loaves	τοὺς πέντε ἄρτους
and the two fish	καὶ τοὺς δύο ἰχθύας
and looking up	ἀναβλέψας
to **heaven**	εἰς τὸν **οὐρανὸν**
He blessed them	εὐλόγησεν αὐτοὺς
and broke them	καὶ κατέκλασεν
and kept giving them to the **disciples**	καὶ ἐδίδου τοῖς **μαθηταῖς**
to set before the people	παραθεῖναι τῷ ὄχλῳ

So He instructed the crowd to sit down on the **ground (γῆς)** and, **taking (λαβὼν)** the seven loaves of bread, He gave thanks, broke them, gave them to His **disciples (μαθηταῖς)** to set before the people, and they set them before the crowd. (MLB)

γῆ	earth, land, soil	249x
gē		S1093

μαθητής ➤ DAY 59	**λαμβάνω** ➤ DAY 60

καὶ παραγγέλλει τῷ ὄχλῳ ἀναπεσεῖν ἐπὶ τῆς **γῆς**· καὶ **λαβὼν** τοὺς ἑπτὰ ἄρτους εὐχαριστήσας ἔκλασεν καὶ ἐδίδου τοῖς **μαθηταῖς** αὐτοῦ ἵνα παρατιθῶσιν καὶ παρέθηκαν τῷ ὄχλῳ.

So He instructed the crowd	καὶ παραγγέλλει τῷ ὄχλῳ
to sit down on the **ground**	ἀναπεσεῖν ἐπὶ τῆς **γῆς**
and, **taking** the seven loaves of bread	καὶ **λαβὼν** τοὺς ἑπτὰ ἄρτους
He gave thanks	εὐχαριστήσας
broke them	ἔκλασεν
gave them to His **disciples**	καὶ ἐδίδου τοῖς **μαθηταῖς** αὐτοῦ
to set before the people	ἵνα παρατιθῶσιν
and they set them before the crowd	καὶ παρέθηκαν τῷ ὄχλῳ

By **faith (Πίστει)** the Israelites [lit., they] crossed the Red Sea
as on dry **land (γῆς)**, and when the Egyptians tried it [lit., **took
(λαβόντες)** the attempt], they were drowned. (MLB)

πίστις	faith, belief, trust	242x
pistis		S4102

λαμβάνω ➢ DAY 60   **γῆ** ➢ DAY 61

Πίστει διέβησαν τὴν Ἐρυθρὰν Θάλασσαν ὡς διὰ ξηρᾶς **γῆς**, ἧς
πεῖραν **λαβόντες** οἱ Αἰγύπτιοι κατεπόθησαν.

By **faith**	**Πίστει**
the Israelites [lit., they] crossed	διέβησαν
the Red Sea	τὴν Ἐρυθρὰν Θάλασσαν
as on	ὡς διὰ
dry **land**	ξηρᾶς **γῆς**
and when the Egyptians	ἧς . . . οἱ Αἰγύπτιοι
tried it [lit., **took** the attempt]	πεῖραν **λαβόντες**
they were drowned	κατεπόθησαν

There remain then, **faith (πίστις)**, hope, love, **these (ταῦτα)** three; but the **greatest (μείζων)** of **these (τούτων)** is love. (MLB)

μέγας	large, great	240x
megas		S3173

οὗτος, αὕτη, τοῦτο ➤ DAY 13   **πίστις** ➤ DAY 62

νυνὶ δὲ μένει **πίστις**, ἐλπίς, ἀγάπη· τὰ τρία **ταῦτα**, **μείζων** δὲ **τούτων** ἡ ἀγάπη.

There remain then	νυνὶ δὲ μένει
faith	**πίστις**
hope	ἐλπίς
love	ἀγάπη
these three	τὰ τρία **ταῦτα**
but the **greatest** of **these**	**μείζων** δὲ **τούτων**
is love	ἡ ἀγάπη

Then Jesus replied to her, "Woman, your **faith (πίστις)** is **great (μεγάλη)**. Let it be done for you as you want." And from **that (ἐκείνης)** moment her daughter was healed. (CSB)

| ἐκεῖνος | that, yonder | 239x |
| *ekeinos* | | S1565 |

　　　πίστις　▷　DAY 62　　　　μέγας　▷　DAY 63

τότε ἀποκριθεὶς ὁ Ἰησοῦς εἶπεν αὐτῇ Ὦ γύναι, **μεγάλη** σου ἡ **πίστις·** γενηθήτω σοι ὡς θέλεις. καὶ ἰάθη ἡ θυγάτηρ αὐτῆς ἀπὸ τῆς ὥρας **ἐκείνης.**

Then Jesus replied to her	τότε ἀποκριθεὶς ὁ Ἰησοῦς εἶπεν αὐτῇ
Woman	Ὦ γύναι
your **faith**	σου ἡ **πίστις**
is **great**	**μεγάλη**
Let it be done for you	γενηθήτω σοι
as you want	ὡς θέλεις
And from **that** moment	καὶ . . . ἀπὸ τῆς ὥρας **ἐκείνης**
her daughter was healed	ἰάθη ἡ θυγάτηρ αὐτῆς

I know (οἶδα) and am persuaded in the Lord Jesus that **nothing (οὐδὲν)** is unclean in itself. Still, to someone who considers a thing to be unclean, to **that one (ἐκείνῳ)** it is unclean. (CSB)

οὐδείς, οὐδεμία, οὐδέν	no, no one, nothing	235x
oudeis, oudemia, ouden		S3762

οἶδα ➤ DAY 56   ἐκεῖνος ➤ DAY 64

οἶδα καὶ πέπεισμαι ἐν κυρίῳ Ἰησοῦ ὅτι **οὐδὲν** κοινὸν δι' ἑαυτοῦ· εἰ μὴ τῷ λογιζομένῳ τι κοινὸν εἶναι, **ἐκείνῳ** κοινόν.

I know and am persuaded	**οἶδα** καὶ πέπεισμαι
in the Lord Jesus	ἐν κυρίῳ Ἰησοῦ
that **nothing** is unclean	ὅτι **οὐδὲν** κοινὸν
in itself	δι' ἑαυτοῦ
Still	εἰ μὴ
to someone who considers a thing	τῷ λογιζομένῳ τι
to be unclean	κοινὸν εἶναι
to **that one** it is unclean	**ἐκείνῳ** κοινόν

Whether **then (οὖν)** it was I or **they (ἐκεῖνοι)**, so we preach and so **you believed (ἐπιστεύσατε)**. (ESV)

πιστεύω	to believe, trust, rely	235x
pisteuō		S4100

οὖν   ➤   DAY 38   ἐκεῖνος   ➤   DAY 64

εἴτε **οὖν** ἐγὼ εἴτε **ἐκεῖνοι**, οὕτως κηρύσσομεν καὶ οὕτως **ἐπιστεύσατε**.

Whether **then**	εἴτε **οὖν**
it was I	ἐγὼ
or **they**	εἴτε **ἐκεῖνοι**
so	οὕτως
we preach	κηρύσσομεν
and so	καὶ οὕτως
you believed	**ἐπιστεύσατε**

We **have come to believe (πεπιστεύκαμεν)** and to know that you
are (εἶ) the **Holy One (ἅγιος)** of God. (NIV)

ἅγιος	holy, sacred, set apart	233x
hagios		S40

εἰμί ➤ DAY 8   πιστεύω ➤ DAY 66

καὶ ἡμεῖς **πεπιστεύκαμεν** καὶ ἐγνώκαμεν ὅτι σὺ **εἶ** ὁ **ἅγιος** τοῦ
θεοῦ.

We **have come to believe**	καὶ ἡμεῖς **πεπιστεύκαμεν**
and to know	καὶ ἐγνώκαμεν
that you **are**	ὅτι σὺ **εἶ**
the **Holy One**	ὁ **ἅγιος**
of God	τοῦ θεοῦ

The angel **answered (ἀποκριθεὶς)** and said to her, "The **Holy (ἅγιον) Spirit (Πνεῦμα)** will come upon you, and the power of the Most High will overshadow you; and for that reason the **holy (ἅγιον)** Child shall be called the Son of God." (NASB)

ἀποκρίνομαι	to answer, reply	231x
apokrinomai		S611

　　πνεῦμα　➤　DAY 47　　　**ἅγιος**　➤　DAY 67

καὶ **ἀποκριθεὶς** ὁ ἄγγελος εἶπεν αὐτῇ **Πνεῦμα ἅγιον** ἐπελεύσεται ἐπὶ σέ, καὶ δύναμις Ὑψίστου ἐπισκιάσει σοι· διὸ καὶ τὸ γεννώμενον **ἅγιον** κληθήσεται, υἱὸς θεοῦ·

The angel **answered** and said to her	καὶ **ἀποκριθεὶς** ὁ ἄγγελος εἶπεν αὐτῇ
The **Holy Spirit** will come upon you	**Πνεῦμα ἅγιον** ἐπελεύσεται ἐπὶ σέ
and the power of the Most High	καὶ δύναμις Ὑψίστου
will overshadow you	ἐπισκιάσει σοι
and for that reason	διὸ καὶ
the **holy** Child	τὸ γεννώμενον **ἅγιον**
shall be called the Son of God	κληθήσεται, υἱὸς θεοῦ

John **answered (Ἀποκριθεὶς)**, "Master, we saw **someone (τινα)** casting out demons in your **name (ὀνόματί)**, and we tried to stop him, because he does not follow with us." (NRSV)

ὄνομα	name, reputation	229x
onoma		S3686

τὶς, τὶ ➤ DAY 35   ἀποκρίνομαι ➤ DAY 68

Ἀποκριθεὶς δὲ Ἰωάνης εἶπεν Ἐπιστάτα, εἴδαμέν **τινα** ἐν τῷ **ὀνόματί** σου ἐκβάλλοντα δαιμόνια, καὶ ἐκωλύομεν αὐτὸν ὅτι οὐκ ἀκολουθεῖ μεθ᾽ ἡμῶν.

John **answered**	**Ἀποκριθεὶς** δὲ Ἰωάνης εἶπεν
Master	Ἐπιστάτα
we saw **someone**	εἴδαμέν **τινα**
casting out demons	ἐκβάλλοντα δαιμόνια
in your **name**	ἐν τῷ **ὀνόματί** σου
and we tried to stop him	καὶ ἐκωλύομεν αὐτὸν
because he does not follow	ὅτι οὐκ ἀκολουθεῖ
with us	μεθ᾽ ἡμῶν

One (εἷς) of them, **named (ὀνόματι)** Cleopas, asked [lit., answering, said to] him, "Are you the only one visiting Jerusalem who **does** not **know (ἔγνως)** the things that have happened there in these days?" (NIV)

γινώσκω	to know, learn, realize	220x
ginōskō		S1097

    εἷς, μία, ἕν ➤ DAY 49   **ὄνομα** ➤ DAY 69

ἀποκριθεὶς δὲ **εἷς ὀνόματι** Κλεόπας εἶπεν πρὸς αὐτόν Σὺ μόνος παροικεῖς Ἰερουσαλὴμ καὶ οὐκ **ἔγνως** τὰ γενόμενα ἐν αὐτῇ ἐν ταῖς ἡμέραις ταύταις;

One of them, **named** Cleopas	δὲ **εἷς ὀνόματι** Κλεόπας
asked [lit., answering, said to] him	ἀποκριθεὶς . . . εἶπεν πρὸς αὐτόν
Are you the only one visiting Jerusalem	Σὺ μόνος παροικεῖς Ἰερουσαλὴμ
who **does** not **know**	καὶ οὐκ **ἔγνως**
the things that have happened	τὰ γενόμενα
there	ἐν αὐτῇ
in these days?	ἐν ταῖς ἡμέραις ταύταις;

Once more Pilate **came out (ἐξῆλθεν)** and addressed them, "See!
I am bringing Him out to **you (ὑμῖν)**, so **you may know (γνῶτε)**
that I do not find Him guilty." (MLB)

ἐξέρχομαι	to go out	218x
exerchomai		S1831

σύ, (pl) **ὑμεῖς** ➤ DAY 4   **γινώσκω** ➤ DAY 70

Καὶ **ἐξῆλθεν** πάλιν ἔξω ὁ Πειλᾶτος καὶ λέγει αὐτοῖς Ἴδε ἄγω **ὑμῖν**
αὐτὸν ἔξω, ἵνα **γνῶτε** ὅτι οὐδεμίαν αἰτίαν εὑρίσκω ἐν αὐτῷ.

Once more	Καὶ . . . πάλιν
Pilate **came out**	**ἐξῆλθεν** . . . ἔξω ὁ Πειλᾶτος
and addressed them	καὶ λέγει αὐτοῖς
See!	Ἴδε
I am bringing Him out	ἄγω . . . αὐτὸν ἔξω
to **you**	**ὑμῖν**
so **you may know** that	ἵνα **γνῶτε** ὅτι
I do not find Him guilty	οὐδεμίαν αἰτίαν εὑρίσκω ἐν αὐτῷ

Then Paul chose Silas and **departed (ἐξῆλθεν)**, after being commended to the grace of the Lord **by (ὑπὸ)** the **brothers (ἀδελφῶν)**. (HCSB)

ὑπό	by, under, about	218x
hupo		S5259

ἀδελφός ➤ DAY 51   **ἐξέρχομαι** ➤ DAY 71

Παῦλος δὲ ἐπιλεξάμενος Σίλαν **ἐξῆλθεν** παραδοθεὶς τῇ χάριτι τοῦ κυρίου **ὑπὸ** τῶν **ἀδελφῶν**,

Then Paul chose Silas	Παῦλος δὲ ἐπιλεξάμενος Σίλαν
and **departed**	**ἐξῆλθεν**
after being commended	παραδοθεὶς
to the grace	τῇ χάριτι
of the Lord	τοῦ κυρίου
by the **brothers**	**ὑπὸ** τῶν **ἀδελφῶν**

Now there were Jews living in Jerusalem, devout **men (ἄνδρες)** from every nation **under (ὑπὸ) heaven (οὐρανόν)**. (NASB)

ἀνήρ	man, husband	216x
anēr		S435

οὐρανός ➤ DAY 58   **ὑπό** ➤ DAY 72

Ἦσαν δὲ ἐν Ἰερουσαλὴμ κατοικοῦντες Ἰουδαῖοι, **ἄνδρες** εὐλαβεῖς ἀπὸ παντὸς ἔθνους τῶν **ὑπὸ** τὸν **οὐρανόν**·

Now there were Jews	Ἦσαν δὲ . . . Ἰουδαῖοι
living	κατοικοῦντες
in Jerusalem	ἐν Ἰερουσαλὴμ
devout **men**	**ἄνδρες** εὐλαβεῖς
from every nation	ἀπὸ παντὸς ἔθνους
under heaven	τῶν **ὑπὸ** τὸν **οὐρανόν**

But a **man (Ἀνὴρ) named (ὀνόματι)** Ananias, with his **wife
(γυναικὶ)** Sapphira, sold a piece of property. (NASB)

γυνή	woman, wife, lady	209x
gunē		S1135

ὄνομα ➤ DAY 69   **ἀνήρ** ➤ DAY 73

Ἀνὴρ δέ τις Ἀνανίας **ὀνόματι** σὺν Σαπφείρῃ τῇ **γυναικὶ** αὐτοῦ
ἐπώλησεν κτῆμα

But a **man**	**Ἀνὴρ** δέ τις
named Ananias	Ἀνανίας **ὀνόματι**
with . . . Sapphira	σὺν Σαπφείρῃ
his **wife**	τῇ **γυναικὶ** αὐτοῦ
sold	ἐπώλησεν
a piece of property	κτῆμα

Another said, "I have married a **wife (Γυναῖκα)** and on that account **I can**not **(δύναμαι) come (ἐλθεῖν)**." (MLB)

δύναμαι	to be able, be powerful	209x
*du*namai		S1410

ἔρχομαι ➢ DAY 30   γυνή ➢ DAY 74

καὶ ἕτερος εἶπεν **Γυναῖκα** ἔγημα καὶ διὰ τοῦτο οὐ **δύναμαι ἐλθεῖν**.

Another said	καὶ ἕτερος εἶπεν
I have married a **wife**	**Γυναῖκα** ἔγημα
and on that account	καὶ διὰ τοῦτο
I cannot	οὐ **δύναμαι**
come	**ἐλθεῖν**

If anyone comes to me and does not hate his own father and mother and **wife (γυναῖκα)** and children and brothers and sisters, yes, **and (τε)** even his own life, **he can**not (**δύναται**) be my disciple. (ESV)

τέ	and	208x
te		S5037

γυνή ➤ DAY 74   **δύναμαι** ➤ DAY 75

Εἴ τις ἔρχεται πρός με καὶ οὐ μισεῖ τὸν πατέρα ἑαυτοῦ καὶ τὴν μητέρα καὶ τὴν **γυναῖκα** καὶ τὰ τέκνα καὶ τοὺς ἀδελφοὺς καὶ τὰς ἀδελφάς, ἔτι **τε** καὶ τὴν ψυχὴν ἑαυτοῦ, οὐ **δύναται** εἶναί μου μαθητής.

If anyone comes to me	Εἴ τις ἔρχεται πρός με
and does not hate	καὶ οὐ μισεῖ
his own father and mother	τὸν πατέρα ἑαυτοῦ καὶ τὴν μητέρα
and **wife** and children	καὶ τὴν **γυναῖκα** καὶ τὰ τέκνα
and brothers and sisters	καὶ τοὺς ἀδελφοὺς καὶ τὰς ἀδελφάς
yes, **and** even his own life	ἔτι **τε** καὶ τὴν ψυχὴν ἑαυτοῦ
he cannot be	οὐ **δύναται** εἶναί
my disciple	μου μαθητής

The same thing happened at Iconium. They went into the Jewish synagogue and **so (οὕτως)** spoke that a large group **both (τε)** of Jews and of Greeks **believed (πιστεῦσαι)**. (MLB)

οὕτως	thus, so, in this way	207x
houtōs		S3779

πιστεύω ➤ DAY 66   **τέ** ➤ DAY 76

Ἐγένετο δὲ ἐν Ἰκονίῳ κατὰ τὸ αὐτὸ εἰσελθεῖν αὐτοὺς εἰς τὴν συναγωγὴν τῶν Ἰουδαίων καὶ λαλῆσαι **οὕτως** ὥστε **πιστεῦσαι** Ἰουδαίων **τε** καὶ Ἑλλήνων πολὺ πλῆθος.

The same thing happened	Ἐγένετο δὲ . . . κατὰ τὸ αὐτὸ
at Iconium	ἐν Ἰκονίῳ
They went into	εἰσελθεῖν αὐτοὺς εἰς
the Jewish synagogue	τὴν συναγωγὴν τῶν Ἰουδαίων
and **so** spoke	καὶ λαλῆσαι **οὕτως**
that a large group . . . **believed**	ὥστε **πιστεῦσαι** . . . πολὺ πλῆθος
both of Jews and of Greeks	Ἰουδαίων **τε** καὶ Ἑλλήνων

So **whatever** (Πάντα . . . ὅσα **ἐὰν**) **you wish** (**θέλητε**) that others would do to you, [**so** (**οὕτως**)] do also to them, for this is the Law and the Prophets. (ESV)

| **θέλω** | to desire, wish, will | 204x |
| *thelō* | | S2309 |

ἐάν ➤ DAY 52   **οὕτως** ➤ DAY 77

Πάντα οὖν ὅσα **ἐὰν θέλητε** ἵνα ποιῶσιν ὑμῖν οἱ ἄνθρωποι, **οὕτως** καὶ ὑμεῖς ποιεῖτε αὐτοῖς· οὗτος γάρ ἐστιν ὁ νόμος καὶ οἱ προφῆται.

So **whatever**	Πάντα οὖν ὅσα **ἐὰν**
you wish	**θέλητε**
that others would do to you	ἵνα ποιῶσιν ὑμῖν οἱ ἄνθρωποι
[**so**] do also to them	**οὕτως** καὶ ὑμεῖς ποιεῖτε αὐτοῖς
for this is	οὗτος γάρ ἐστιν
the Law	ὁ νόμος
and the Prophets	καὶ οἱ προφῆται

And [**behold (ἰδοὺ)**] a leper came up and knelt before Him
saying: "Lord, if **You are willing (θέλῃς)**, **You are able (δύνασαί)**
to cleanse me." (MLB)

ἰδού	behold!	199x
idou		S2400

δύναμαι ➤ DAY 75   **θέλω** ➤ DAY 78

Καὶ **ἰδοὺ** λεπρὸς προσελθὼν προσεκύνει αὐτῷ λέγων Κύριε, ἐὰν
θέλῃς δύνασαί με καθαρίσαι.

And [**behold**]	Καὶ **ἰδοὺ**
a leper came up	λεπρὸς προσελθὼν
and knelt before Him	προσεκύνει αὐτῷ
saying	λέγων
Lord	Κύριε
if **You are willing**	ἐὰν **θέλῃς**
You are able	**δύνασαί**
to cleanse me	με καθαρίσαι

Tell me, you who **want (θέλοντες)** to be **under (ὑπὸ)** the **Law (νόμον)**, do you not listen to the **Law (νόμον)**? (MLB)

νόμος	law, Law, ordinance	194x
nomos		S3551

ὑπό ➢ DAY 72 θέλω ➢ DAY 78

Λέγετέ μοι, οἱ **ὑπὸ νόμον θέλοντες** εἶναι, τὸν **νόμον** οὐκ ἀκούετε;

Tell me	Λέγετέ μοι
you who **want** to be	οἱ . . . **θέλοντες** εἶναι
under the Law	**ὑπὸ νόμον**
do you not listen to	οὐκ ἀκούετε;
the **Law?**	τὸν **νόμον**

And **behold (ἰδοὺ)**, there were two blind men sitting **by (παρὰ)** the roadside, and when **they heard (ἀκούσαντες)** that Jesus was passing by, they cried out, "Lord, have mercy on us, Son of David!" (ESV)

παρά	by, near, beside, from	193x
para		S3844

ἀκούω ➤ DAY 42   **ἰδού** ➤ DAY 79

καὶ **ἰδοὺ** δύο τυφλοὶ καθήμενοι **παρὰ** τὴν ὁδόν, **ἀκούσαντες** ὅτι Ἰησοῦς παράγει, ἔκραξαν λέγοντες Κύριε, ἐλέησον ἡμᾶς, υἱὸς Δαυείδ.

And **behold**	καὶ **ἰδοὺ**
there were two blind men	δύο τυφλοὶ
sitting **by** the roadside	καθήμενοι **παρὰ** τὴν ὁδόν
and when **they heard** that	**ἀκούσαντες** ὅτι
Jesus was passing by	Ἰησοῦς παράγει
they cried out	ἔκραξαν λέγοντες
Lord, have mercy on us	Κύριε, ἐλέησον ἡμᾶς
Son of David!	υἱὸς Δαυείδ

Just then [lit., and **behold (ἰδού)**] there came a man named Jairus, a leader of the synagogue. He fell **at (παρὰ)** Jesus' feet and begged him to come to [lit., **to enter (εἰσελθεῖν)** into] his house. (NRSV)

εἰσέρχομαι	to enter, go in	191x
eiserchomai		S1525

ἰδού　➤　DAY 79　　　　**παρά**　➤　DAY 81

Καὶ **ἰδοὺ** ἦλθεν ἀνὴρ ᾧ ὄνομα Ἰάειρος, καὶ οὗτος ἄρχων τῆς συναγωγῆς ὑπῆρχεν, καὶ πεσὼν **παρὰ** τοὺς πόδας Ἰησοῦ παρεκάλει αὐτὸν **εἰσελθεῖν** εἰς τὸν οἶκον αὐτοῦ,

Just then [lit., and **behold**]	Καὶ **ἰδού**
there came a man	ἦλθεν ἀνὴρ
named Jairus	ᾧ ὄνομα Ἰάειρος
a leader of the synagogue	καὶ οὗτος ἄρχων τῆς συναγωγῆς ὑπῆρχεν
He fell	καὶ πεσὼν
at Jesus' feet	**παρὰ** τοὺς πόδας Ἰησοῦ
and begged him	παρεκάλει αὐτὸν
to come to [lit., **to enter** into] his house	**εἰσελθεῖν** εἰς τὸν οἶκον αὐτοῦ

Therefore Pilate **entered (Εἰσῆλθεν)** again into the Praetorium, and summoned Jesus and **said (εἶπεν)** to Him, "Are You the King of the **Jews (Ἰουδαίων)**?" (NASB)

Ἰουδαῖος	Jew, Jewish, Judean	190x
Ioudaios		S2453

λέγω ➤ DAY 9   εἰσέρχομαι ➤ DAY 82

Εἰσῆλθεν οὖν πάλιν εἰς τὸ πραιτώριον ὁ Πειλᾶτος καὶ ἐφώνησεν τὸν Ἰησοῦν καὶ **εἶπεν** αὐτῷ Σὺ εἶ ὁ βασιλεὺς τῶν **Ἰουδαίων**;

Therefore Pilate **entered**	**Εἰσῆλθεν** οὖν . . . ὁ Πειλᾶτος
again	πάλιν
into the Praetorium	εἰς τὸ πραιτώριον
and summoned Jesus	καὶ ἐφώνησεν τὸν Ἰησοῦν
and **said** to Him	καὶ **εἶπεν** αὐτῷ
Are You	Σὺ εἶ
the King of the **Jews**?	ὁ βασιλεὺς τῶν **Ἰουδαίων**;

Over His head they placed the **written (γεγραμμένην)** charge against Him, **THIS (Οὗτός)** IS JESUS, THE KING OF THE **JEWS** (**Ἰουδαίων**). (MLB)

γράφω	to write	189x
graphō		S1125

οὗτος, αὕτη, τοῦτο   ➤   DAY 13   Ἰουδαῖος   ➤   DAY 83

καὶ ἐπέθηκαν ἐπάνω τῆς κεφαλῆς αὐτοῦ τὴν αἰτίαν αὐτοῦ **γεγραμμένην Οὗτός** ἐστιν Ἰησοῦς ὁ βασιλεὺς τῶν **Ἰουδαίων**.

Over His head	καὶ . . . ἐπάνω τῆς κεφαλῆς αὐτοῦ
they placed	ἐπέθηκαν
the **written** charge against Him	τὴν αἰτίαν αὐτοῦ **γεγραμμένην**
THIS IS JESUS	**Οὗτός** ἐστιν Ἰησοῦς
THE KING OF THE **JEWS**	ὁ βασιλεὺς τῶν **Ἰουδαίων**

But there are also many other things that Jesus **did (ἐποίησεν)**; if every one of them **were written down (γράφηται)**, I suppose that the **world (κόσμον)** itself could not contain the books **that would be written (γραφόμενα)**. (NRSV)

κόσμος	world, universe	185x
kosmos		S2889

ποιέω ➤ DAY 31   **γράφω** ➤ DAY 84

Ἔστιν δὲ καὶ ἄλλα πολλὰ ἃ **ἐποίησεν** ὁ Ἰησοῦς, ἅτινα ἐὰν **γράφηται** καθ᾽ ἕν, οὐδ᾽ αὐτὸν οἶμαι τὸν **κόσμον** χωρήσειν τὰ **γραφόμενα** βιβλία.

But there are also many other things	Ἔστιν δὲ καὶ ἄλλα πολλὰ
that Jesus **did**	ἃ **ἐποίησεν** ὁ Ἰησοῦς
if every one of them **were written down**	ἅτινα ἐὰν **γράφηται** καθ᾽ ἕν
I suppose that	οἶμαι
the **world** itself	αὐτὸν . . . τὸν **κόσμον**
could not contain	οὐδ᾽ . . . χωρήσειν
the books **that would be written**	τὰ **γραφόμενα** βιβλία

First (Πρῶτον **μὲν**), I thank my God through Jesus Christ for all of you, because your **faith (πίστις)** is being reported all over the **world (κόσμῳ)**. (NIV)

μέν	(particle that is usually left untranslated), on the one hand	181x
men		S3303a

πίστις ➤ DAY 62   **κόσμος** ➤ DAY 85

Πρῶτον **μὲν** εὐχαριστῶ τῷ θεῷ μου διὰ Ἰησοῦ Χριστοῦ περὶ πάντων ὑμῶν, ὅτι ἡ **πίστις** ὑμῶν καταγγέλλεται ἐν ὅλῳ τῷ **κόσμῳ**.

First	Πρῶτον **μὲν**
I thank my God	εὐχαριστῶ τῷ θεῷ μου
through Jesus Christ	διὰ Ἰησοῦ Χριστοῦ
for all of you	περὶ πάντων ὑμῶν
because your **faith**	ὅτι ἡ **πίστις** ὑμῶν
is being reported	καταγγέλλεται
all over the **world**	ἐν ὅλῳ τῷ **κόσμῳ**

For the (ὁ **μὲν**) Son of Man goes **as (καθὼς)** it is written of him, but woe to **that (ἐκείνῳ)** man by whom the Son of Man is betrayed! (ESV)

καθώς	as, just as, even as	178x
kathōs		S2531

ἐκεῖνος   ➤   DAY 64   **μέν**   ➤   DAY 86

ὅτι ὁ **μὲν** υἱὸς τοῦ ἀνθρώπου ὑπάγει **καθὼς** γέγραπται περὶ αὐτοῦ, οὐαὶ δὲ τῷ ἀνθρώπῳ **ἐκείνῳ** δι᾽ οὗ ὁ υἱὸς τοῦ ἀνθρώπου παραδίδοται·

For the Son of Man	ὅτι ὁ **μὲν** υἱὸς τοῦ ἀνθρώπου
goes	ὑπάγει
as it is written	**καθὼς** γέγραπται
of him	περὶ αὐτοῦ
but woe	οὐαὶ δὲ
to **that** man	τῷ ἀνθρώπῳ **ἐκείνῳ**
by whom	δι᾽ οὗ
the Son of Man	ὁ υἱὸς τοῦ ἀνθρώπου
is betrayed!	παραδίδοται

Look at my **hands (χεῖράς)** and my feet. It is I myself! Touch me and see; a **ghost (πνεῦμα)** does not have flesh and bones, **as (καθὼς)** you see I have. (NIV)

χείρ	hand	178x
cheir		S5495

πνεῦμα ➤ DAY 47   **καθώς** ➤ DAY 87

ἴδετε τὰς **χεῖράς** μου καὶ τοὺς πόδας μου ὅτι ἐγώ εἰμι αὐτός· ψηλαφήσατέ με καὶ ἴδετε, ὅτι **πνεῦμα** σάρκα καὶ ὀστέα οὐκ ἔχει **καθὼς** ἐμὲ θεωρεῖτε ἔχοντα.

Look at my **hands**	ἴδετε τὰς **χεῖράς** μου
and my feet	καὶ τοὺς πόδας μου
It is I myself!	ὅτι ἐγώ εἰμι αὐτός
Touch me	ψηλαφήσατέ με
and see	καὶ ἴδετε
a **ghost** does not have	ὅτι **πνεῦμα** . . . οὐκ ἔχει
flesh and bones	σάρκα καὶ ὀστέα
as you see	**καθὼς** . . . θεωρεῖτε
I have	ἐμὲ . . . ἔχοντα

Why then the **law (νόμος)**? It was added because of
transgressions, until (ἄχρις **ἄν**) the offspring would come to
whom the promise had been made; and it was ordained through
angels by [lit., in the **hand (χειρὶ)** of] a mediator. (NRSV)

ἄν	(particle that is usually left untranslated; indicates	174x
an	contingency or dependence)	S302

νόμος ➤ DAY 80   **χείρ** ➤ DAY 88

Τί οὖν ὁ **νόμος**; τῶν παραβάσεων χάριν προσετέθη, ἄχρις **ἄν** ἔλθῃ
τὸ σπέρμα ᾧ ἐπήγγελται, διαταγεὶς δι' ἀγγέλων ἐν **χειρὶ** μεσίτου·

Why then the **law**?	Τί οὖν ὁ **νόμος**;
It was added	προσετέθη
because of transgressions	τῶν παραβάσεων χάριν
until the offspring	ἄχρις **ἄν** . . . τὸ σπέρμα
would come	ἔλθῃ
to whom the promise had been made	ᾧ ἐπήγγελται
and it was ordained	διαταγεὶς
through angels	δι' ἀγγέλων
by [lit., in the **hand** of] a mediator	ἐν **χειρὶ** μεσίτου

But when the **crowd (ὄχλος)** had been put outside, **he went in (εἰσελθὼν)** and took her by the **hand (χειρὸς)**, and the girl got up. (NRSV)

ὄχλος	crowd, multitude, mob	174x
*och*los		S3793

     εἰσέρχομαι ➤ DAY 82   **χείρ** ➤ DAY 88

ὅτε δὲ ἐξεβλήθη ὁ **ὄχλος**, **εἰσελθὼν** ἐκράτησεν τῆς **χειρὸς** αὐτῆς, καὶ ἠγέρθη τὸ κοράσιον.

But when	ὅτε δὲ
the **crowd**	ὁ **ὄχλος**
had been put outside	ἐξεβλήθη
he went in	**εἰσελθὼν**
and took her by the **hand**	ἐκράτησεν τῆς **χειρὸς** αὐτῆς
and the girl	καὶ . . . τὸ κοράσιον
got up	ἠγέρθη

Jesus said to them, "**If (Ei)** you were blind, you would not have (οὐκ **ἂν** εἴχετε) **sin (ἁμαρτίαν)**. But now that you say, 'We see,' your **sin (ἁμαρτία)** remains." (NRSV)

| **ἁμαρτία** | sin | 173x |
| *hamartia* | | S266 |

εἰ ➤ DAY 37   ἂν ➤ DAY 89

εἶπεν αὐτοῖς [ὁ] Ἰησοῦς **Εἰ** τυφλοὶ ἦτε, οὐκ **ἂν** εἴχετε **ἁμαρτίαν·** νῦν δὲ λέγετε ὅτι Βλέπομεν· ἡ **ἁμαρτία** ὑμῶν μένει.

Jesus said to them	εἶπεν αὐτοῖς [ὁ] Ἰησοῦς
If you were	**Εἰ** . . . ἦτε
blind	τυφλοὶ
you would not have	οὐκ **ἂν** εἴχετε
sin	**ἁμαρτίαν**
But now that you say	νῦν δὲ λέγετε ὅτι
We see	Βλέπομεν
your **sin**	ἡ **ἁμαρτία** ὑμῶν
remains	μένει

For by **works (ἔργων)** of the law no human being will be justified [lit., **all (πᾶσα)** flesh will not be justified] in his sight, since through the law comes knowledge of **sin (ἁμαρτίας)**. (ESV)

ἔργον	work, deed, action, labor	170x
ergon		S2041

πᾶς ➤ DAY 16   ἁμαρτία ➤ DAY 91

διότι ἐξ **ἔργων** νόμου οὐ δικαιωθήσεται **πᾶσα** σὰρξ ἐνώπιον αὐτοῦ, διὰ γὰρ νόμου ἐπίγνωσις **ἁμαρτίας**.

For	διότι
by **works** of the law	ἐξ **ἔργων** νόμου
no human being will be justified [lit., **all** flesh will not be justified]	οὐ δικαιωθήσεται **πᾶσα** σὰρξ
in his sight	ἐνώπιον αὐτοῦ
since through the law	διὰ γὰρ νόμου
comes knowledge of **sin**	ἐπίγνωσις **ἁμαρτίας**

Be alert and strengthen what remains, which is about to die, **for (γὰρ) I have** not **found (εὕρηκά)** your **works (ἔργα)** complete before my God. (CSB)

εὑρίσκω	to find	170x
heuriskō		S2147

γάρ ➤ DAY 18   **ἔργον** ➤ DAY 92

γίνου γρηγορῶν, καὶ στήρισον τὰ λοιπὰ ἃ ἔμελλον ἀποθανεῖν, οὐ **γὰρ εὕρηκά** σου **ἔργα** πεπληρωμένα ἐνώπιον τοῦ θεοῦ μου·

Be	γίνου
alert	γρηγορῶν
and strengthen	καὶ στήρισον
what remains	τὰ λοιπὰ
which is about	ἃ ἔμελλον
to die	ἀποθανεῖν
for I have not **found**	οὐ **γὰρ εὕρηκά**
your **works**	σου **ἔργα**
complete	πεπληρωμένα
before my God	ἐνώπιον τοῦ θεοῦ μου

And the **angel (ἄγγελος)** said to her, "Do not be afraid, Mary, for **you have found (εὗρες)** favor **with (παρὰ)** God." (ESV)

ἄγγελος	messenger, angel	169x
angelos		S32a

παρά ➤ DAY 81   **εὑρίσκω** ➤ DAY 93

καὶ εἶπεν ὁ **ἄγγελος** αὐτῇ Μὴ φοβοῦ, Μαριάμ, **εὗρες** γὰρ χάριν **παρὰ** τῷ θεῷ·

And the **angel** said to her	καὶ εἶπεν ὁ **ἄγγελος** αὐτῇ
Do not be afraid	Μὴ φοβοῦ
Mary	Μαριάμ
for **you have found**	**εὗρες** γὰρ
favor	χάριν
with God	**παρὰ** τῷ θεῷ

After these things I saw another **angel (ἄγγελον)** coming down from **heaven (οὐρανοῦ)**, having great authority, and the earth was illumined with his **glory (δόξης)**. (NASB)

δόξα	glory	166x
doxa		S1391

οὐρανός ➤ DAY 58   ἄγγελος ➤ DAY 94

Μετὰ ταῦτα εἶδον ἄλλον **ἄγγελον** καταβαίνοντα ἐκ τοῦ **οὐρανοῦ**, ἔχοντα ἐξουσίαν μεγάλην, καὶ ἡ γῆ ἐφωτίσθη ἐκ τῆς **δόξης** αὐτοῦ.

After these things	Μετὰ ταῦτα
I saw another **angel**	εἶδον ἄλλον **ἄγγελον**
coming down	καταβαίνοντα
from **heaven**	ἐκ τοῦ **οὐρανοῦ**
having	ἔχοντα
great authority	ἐξουσίαν μεγάλην
and the earth was illumined	καὶ ἡ γῆ ἐφωτίσθη
with his **glory**	ἐκ τῆς **δόξης** αὐτοῦ

The **city (πόλις)** has no need of the sun or of the moon to shine on **it (αὐτῇ)**, because God's **glory (δόξα)** illumines **it (αὐτήν)** and the Lamb is **its (αὐτῆς)** light. (MLB)

πόλις	city, city-state	164x
polis		S4172

αὐτός, αὐτή, αὐτό ➤ DAY 3	**δόξα** ➤ DAY 95

καὶ ἡ **πόλις** οὐ χρείαν ἔχει τοῦ ἡλίου οὐδὲ τῆς σελήνης, ἵνα φαίνωσιν **αὐτῇ**, ἡ γὰρ **δόξα** τοῦ θεοῦ ἐφώτισεν **αὐτήν**, καὶ ὁ λύχνος **αὐτῆς** τὸ ἀρνίον.

The **city**	καὶ ἡ **πόλις**
has no need	οὐ χρείαν ἔχει
of the sun	τοῦ ἡλίου
or of the moon	οὐδὲ τῆς σελήνης
to shine on **it**	ἵνα φαίνωσιν **αὐτῇ**
because God's **glory**	ἡ γὰρ **δόξα** τοῦ θεοῦ
illumines **it**	ἐφώτισεν **αὐτήν**
and the Lamb	καὶ . . . τὸ ἀρνίον
is **its** light	ὁ λύχνος **αὐτῆς**

Knowing their thoughts, he said to them, "Every **kingdom** (βασιλεία) divided **against (καθ᾽)** itself is laid waste, and no **city** (πόλις) or house divided **against (καθ᾽)** itself will stand." (ESV)

βασιλεία *basileia*	kingdom, kingship, rule	162x S932

κατά ➤ DAY 39   **πόλις** ➤ DAY 96

Εἰδὼς δὲ τὰς ἐνθυμήσεις αὐτῶν εἶπεν αὐτοῖς Πᾶσα **βασιλεία** μερισθεῖσα **καθ᾽** ἑαυτῆς ἐρημοῦται, καὶ πᾶσα **πόλις** ἢ οἰκία μερισθεῖσα **καθ᾽** ἑαυτῆς οὐ σταθήσεται.

Knowing	Εἰδὼς δὲ
their thoughts	τὰς ἐνθυμήσεις αὐτῶν
he said to them	εἶπεν αὐτοῖς
Every **kingdom**	Πᾶσα **βασιλεία**
divided **against** itself	μερισθεῖσα **καθ᾽** ἑαυτῆς
is laid waste	ἐρημοῦται
and no **city** or house . . . will stand	καὶ πᾶσα **πόλις** ἢ οἰκία . . . οὐ σταθήσεται
divided **against** itself	μερισθεῖσα **καθ᾽** ἑαυτῆς

I tell you, therefore, that the **kingdom (βασιλεία)** of God will be taken from you and **will be given (δοθήσεται)** to a **people (ἔθνει)** that produces its fruits. (MLB)

ἔθνος	people, nation, race; (pl) nations, gentiles	162x
ethnos		S1484

δίδωμι ➤ DAY 43　　　　**βασιλεία** ➤ DAY 97

διὰ τοῦτο λέγω ὑμῖν ὅτι ἀρθήσεται ἀφ᾽ ὑμῶν ἡ **βασιλεία** τοῦ θεοῦ καὶ **δοθήσεται ἔθνει** ποιοῦντι τοὺς καρποὺς αὐτῆς.

I tell you . . . that	λέγω ὑμῖν ὅτι
therefore	διὰ τοῦτο
the **kingdom** of God	ἡ **βασιλεία** τοῦ θεοῦ
will be taken from you	ἀρθήσεται ἀφ᾽ ὑμῶν
and **will be given**	καὶ **δοθήσεται**
to a **people**	**ἔθνει**
that produces	ποιοῦντι
its fruits	τοὺς καρποὺς αὐτῆς

Then (Τότε) He told them: "**Nation (ἔθνος)** will rise against **nation (ἔθνος)** and **kingdom (βασιλεία)** against **kingdom (βασιλείαν)**." (MLB)

τότε	then, at that time	161x
tote		S5119

βασιλεία ➤ DAY 97   **ἔθνος** ➤ DAY 98

Τότε ἔλεγεν αὐτοῖς Ἐγερθήσεται **ἔθνος** ἐπ' **ἔθνος** καὶ **βασιλεία** ἐπὶ **βασιλείαν**,

Then He told them	**Τότε** ἔλεγεν αὐτοῖς
Nation will rise	Ἐγερθήσεται **ἔθνος**
against **nation**	ἐπ' **ἔθνος**
and **kingdom**	καὶ **βασιλεία**
against **kingdom**	ἐπὶ **βασιλείαν**

that **you may eat (ἔσθητε)** and drink **at (ἐπὶ)** My table in My **kingdom (βασιλείᾳ)**, and you will be seated **on (ἐπὶ)** thrones judging the twelve tribes of Israel. (MLB)

| ἐσθίω | to eat | 158x |
| *esthiō* | | S2068 |

ἐπί ➤ DAY 21   **βασιλεία** ➤ DAY 97

ἵνα **ἔσθητε** καὶ πίνητε **ἐπὶ** τῆς τραπέζης μου ἐν τῇ **βασιλείᾳ** μου, καὶ καθῆσθε **ἐπὶ** θρόνων τὰς δώδεκα φυλὰς κρίνοντες τοῦ Ἰσραήλ.

that **you may eat**	ἵνα **ἔσθητε**
and drink	καὶ πίνητε
at My table	**ἐπὶ** τῆς τραπέζης μου
in My **kingdom**	ἐν τῇ **βασιλείᾳ** μου
and you will be seated	καὶ καθῆσθε
on thrones	**ἐπὶ** θρόνων
judging	κρίνοντες
the twelve tribes	τὰς δώδεκα φυλὰς
of Israel	τοῦ Ἰσραήλ

Agrippa said to **Paul (Παῦλον)**, "You have permission to speak for yourself." **Then (τότε) Paul (Παῦλος)** stretched out his **hand (χεῖρα)** and began to defend himself. (NRSV)

Παῦλος	Paul	158x
Paulos		S3972

χείρ ➤ DAY 88   **τότε** ➤ DAY 99

Ἀγρίππας δὲ πρὸς τὸν **Παῦλον** ἔφη Ἐπιτρέπεταί σοι ὑπὲρ σεαυτοῦ λέγειν. **τότε** ὁ **Παῦλος** ἐκτείνας τὴν **χεῖρα** ἀπελογεῖτο

Agrippa said to **Paul**	Ἀγρίππας δὲ πρὸς τὸν **Παῦλον** ἔφη
You have permission	Ἐπιτρέπεταί σοι
to speak for yourself	ὑπὲρ σεαυτοῦ λέγειν
Then Paul	**τότε** ὁ **Παῦλος**
stretched out his **hand**	ἐκτείνας τὴν **χεῖρα**
and began to defend himself	ἀπελογεῖτο

A woman named Lydia, a dealer in purple cloth from the city of Thyatira, who worshiped God, was listening. The Lord opened her **heart (καρδίαν)** to pay attention to **what was spoken (λαλουμένοις)** by **Paul (Παύλου)**. (HCSB)

καρδία	heart	156x
kardia		S2588

λαλέω ➤ DAY 57   **Παῦλος** ➤ DAY 101

καί τις γυνὴ ὀνόματι Λυδία, πορφυρόπωλις πόλεως Θυατείρων σεβομένη τὸν θεόν, ἤκουεν, ἧς ὁ κύριος διήνοιξεν τὴν **καρδίαν** προσέχειν τοῖς **λαλουμένοις** ὑπὸ **Παύλου**.

A woman named Lydia	καί τις γυνὴ ὀνόματι Λυδία
a dealer in purple cloth	πορφυρόπωλις
from the city of Thyatira	πόλεως Θυατείρων
who worshiped God	σεβομένη τὸν θεόν
was listening	ἤκουεν
The Lord opened her **heart**	ἧς ὁ κύριος διήνοιξεν τὴν **καρδίαν**
to pay attention	προσέχειν
to **what was spoken** by **Paul**	τοῖς **λαλουμένοις** ὑπὸ **Παύλου**

Now when they heard this, they were cut to the **heart (καρδίαν)** and said to **Peter (Πέτρον)** and to the other apostles, "Brothers [lit., **men (ἄνδρες)**, brothers], what should we do?" (NRSV)

Πέτρος	Peter	156x
Petros		S4074

ἀνήρ ➤ DAY 73   **καρδία** ➤ DAY 102

Ἀκούσαντες δὲ κατενύγησαν τὴν **καρδίαν**, εἶπάν τε πρὸς τὸν **Πέτρον** καὶ τοὺς λοιποὺς ἀποστόλους Τί ποιήσωμεν, **ἄνδρες** ἀδελφοί;

Now when they heard this	Ἀκούσαντες δὲ
they were cut to the **heart**	κατενύγησαν τὴν **καρδίαν**
and said to **Peter**	εἶπάν τε πρὸς τὸν **Πέτρον**
and to the other apostles	καὶ τοὺς λοιποὺς ἀποστόλους
Brothers [lit., **men**, brothers]	**ἄνδρες** ἀδελφοί;
what should we do?	Τί ποιήσωμεν

Meanwhile (δὲ), Simon **Peter (Πέτρος)** was following Jesus, as was **another (ἄλλος)** disciple. That disciple (ὁ **δὲ** μαθητὴς) was an acquaintance of the high priest; so he went with Jesus into the high priest's courtyard. (HCSB)

| ἄλλος | other, another, different | 154x |
| *allos* | | S243 |

δέ ➤ DAY 5   **Πέτρος** ➤ DAY 103

Ἠκολούθει **δὲ** τῷ Ἰησοῦ Σίμων **Πέτρος** καὶ **ἄλλος** μαθητής. ὁ **δὲ** μαθητὴς ἐκεῖνος ἦν γνωστὸς τῷ ἀρχιερεῖ, καὶ συνεισῆλθεν τῷ Ἰησοῦ εἰς τὴν αὐλὴν τοῦ ἀρχιερέως,

Meanwhile, Simon **Peter** was following Jesus	Ἠκολούθει **δὲ** τῷ Ἰησοῦ Σίμων **Πέτρος**
as was **another** disciple	καὶ **ἄλλος** μαθητής
That disciple	ὁ **δὲ** μαθητὴς ἐκεῖνος
was an acquaintance of the high priest	ἦν γνωστὸς τῷ ἀρχιερεῖ
so he went with Jesus	καὶ συνεισῆλθεν τῷ Ἰησοῦ
into the high priest's courtyard	εἰς τὴν αὐλὴν τοῦ ἀρχιερέως

The man **who had received (λαβὼν)** five talents **went
(πορευθεὶς)**, put them to work, and earned five **more (ἄλλα)**.
(CSB)

πορεύομαι	to go, depart, travel, journey	154x
poreuomai		S4198

λαμβάνω　➤　DAY 60　　　　**ἄλλος**　➤　DAY 104

πορευθεὶς ὁ τὰ πέντε τάλαντα **λαβὼν** ἠργάσατο ἐν αὐτοῖς καὶ
ἐκέρδησεν **ἄλλα** πέντε·

The man **who had received** five talents	ὁ τὰ πέντε τάλαντα **λαβὼν**
went	**πορευθεὶς**
put them to work	ἠργάσατο ἐν αὐτοῖς
and earned	καὶ ἐκέρδησεν
five **more**	**ἄλλα** πέντε

According to the **grace (χάριν)** of God **given (δοθεῖσάν)** to me, like a skilled master builder I laid a foundation, and **someone else (ἄλλος)** is building on it. Each builder must choose with care how to build on it. (NRSV)

χάρις	grace, favor	153x
charis		S5485

δίδωμι ➤ DAY 43   **ἄλλος** ➤ DAY 104

Κατὰ τὴν **χάριν** τοῦ θεοῦ τὴν **δοθεῖσάν** μοι ὡς σοφὸς ἀρχιτέκτων θεμέλιον ἔθηκα, **ἄλλος** δὲ ἐποικοδομεῖ. ἕκαστος δὲ βλεπέτω πῶς ἐποικοδομεῖ·

According to the **grace** of God	Κατὰ τὴν **χάριν** τοῦ θεοῦ
given to me	τὴν **δοθεῖσάν** μοι
like a skilled master builder	ὡς σοφὸς ἀρχιτέκτων
I laid a foundation	θεμέλιον ἔθηκα
and **someone else** is building on it	**ἄλλος** δὲ ἐποικοδομεῖ
Each builder must choose with care	ἕκαστος δὲ βλεπέτω
how to build on it	πῶς ἐποικοδομεῖ

When I partake with **gratitude (χάριτι)**, **why (τί)** should I be
denounced **on account of (ὑπὲρ)** that for which I give thanks?
(MLB)

ὑπέρ	for, for the sake of, on behalf of, about, over,	150x
huper	beyond, more	S5228

τίς, τί ➤ DAY 32   **χάρις** ➤ DAY 106

εἰ ἐγὼ **χάριτι** μετέχω, **τί** βλασφημοῦμαι **ὑπὲρ** οὗ ἐγὼ εὐχαριστῶ;

When I partake	εἰ ἐγὼ . . . μετέχω
with **gratitude**	χάριτι
why should I be denounced	τί βλασφημοῦμαι
on account of that for which	ὑπὲρ οὗ
I give thanks?	ἐγὼ εὐχαριστῶ;

I no longer live as I myself, but Christ lives within me; the life I
now (νῦν) live in the flesh I live by **faith (πίστει)** in the Son of
God, who loved me and gave Himself **for (ὑπὲρ)** me. (MLB)

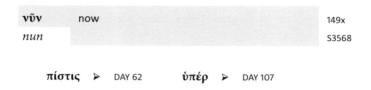

| νῦν | now | | 149x |
| *nun* | | | S3568 |

πίστις ➤ DAY 62   **ὑπέρ** ➤ DAY 107

ζῶ δὲ οὐκέτι ἐγώ, ζῇ δὲ ἐν ἐμοὶ Χριστός· ὃ δὲ **νῦν** ζῶ ἐν σαρκί,
ἐν **πίστει** ζῶ τῇ τοῦ υἱοῦ τοῦ θεοῦ τοῦ ἀγαπήσαντός με καὶ
παραδόντος ἑαυτὸν **ὑπὲρ** ἐμοῦ.

I no longer live as I myself	ζῶ δὲ οὐκέτι ἐγώ
but Christ lives within me	ζῇ δὲ ἐν ἐμοὶ Χριστός
the life I **now** live in the flesh	ὃ δὲ **νῦν** ζῶ ἐν σαρκί
I live by **faith** in the Son of God	ἐν **πίστει** ζῶ τῇ τοῦ υἱοῦ τοῦ θεοῦ
who loved me	τοῦ ἀγαπήσαντός με
and gave Himself **for** me	καὶ παραδόντος ἑαυτὸν **ὑπὲρ** ἐμοῦ

And **now (νῦν) I stand (ἕστηκα)** here on trial on account of my hope in the promise made by God to our **ancestors (πατέρας)**.

(NRSV)

ἵστημι	to stand, set up, make stand	148x
histēmi		S2476

πατήρ ➤ DAY 44　　　**νῦν** ➤ DAY 108

καὶ **νῦν** ἐπ᾽ ἐλπίδι τῆς εἰς τοὺς **πατέρας** ἡμῶν ἐπαγγελίας γενομένης ὑπὸ τοῦ θεοῦ **ἕστηκα** κρινόμενος,

And **now**	καὶ **νῦν**
I stand here on trial	**ἕστηκα** κρινόμενος
on account of my hope in the promise	ἐπ᾽ ἐλπίδι τῆς . . . ἐπαγγελίας
made by God	γενομένης ὑπὸ τοῦ θεοῦ
to our **ancestors**	εἰς τοὺς **πατέρας** ἡμῶν

Now (Νῦν) I rejoice in what I am suffering **for (ὑπὲρ)** you, and I fill up in my **flesh (σαρκί)** what is still lacking in regard to Christ's afflictions, **for the sake of (ὑπὲρ)** his body, which is the church. (NIV)

σάρξ	flesh, body	147x
sarx		S4561

ὑπέρ ➤ DAY 107   νῦν ➤ DAY 108

Νῦν χαίρω ἐν τοῖς παθήμασιν **ὑπὲρ** ὑμῶν, καὶ ἀνταναπληρῶ τὰ ὑστερήματα τῶν θλίψεων τοῦ χριστοῦ ἐν τῇ **σαρκί** μου **ὑπὲρ** τοῦ σώματος αὐτοῦ, ὅ ἐστιν ἡ ἐκκλησία,

Now I rejoice	**Νῦν** χαίρω
in what I am suffering **for** you	ἐν τοῖς παθήμασιν **ὑπὲρ** ὑμῶν
and I fill up in my **flesh**	καὶ ἀνταναπληρῶ . . . ἐν τῇ **σαρκί** μου
what is still lacking	τὰ ὑστερήματα
in regard to Christ's afflictions	τῶν θλίψεων τοῦ χριστοῦ
for the sake of his body	**ὑπὲρ** τοῦ σώματος αὐτοῦ
which is the church	ὅ ἐστιν ἡ ἐκκλησία

But I tell you truly, there are some **standing (ἑστηκότων)** here who will not taste death **until (ἕως) they see (ἴδωσιν)** the kingdom of God. (ESV)

ἕως	until, as far as, up to, as much as	146x
heōs		S2193

ὁράω ➤ DAY 40   **ἵστημι** ➤ DAY 109

Λέγω δὲ ὑμῖν ἀληθῶς, εἰσίν τινες τῶν αὐτοῦ **ἑστηκότων** οἳ οὐ μὴ γεύσωνται θανάτου **ἕως** ἂν **ἴδωσιν** τὴν βασιλείαν τοῦ θεοῦ.

But I tell you truly	Λέγω δὲ ὑμῖν ἀληθῶς
there are some **standing** here	εἰσίν τινες τῶν αὐτοῦ **ἑστηκότων**
who will not taste death	οἳ οὐ μὴ γεύσωνται θανάτου
until they see	**ἕως** ἂν **ἴδωσιν**
the kingdom of God	τὴν βασιλείαν τοῦ θεοῦ

Therefore **that (ἐκεῖνος)** field **has been called (ἐκλήθη)** the Field of Blood **to (ἕως)** this day. (ESV)

καλέω	to call, name, summon, invite	145x
kaleō		S2564

ἐκεῖνος ➤ DAY 64   ἕως ➤ DAY 111

διὸ **ἐκλήθη** ὁ ἀγρὸς **ἐκεῖνος** Ἀγρὸς Αἵματος **ἕως** τῆς σήμερον.

Therefore	διὸ
that field	ὁ ἀγρὸς **ἐκεῖνος**
has been called	**ἐκλήθη**
the Field of Blood	Ἀγρὸς Αἵματος
to this day	**ἕως** τῆς σήμερον

He stayed there **until (ἕως)** Herod's death, so that what was spoken by the Lord through the **prophet (προφήτου)** might be fulfilled: Out of Egypt **I called (ἐκάλεσα)** my Son. (CSB)

| προφήτης | prophet | 144x |
| *prophētēs* | | S4396 |

| ἕως | ➤ | DAY 111 | καλέω | ➤ | DAY 112 |

καὶ ἦν ἐκεῖ **ἕως** τῆς τελευτῆς Ἡρῴδου· ἵνα πληρωθῇ τὸ ῥηθὲν ὑπὸ Κυρίου διὰ τοῦ **προφήτου** λέγοντος Ἐξ Αἰγύπτου **ἐκάλεσα** τὸν υἱόν μου.

He stayed there	καὶ ἦν ἐκεῖ
until Herod's death	**ἕως** τῆς τελευτῆς Ἡρῴδου
so that what was spoken	ἵνα . . . τὸ ῥηθὲν . . . λέγοντος
by the Lord	ὑπὸ Κυρίου
through the **prophet**	διὰ τοῦ **προφήτου**
might be fulfilled	πληρωθῇ
Out of Egypt	Ἐξ Αἰγύπτου
I called my Son	**ἐκάλεσα** τὸν υἱόν μου

Now (νῦν) I ask you, lady, not as though **I were writing (γράφων)** to you a new commandment, but the one which we have had from the beginning, that **we love (ἀγαπῶμεν)** one another. (NASB)

ἀγαπάω	to love	143x
agapaō		S25

γράφω ➤ DAY 84   **νῦν** ➤ DAY 108

καὶ **νῦν** ἐρωτῶ σε, κυρία, οὐχ ὡς ἐντολὴν **γράφων** σοι καινὴν ἀλλὰ ἣν εἴχαμεν ἀπ᾽ ἀρχῆς, ἵνα **ἀγαπῶμεν** ἀλλήλους.

Now I ask you	καὶ **νῦν** ἐρωτῶ σε
lady	κυρία
not as though **I were writing** to you	οὐχ ὡς . . . **γράφων** σοι
a new commandment	ἐντολὴν . . . καινὴν
but the one which we have had	ἀλλὰ ἣν εἴχαμεν
from the beginning	ἀπ᾽ ἀρχῆς
that **we love** one another	ἵνα **ἀγαπῶμεν** ἀλλήλους

Therefore I tell you, her many **sins (ἁμαρτίαι) have been forgiven (ἀφέωνται)**; that's why **she loved (ἠγάπησεν)** much. But the one who **is forgiven (ἀφίεται)** little, **loves (ἀγαπᾷ)** little. (CSB)

ἀφίημι *aphiēmi*	to send away, let go, release, forgive, permit	143x S863

ἁμαρτία ➤ DAY 91   **ἀγαπάω** ➤ DAY 114

οὗ χάριν, λέγω σοι, **ἀφέωνται** αἱ **ἁμαρτίαι** αὐτῆς αἱ πολλαί, ὅτι **ἠγάπησεν** πολύ· ᾧ δὲ ὀλίγον **ἀφίεται**, ὀλίγον **ἀγαπᾷ**.

Therefore	οὗ χάριν
I tell you	λέγω σοι
her many **sins**	αἱ **ἁμαρτίαι** αὐτῆς αἱ πολλαί
have been forgiven	**ἀφέωνται**
that's why **she loved** much	ὅτι **ἠγάπησεν** πολύ
But the one who **is forgiven** little	ᾧ δὲ ὀλίγον **ἀφίεται**
loves little	ὀλίγον **ἀγαπᾷ**

Those from the **peoples (λαῶν)** and tribes and tongues and **nations (ἐθνῶν)** will look at their dead bodies for three and a half days, and **will** not **permit (ἀφίουσιν)** their dead bodies to be laid in a tomb. (NASB)

λαός	people, crowd	142x
laos		S2992

ἔθνος ➤ DAY 98   **ἀφίημι** ➤ DAY 115

καὶ βλέπουσιν ἐκ τῶν **λαῶν** καὶ φυλῶν καὶ γλωσσῶν καὶ **ἐθνῶν** τὸ πτῶμα αὐτῶν ἡμέρας τρεῖς καὶ ἥμισυ, καὶ τὰ πτώματα αὐτῶν οὐκ **ἀφίουσιν** τεθῆναι εἰς μνῆμα.

Those from the **peoples** and tribes and tongues and **nations**	καὶ . . . ἐκ τῶν **λαῶν** καὶ φυλῶν καὶ γλωσσῶν καὶ **ἐθνῶν**
will look at their dead bodies	βλέπουσιν . . . τὸ πτῶμα αὐτῶν
for three and a half days	ἡμέρας τρεῖς καὶ ἥμισυ
and **will** not **permit**	καὶ . . . οὐκ **ἀφίουσιν**
their dead bodies	τὰ πτώματα αὐτῶν
to be laid in a tomb	τεθῆναι εἰς μνῆμα

For (γὰρ) if you live according to the **flesh (σάρκα)**, you are going to die. But if by the Spirit you put to death the deeds of the **body (σώματος)**, you will live. (HCSB)

σῶμα	body	142x
sōma		S4983

γάρ ➤ DAY 18   σάρξ ➤ DAY 110

εἰ **γὰρ** κατὰ **σάρκα** ζῆτε μέλλετε ἀποθνήσκειν, εἰ δὲ πνεύματι τὰς πράξεις τοῦ **σώματος** θανατοῦτε ζήσεσθε.

For if you live	εἰ **γὰρ** . . . ζῆτε
according to the **flesh**	κατὰ **σάρκα**
you are going to die	μέλλετε ἀποθνήσκειν
But if by the Spirit	εἰ δὲ πνεύματι
you put to death	θανατοῦτε
the deeds of the **body**	τὰς πράξεις τοῦ **σώματος**
you will live	ζήσεσθε

But **someone (τις)** will ask, "How **are** the dead **raised (ἐγείρονται)**? With what kind of **body (σώματι)** will they come?" (NIV)

ἐγείρω	to wake, arouse, rise, raise up	141x
egeirō		S1453

τὶς, τὶ ➤ DAY 35   **σῶμα** ➤ DAY 117

Ἀλλὰ ἐρεῖ **τις** Πῶς **ἐγείρονται** οἱ νεκροί, ποίῳ δὲ **σώματι** ἔρχονται;

But **someone** will ask	Ἀλλὰ ἐρεῖ **τις**
How **are** the dead **raised**?	Πῶς **ἐγείρονται** οἱ νεκροί
With what kind of **body**	ποίῳ δὲ **σώματι**
will they come?	ἔρχονται;

But **if (εἰ)** there is no resurrection of the dead, **not even (οὐδὲ)** Christ **has been raised (ἐγήγερται).** (NASB)

οὐδέ	not even, nor, neither	141x
oude		S3761

εἰ ➤ DAY 37   ἐγείρω ➤ DAY 118

εἰ δὲ ἀνάστασις νεκρῶν οὐκ ἔστιν, **οὐδὲ** Χριστὸς **ἐγήγερται·**

But **if**	**εἰ** δὲ
there is no	οὐκ ἔστιν
resurrection of the dead	ἀνάστασις νεκρῶν
not even Christ	**οὐδὲ** Χριστὸς
has been raised	**ἐγήγερται**

For there is no good tree **which produces (ποιοῦν)** bad fruit, **nor (οὐδὲ), on the other hand (πάλιν)**, a bad tree **which produces (ποιοῦν)** good fruit. (NASB)

πάλιν	again	141x
palin		S3825

ποιέω ➤ DAY 31   **οὐδέ** ➤ DAY 119

Οὐ γὰρ ἔστιν δένδρον καλὸν **ποιοῦν** καρπὸν σαπρόν, **οὐδὲ πάλιν** δένδρον σαπρὸν **ποιοῦν** καρπὸν καλόν.

For there is no good tree	Οὐ γὰρ ἔστιν δένδρον καλὸν
which produces bad fruit	**ποιοῦν** καρπὸν σαπρόν
nor, **on the other hand**	**οὐδὲ πάλιν**
a bad tree	δένδρον σαπρὸν
which produces good fruit	**ποιοῦν** καρπὸν καλόν

Now if I **live on (ζῆν)** in the **flesh (σαρκί)**, this means fruitful
work (ἔργου) for me; and I don't know which one I should
choose. (CSB)

ζάω	to live	140x
zaō		S2198

ἔργον ➤ DAY 92   **σάρξ** ➤ DAY 110

εἰ δὲ τὸ **ζῆν** ἐν **σαρκί**, τοῦτό μοι καρπὸς **ἔργου**,—καὶ τί αἱρήσομαι
οὐ γνωρίζω·

Now if I **live on**	εἰ δὲ τὸ **ζῆν**
in the **flesh**	ἐν **σαρκί**
this means . . . for me	τοῦτό μοι
fruitful **work**	καρπὸς **ἔργου**
and I don't know	καὶ . . . οὐ γνωρίζω
which one I should choose	τί αἱρήσομαι

Yet today, tomorrow, and the next day I must **be on my way** (**πορεύεσθαι**), because it is impossible for a **prophet** (**προφήτην**) to be killed outside of **Jerusalem** (Ἰερουσαλήμ). (NRSV)

Ἰερουσαλήμ / Ἰεροσόλυμα	Jerusalem	139x
Ierousalēm / *Hierosoluma*		S2419 + S2414

πορεύομαι ➤ DAY 105	**προφήτης** ➤ DAY 113

πλὴν δεῖ με σήμερον καὶ αὔριον καὶ τῇ ἐχομένῃ **πορεύεσθαι**, ὅτι οὐκ ἐνδέχεται **προφήτην** ἀπολέσθαι ἔξω Ἰερουσαλήμ.

Yet . . . I must **be on my way**	πλὴν δεῖ με . . . **πορεύεσθαι**
today	σήμερον
tomorrow	καὶ αὔριον
and the next day	καὶ τῇ ἐχομένῃ
because it is impossible for a **prophet**	ὅτι οὐκ ἐνδέχεται **προφήτην**
to be killed	ἀπολέσθαι
outside of **Jerusalem**	ἔξω Ἰερουσαλήμ

Truly, truly, I say to you, an hour **is coming (ἔρχεται)** and now is, when the dead will hear the **voice (φωνῆς)** of the Son of God, and those who hear **will live (ζήσουσιν)**. (NASB)

φωνή	voice, sound	139x
phōnē		S5456

ἔρχομαι ➤ DAY 30   **ζάω** ➤ DAY 121

ἀμὴν ἀμὴν λέγω ὑμῖν ὅτι **ἔρχεται** ὥρα καὶ νῦν ἐστιν ὅτε οἱ νεκροὶ ἀκούσουσιν τῆς **φωνῆς** τοῦ υἱοῦ τοῦ θεοῦ καὶ οἱ ἀκούσαντες **ζήσουσιν**.

Truly, truly	ἀμὴν ἀμὴν
I say to you	λέγω ὑμῖν ὅτι
an hour **is coming**	**ἔρχεται** ὥρα
and now is	καὶ νῦν ἐστιν
when the dead	ὅτε οἱ νεκροὶ
will hear	ἀκούσουσιν
the **voice** of the Son of God	τῆς **φωνῆς** τοῦ υἱοῦ τοῦ θεοῦ
and those who hear	καὶ οἱ ἀκούσαντες
will live	**ζήσουσιν**

But when they realized he was a Jew, they all shouted in unison [lit., there was one **voice (φωνὴ)** from all of them . . . shouting] for about **two (δύο)** hours: "**Great (Μεγάλη)** is Artemis of the Ephesians!" (NIV)

δύο	two	137x
duo		S1417

     μέγας ➤ DAY 63   **φωνή** ➤ DAY 123

ἐπιγνόντες δὲ ὅτι Ἰουδαῖός ἐστιν **φωνὴ** ἐγένετο μία ἐκ πάντων ὡσεὶ ἐπὶ ὥρας **δύο** κραζόντων **Μεγάλη** ἡ Ἄρτεμις Ἐφεσίων.

But when they realized	ἐπιγνόντες δὲ ὅτι
he was a Jew	Ἰουδαῖός ἐστιν
they all shouted in unison [lit., there was one **voice** from all of them . . . shouting]	**φωνὴ** ἐγένετο μία ἐκ πάντων . . . κραζόντων
for about **two** hours	ὡσεὶ ἐπὶ ὥρας **δύο**
Great is	**Μεγάλη**
Artemis of the Ephesians!	ἡ Ἄρτεμις Ἐφεσίων

And if your eye causes you to stumble, tear it out and throw it away; it is better for you to enter **life (ζωὴν)** with one eye **than (ἤ)** to have **two (δύο)** eyes and to be thrown into the hell of fire. (NRSV)

| **ζωή** | life | | 135x |
| *zōē* | | | S2222 |

| **ἤ** ➤ DAY 50 | **δύο** ➤ DAY 124 |

καὶ εἰ ὁ ὀφθαλμός σου σκανδαλίζει σε, ἔξελε αὐτὸν καὶ βάλε ἀπὸ σοῦ· καλόν σοί ἐστιν μονόφθαλμον εἰς τὴν **ζωὴν** εἰσελθεῖν, **ἤ δύο** ὀφθαλμοὺς ἔχοντα βληθῆναι εἰς τὴν γέενναν τοῦ πυρός.

And if your eye	καὶ εἰ ὁ ὀφθαλμός σου
causes you to stumble	σκανδαλίζει σε
tear it out	ἔξελε αὐτὸν
and throw it away	καὶ βάλε ἀπὸ σοῦ
it is better for you	καλόν σοί ἐστιν
to enter **life**	εἰς τὴν **ζωὴν** εἰσελθεῖν
with one eye	μονόφθαλμον
than to have **two** eyes	**ἤ δύο** ὀφθαλμοὺς ἔχοντα
and to be thrown into the hell of fire	βληθῆναι εἰς τὴν γέενναν τοῦ πυρός

The next day **again (πάλιν) John (Ἰωάνης)** was standing with **two (δύο)** of his disciples. (ESV)

Ἰωάννης	John	134x
Iōannēs		S2491

πάλιν ➤ DAY 120 **δύο** ➤ DAY 124

Τῇ ἐπαύριον **πάλιν** ἱστήκει Ἰωάνης καὶ ἐκ τῶν μαθητῶν αὐτοῦ **δύο**,

The next day	Τῇ ἐπαύριον
again	**πάλιν**
John was standing	ἱστήκει Ἰωάνης
with **two** of his disciples	καὶ ἐκ τῶν μαθητῶν αὐτοῦ **δύο**

And **whoever (ὅστις)** forces you to go **one (ἕν)** mile, go **with (μετ')** him two miles. (MLB)

ὅστις, ἥτις, ὅ τι	who, which	134x
*hos*tis, *hē*tis, *ho* ti		S3748

μετά ➤ DAY 41   **εἷς, μία, ἕν** ➤ DAY 49

καὶ **ὅστις** σε ἀγγαρεύσει μίλιον **ἕν**, ὕπαγε **μετ'** αὐτοῦ δύο.

And **whoever**	καὶ **ὅστις**
forces you to go	σε ἀγγαρεύσει
one mile	μίλιον **ἕν**
go **with** him	ὕπαγε **μετ'** αὐτοῦ
two miles	δύο

I turned around **to see (βλέπειν)** the **voice (φωνὴν) that (ἥτις)** was speaking to me. And when I turned I saw seven golden lampstands. (NIV)

βλέπω	to look, see	133x
blepō		S991

φωνή ➢ DAY 123   ὅστις, ἥτις, ὅ τι ➢ DAY 127

Καὶ ἐπέστρεψα **βλέπειν** τὴν **φωνὴν ἥτις** ἐλάλει μετ᾽ ἐμοῦ· καὶ ἐπιστρέψας εἶδον ἑπτὰ λυχνίας χρυσᾶς,

I turned around	Καὶ ἐπέστρεψα
to see the **voice**	**βλέπειν** τὴν **φωνὴν**
that was speaking	**ἥτις** ἐλάλει
to me	μετ᾽ ἐμοῦ
And when I turned	καὶ ἐπιστρέψας
I saw	εἶδον
seven golden lampstands	ἑπτὰ λυχνίας χρυσᾶς

Now Herod the tetrarch heard about all that was happening, and he was perplexed, because it was said by some that **John (Ἰωάνης) had been raised (ἠγέρθη)** from the **dead (νεκρῶν)**.

(ESV)

| **νεκρός** | dead | 130x |
| *nekros* | | S3498 |

ἐγείρω ➤ DAY 118   **Ἰωάννης** ➤ DAY 126

Ἤκουσεν δὲ Ἡρῴδης ὁ τετραάρχης τὰ γινόμενα πάντα, καὶ διηπόρει διὰ τὸ λέγεσθαι ὑπὸ τινῶν ὅτι **Ἰωάνης ἠγέρθη** ἐκ **νεκρῶν**,

Now Herod the tetrarch heard about	Ἤκουσεν δὲ Ἡρῴδης ὁ τετραάρχης
all that was happening	τὰ γινόμενα πάντα
and he was perplexed	καὶ διηπόρει
because it was said by some that	διὰ τὸ λέγεσθαι ὑπὸ τινῶν ὅτι
John had been raised	**Ἰωάνης ἠγέρθη**
from the **dead**	ἐκ **νεκρῶν**

And when you were **dead (νεκροὺς)** in trespasses and the uncircumcision of your **flesh (σαρκὸς)**, God [lit., he] made you alive together **with (σὺν)** him, when he forgave us all our trespasses. (NRSV)

σύν	with, plus, including	128x
sun		S4862

σάρξ ➢ DAY 110　　　　**νεκρός** ➢ DAY 129

καὶ ὑμᾶς **νεκροὺς** ὄντας τοῖς παραπτώμασιν καὶ τῇ ἀκροβυστίᾳ τῆς **σαρκὸς** ὑμῶν, συνεζωοποίησεν ὑμᾶς **σὺν** αὐτῷ· χαρισάμενος ἡμῖν πάντα τὰ παραπτώματα,

And when you were **dead**	καὶ ὑμᾶς **νεκροὺς** ὄντας
in trespasses	τοῖς παραπτώμασιν
and the uncircumcision	καὶ τῇ ἀκροβυστίᾳ
of your **flesh**	τῆς **σαρκὸς** ὑμῶν
God [lit., he] made you alive together **with** him	συνεζωοποίησεν ὑμᾶς **σὺν** αὐτῷ
when he forgave us	χαρισάμενος ἡμῖν
all our trespasses	πάντα τὰ παραπτώματα

Now (ἀλλὰ) get up, go down, and go **with (σὺν)** them without hesitation; for I **have sent (ἀπέσταλκα)** them. (NRSV)

ἀποστέλλω	to send away, send out	127x
apostellō		S649

ἀλλά ➤ DAY 29　　　σύν ➤ DAY 130

ἀλλὰ ἀναστὰς κατάβηθι καὶ πορεύου **σὺν** αὐτοῖς μηδὲν διακρινόμενος, ὅτι ἐγὼ **ἀπέσταλκα** αὐτούς.

Now get up	**ἀλλὰ** ἀναστὰς
go down	κατάβηθι
and go	καὶ πορεύου
with them	**σὺν** αὐτοῖς
without hesitation	μηδὲν διακρινόμενος
for I **have sent** them	ὅτι ἐγὼ **ἀπέσταλκα** αὐτούς

And He said to them, "**Do you** not **see (βλέπετε)** all these things? **Truly (ἀμὴν)** I say to you, not one stone here **will be left (ἀφεθῇ)** upon another, which will not be torn down." (NASB)

ἀμήν	truly, so let it be	126x
amēn		S281

ἀφίημι ➤ DAY 115   **βλέπω** ➤ DAY 128

ὁ δὲ ἀποκριθεὶς εἶπεν αὐτοῖς Οὐ **βλέπετε** ταῦτα πάντα; **ἀμὴν** λέγω ὑμῖν, οὐ μὴ **ἀφεθῇ** ὧδε λίθος ἐπὶ λίθον ὃς οὐ καταλυθήσεται.

And He said to them	ὁ δὲ ἀποκριθεὶς εἶπεν αὐτοῖς
Do you not **see**	Οὐ **βλέπετε**
all these things?	ταῦτα πάντα;
Truly I say to you	**ἀμὴν** λέγω ὑμῖν
not one stone here **will be left** upon another	οὐ μὴ **ἀφεθῇ** ὧδε λίθος ἐπὶ λίθον
which will not be torn down	ὃς οὐ καταλυθήσεται

Then (οὖν) Annas **sent (Ἀπέστειλεν)** him bound to Caiaphas the **high priest (ἀρχιερέα).** (NIV)

ἀρχιερεύς	high priest, chief priest	123x
archie**reus**		S749

οὖν ➤ DAY 38   **ἀποστέλλω** ➤ DAY 131

Ἀπέστειλεν **οὖν** αὐτὸν ὁ Ἄννας δεδεμένον πρὸς Καιάφαν τὸν ἀρχιερέα.

Then	**οὖν**
Annas **sent** him	**Ἀπέστειλεν** . . . αὐτὸν ὁ Ἄννας
bound	δεδεμένον
to Caiaphas	πρὸς Καιάφαν
the **high priest**	τὸν **ἀρχιερέα**

The **chief priests (ἀρχιερεῖς) picked up (λαβόντες)** the money and said, "It is not right **to put (βαλεῖν)** this in the treasury, since it is blood money." (MLB)

βάλλω	to throw, cast, put, place	123x
ballō		S906

λαμβάνω ➤ DAY 60   **ἀρχιερεύς** ➤ DAY 133

Οἱ δὲ **ἀρχιερεῖς λαβόντες** τὰ ἀργύρια εἶπαν Οὐκ ἔξεστιν **βαλεῖν** αὐτὰ εἰς τὸν κορβανᾶν, ἐπεὶ τιμὴ αἵματός ἐστιν·

The **chief priests**	Οἱ δὲ **ἀρχιερεῖς**
picked up the money	**λαβόντες** τὰ ἀργύρια
and said	εἶπαν
It is not right	Οὐκ ἔξεστιν
to put this	**βαλεῖν** αὐτὰ
in the treasury	εἰς τὸν κορβανᾶν
since it is	ἐπεὶ . . . ἐστιν
blood money	τιμὴ αἵματός

The sick man answered him, "Sir, I have no **one (ἄνθρωπον)** to **put (βάλῃ)** me into the pool **when (ὅταν)** the water is stirred up; and while I am making my way, someone else steps down ahead of me." (NRSV)

ὅταν	whenever, as often as	122x
hotan		S3752

ἄνθρωπος ➤ DAY 33   **βάλλω** ➤ DAY 134

ἀπεκρίθη αὐτῷ ὁ ἀσθενῶν Κύριε, **ἄνθρωπον** οὐκ ἔχω ἵνα **ὅταν** ταραχθῇ τὸ ὕδωρ **βάλῃ** με εἰς τὴν κολυμβήθραν· ἐν ᾧ δὲ ἔρχομαι ἐγὼ ἄλλος πρὸ ἐμοῦ καταβαίνει.

The sick man answered him	ἀπεκρίθη αὐτῷ ὁ ἀσθενῶν
Sir	Κύριε
I have no **one**	**ἄνθρωπον** οὐκ ἔχω
to **put** me	ἵνα . . . **βάλῃ** με
into the pool	εἰς τὴν κολυμβήθραν
when the water is stirred up	**ὅταν** ταραχθῇ τὸ ὕδωρ
and while I am making my way	ἐν ᾧ δὲ ἔρχομαι ἐγὼ
someone else steps down	ἄλλος . . . καταβαίνει
ahead of me	πρὸ ἐμοῦ

And **when (ὅταν)** the living creatures give glory and honor and thanks to Him who sits on the throne, to Him **who lives (ζῶντι)** forever and ever [lit., for the **ages (αἰῶνας)** of **ages (αἰώνων)**], . . .
(NASB)

αἰών	age, eternity	121x
aiōn		S165

ζάω ➤ DAY 121   ὅταν ➤ DAY 135

Καὶ **ὅταν** δώσουσιν τὰ ζῷα δόξαν καὶ τιμὴν καὶ εὐχαριστίαν τῷ καθημένῳ ἐπὶ τοῦ θρόνου, τῷ **ζῶντι** εἰς τοὺς **αἰῶνας** τῶν **αἰώνων**,

And **when** the living creatures	Καὶ **ὅταν** . . . τὰ ζῷα
give	δώσουσιν
glory and honor	δόξαν καὶ τιμὴν
and thanks	καὶ εὐχαριστίαν
to Him who sits	τῷ καθημένῳ
on the throne	ἐπὶ τοῦ θρόνου
to Him **who lives**	τῷ **ζῶντι**
forever and ever [lit., for the **ages** of **ages**]	εἰς τοὺς **αἰῶνας** τῶν **αἰώνων**

So (οὕτως) you also, **when (ὅταν)** you have done all that you were ordered to do, say, 'We are worthless **slaves (Δοῦλοι)**; we have done only what we ought to have done!'" (NRSV)

δοῦλος	slave, servant	121x
doulos		S1401

οὕτως ➤ DAY 77   **ὅταν** ➤ DAY 135

οὕτως καὶ ὑμεῖς, **ὅταν** ποιήσητε πάντα τὰ διαταχθέντα ὑμῖν, λέγετε ὅτι **Δοῦλοι** ἀχρεῖοί ἐσμεν, ὃ ὠφείλομεν ποιῆσαι πεποιήκαμεν.

So you also	**οὕτως** καὶ ὑμεῖς
when you have done all	**ὅταν** ποιήσητε πάντα
that you were ordered to do	τὰ διαταχθέντα ὑμῖν
say	λέγετε ὅτι
We are	ἐσμεν
worthless **slaves**	**Δοῦλοι** ἀχρεῖοί
we have done	πεποιήκαμεν
only what we ought	ὃ ὠφείλομεν
to have done!	ποιῆσαι

Do you not **know (οἴδατε)** that if you present yourselves to anyone as obedient **slaves (δούλους)**, you are **slaves (δοῦλοί)** of the one whom you obey, either of sin, which leads to **death (θάνατον)**, or of obedience, which leads to righteousness? (ESV)

θάνατος	death	120x
thanatos		S2288

οἶδα ➤ DAY 56   **δοῦλος** ➤ DAY 137

οὐκ **οἴδατε** ὅτι ᾧ παριστάνετε ἑαυτοὺς **δούλους** εἰς ὑπακοήν, **δοῦλοί** ἐστε ᾧ ὑπακούετε, ἤτοι ἁμαρτίας εἰς **θάνατον** ἢ ὑπακοῆς εἰς δικαιοσύνην;

Do you not **know** that	οὐκ **οἴδατε** ὅτι
if you present yourselves to anyone	ᾧ παριστάνετε ἑαυτοὺς
as obedient **slaves**	**δούλους** εἰς ὑπακοήν
you are **slaves**	**δοῦλοί** ἐστε
of the one whom you obey	ᾧ ὑπακούετε
either of sin	ἤτοι ἁμαρτίας
which leads to **death**	εἰς **θάνατον**
or of obedience	ἢ ὑπακοῆς
which leads to righteousness?	εἰς δικαιοσύνην;

The **slave (δοῦλος) does** not **remain (μένει)** in the house **forever** (εἰς τὸν **αἰῶνα**); the son **remains (μένει) forever** (εἰς τὸν **αἰῶνα**).
(ESV)

| **μένω** | to stay, remain, wait (for), abide | 118x |
| *menō* | | S3306 |

αἰών ➤ DAY 136   **δοῦλος** ➤ DAY 137

ὁ δὲ **δοῦλος** οὐ **μένει** ἐν τῇ οἰκίᾳ εἰς τὸν **αἰῶνα**· ὁ υἱὸς **μένει** εἰς τὸν **αἰῶνα**.

The **slave**	ὁ δὲ **δοῦλος**
does not **remain**	οὐ **μένει**
in the house	ἐν τῇ οἰκίᾳ
forever	εἰς τὸν **αἰῶνα**
the son	ὁ υἱὸς
remains	**μένει**
forever	εἰς τὸν **αἰῶνα**

and how the **chief priests (ἀρχιερεῖς)** and our rulers **delivered (παρέδωκαν)** Him to the sentence of **death (θανάτου)**, and crucified Him. (NASB)

παραδίδωμι	to deliver, hand over, betray	118x
paradidōmi		S3860

ἀρχιερεύς ➤ DAY 133   **θάνατος** ➤ DAY 138

ὅπως τε **παρέδωκαν** αὐτὸν οἱ **ἀρχιερεῖς** καὶ οἱ ἄρχοντες ἡμῶν εἰς κρίμα **θανάτου** καὶ ἐσταύρωσαν αὐτόν.

and how	ὅπως τε
the **chief priests**	οἱ **ἀρχιερεῖς**
and our rulers	καὶ οἱ ἄρχοντες ἡμῶν
delivered Him	**παρέδωκαν** αὐτὸν
to the sentence of **death**	εἰς κρίμα **θανάτου**
and crucified Him	καὶ ἐσταύρωσαν αὐτόν

And you, Capernaum, will you be exalted to heaven? You will go down to Hades. For if the **miracles (δυνάμεις)** that **were done (γενόμεναι)** in you **had been done (ἐγενήθησαν)** in Sodom, **it would have remained (ἔμεινεν)** until today. (HCSB)

δύναμις	power, force, might	117x
dunamis		S1411

γίνομαι ➤ DAY 27   **μένω** ➤ DAY 139

Καὶ σύ, Καφαρναούμ, μὴ ἕως οὐρανοῦ ὑψωθήσῃ; ἕως ᾅδου καταβήσῃ. ὅτι εἰ ἐν Σοδόμοις **ἐγενήθησαν** αἱ **δυνάμεις** αἱ **γενόμεναι** ἐν σοί, **ἔμεινεν** ἂν μέχρι τῆς σήμερον.

And you, Capernaum	Καὶ σύ, Καφαρναούμ
will you be exalted to heaven?	μὴ ἕως οὐρανοῦ ὑψωθήσῃ;
You will go down to Hades	ἕως ᾅδου καταβήσῃ
For if the **miracles**	ὅτι εἰ . . . αἱ **δυνάμεις**
that **were done** in you	αἱ **γενόμεναι** ἐν σοί
had been done in Sodom	ἐν Σοδόμοις **ἐγενήθησαν**
it would have remained	**ἔμεινεν** ἂν
until today	μέχρι τῆς σήμερον

But when **they hand** you **over (παραδῶσιν)**, don't worry about **how (πῶς)** or what **you should speak (λαλήσητε)**. For you will be given what **to say (λαλήσητε)** at that hour. (HCSB)

πῶς	how?		117x
pōs			S4459

λαλέω ➤ DAY 57   **παραδίδωμι** ➤ DAY 140

ὅταν δὲ **παραδῶσιν** ὑμᾶς, μὴ μεριμνήσητε **πῶς** ἢ τί **λαλήσητε**· δοθήσεται γὰρ ὑμῖν ἐν ἐκείνῃ τῇ ὥρᾳ τί **λαλήσητε**·

But when	ὅταν δὲ
they hand you **over**	**παραδῶσιν** ὑμᾶς
don't worry about	μὴ μεριμνήσητε
how or what	**πῶς** ἢ τί
you should speak	**λαλήσητε**
For you will be given	δοθήσεται γὰρ ὑμῖν
what **to say**	τί **λαλήσητε**
at that hour	ἐν ἐκείνῃ τῇ ὥρᾳ

And **he went off (ἀπελθὼν)** to confer with the chief priests and
officers **how (πῶς) he might deliver (παραδῷ)** Him to them.

(MLB)

ἀπέρχομαι	to go away from	116x
aperchomai		S565

παραδίδωμι ➢ DAY 140   **πῶς** ➢ DAY 142

καὶ **ἀπελθὼν** συνελάλησεν τοῖς ἀρχιερεῦσιν καὶ στρατηγοῖς τὸ
πῶς αὐτοῖς **παραδῷ** αὐτόν.

And **he went off**	καὶ **ἀπελθὼν**
to confer	συνελάλησεν
with the chief priests	τοῖς ἀρχιερεῦσιν
and officers	καὶ στρατηγοῖς
how	τὸ **πῶς**
he might deliver Him	**παραδῷ** αὐτόν
to them	αὐτοῖς

Immediately the **king (βασιλεὺς) sent (ἀποστείλας)** an executioner and commanded him to bring back his head. And **he went (ἀπελθὼν)** and had him beheaded in the prison. (NASB)

βασιλεύς	king, emperor	115x
basileus		S935

    ἀποστέλλω ➤ DAY 131   **ἀπέρχομαι** ➤ DAY 143

καὶ εὐθὺς **ἀποστείλας** ὁ **βασιλεὺς** σπεκουλάτορα ἐπέταξεν ἐνέγκαι τὴν κεφαλὴν αὐτοῦ. καὶ **ἀπελθὼν** ἀπεκεφάλισεν αὐτὸν ἐν τῇ φυλακῇ

Immediately	καὶ εὐθὺς
the **king sent**	**ἀποστείλας** ὁ **βασιλεὺς**
an executioner	σπεκουλάτορα
and commanded him	ἐπέταξεν
to bring back	ἐνέγκαι
his head	τὴν κεφαλὴν αὐτοῦ
And **he went**	καὶ **ἀπελθὼν**
and had him beheaded	ἀπεκεφάλισεν αὐτὸν
in the prison	ἐν τῇ φυλακῇ

For God has not given us a **spirit (πνεῦμα)** of cowardice, but of **power (δυνάμεως)** and **love (ἀγάπης)** and self-control. (MLB)

ἀγάπη	love, charity	114x
agapē		S26

πνεῦμα ➤ DAY 47   **δύναμις** ➤ DAY 141

οὐ γὰρ ἔδωκεν ἡμῖν ὁ θεὸς **πνεῦμα** δειλίας, ἀλλὰ **δυνάμεως** καὶ **ἀγάπης** καὶ σωφρονισμοῦ.

For God has not given us	οὐ γὰρ ἔδωκεν ἡμῖν ὁ θεὸς
a **spirit** of cowardice	**πνεῦμα** δειλίας
but of **power**	ἀλλὰ **δυνάμεως**
and **love**	καὶ **ἀγάπης**
and self-control	καὶ σωφρονισμοῦ

They have testified to your **love (ἀγάπη)** before the **church (ἐκκλησίας)**. **You will do (ποιήσεις)** well to send them on in a manner worthy of God. (NRSV)

ἐκκλησία	assembly, congregation, church	114x
ekklēsia		S1577

ποιέω · ➤ DAY 31   **ἀγάπη** ➤ DAY 145

οἳ ἐμαρτύρησάν σου τῇ **ἀγάπῃ** ἐνώπιον **ἐκκλησίας**, οὓς καλῶς **ποιήσεις** προπέμψας ἀξίως τοῦ θεοῦ·

They have testified	οἳ ἐμαρτύρησάν
to your **love**	σου τῇ **ἀγάπῃ**
before the **church**	ἐνώπιον **ἐκκλησίας**
You will do well	καλῶς **ποιήσεις**
to send them on	οὓς . . . προπέμψας
in a manner worthy	ἀξίως
of God	τοῦ θεοῦ

For if someone **does** not **know (οἶδεν)** how to manage his own **household (οἴκου)**, how can he take care of God's **church (ἐκκλησίας)**? (NRSV)

οἶκος	house, household, family	113x
oikos		S3624

οἶδα ➤ DAY 56   ἐκκλησία ➤ DAY 146

εἰ δέ τις τοῦ ἰδίου **οἴκου** προστῆναι οὐκ **οἶδεν**, πῶς **ἐκκλησίας** θεοῦ ἐπιμελήσεται;

For if someone	εἰ δέ τις
does not **know**	οὐκ **οἶδεν**
how to manage	προστῆναι
his own **household**	τοῦ ἰδίου **οἴκου**
how	πῶς
can he take care of	ἐπιμελήσεται;
God's **church**?	**ἐκκλησίας** θεοῦ

But **God (θεὸς)** demonstrates his own **love (ἀγάπην)** for us in this: While we were still sinners, Christ **died (ἀπέθανεν)** for us. (NIV)

ἀποθνῄσκω	to die	112x
apothnēskō		S599

θεός ➤ DAY 14   **ἀγάπη** ➤ DAY 145

συνίστησιν δὲ τὴν ἑαυτοῦ **ἀγάπην** εἰς ἡμᾶς ὁ **θεὸς** ὅτι ἔτι ἁμαρτωλῶν ὄντων ἡμῶν Χριστὸς ὑπὲρ ἡμῶν **ἀπέθανεν**.

But **God** demonstrates	συνίστησιν δὲ . . . ὁ **θεὸς**
his own **love**	τὴν ἑαυτοῦ **ἀγάπην**
for us	εἰς ἡμᾶς
in this	ὅτι
While we were still	ἔτι . . . ὄντων ἡμῶν
sinners	ἁμαρτωλῶν
Christ **died**	Χριστὸς . . . **ἀπέθανεν**
for us	ὑπὲρ ἡμῶν

For the **love (ἀγάπη)** of Christ urges us on, because we are
convinced [lit., **being convinced (κρίναντας)** of this] that one
has died (ἀπέθανεν) for all; therefore all **have died (ἀπέθανον)**.

(NRSV)

κρίνω	to judge, decide	112x
krinō		S2919

ἀγάπη ➤ DAY 145   **ἀποθνῄσκω** ➤ DAY 148

ἡ γὰρ **ἀγάπη** τοῦ χριστοῦ συνέχει ἡμᾶς, **κρίναντας** τοῦτο ὅτι εἷς
ὑπὲρ πάντων **ἀπέθανεν**· ἄρα οἱ πάντες **ἀπέθανον**·

For the **love** of Christ	ἡ γὰρ **ἀγάπη** τοῦ χριστοῦ
urges us on	συνέχει ἡμᾶς
because we are convinced [lit., **being convinced** of this]	**κρίναντας** τοῦτο
that one	ὅτι εἷς
has died	**ἀπέθανεν**
for all	ὑπὲρ πάντων
therefore	ἄρα
all	οἱ πάντες
have died	**ἀπέθανον**

But I **do** not **seek (ζητῶ)** My **glory (δόξαν)**; there is One **who seeks (ζητῶν)** and **judges (κρίνων)**. (NASB)

ζητέω	to seek, search for	110x
zēteō		S2212

δόξα ➢ DAY 95　　　　**κρίνω** ➢ DAY 149

ἐγὼ δὲ οὐ **ζητῶ** τὴν **δόξαν** μου· ἔστιν ὁ **ζητῶν** καὶ **κρίνων**.

But I **do** not **seek**	ἐγὼ δὲ οὐ **ζητῶ**
My **glory**	τὴν **δόξαν** μου
there is One **who seeks**	ἔστιν ὁ **ζητῶν**
and **judges**	καὶ **κρίνων**

For this reason the Jews **were seeking (ἐζήτουν)** all the more to kill him, because he was not only breaking the sabbath, but was also calling God his **own (ἴδιον)** Father, thereby making **himself (ἑαυτὸν)** equal to God. (NRSV)

ἴδιος	one's own, private, personal	110x
idios		S2398

ἑαυτοῦ ➤ DAY 55   **ζητέω** ➤ DAY 150

διὰ τοῦτο οὖν μᾶλλον **ἐζήτουν** αὐτὸν οἱ Ἰουδαῖοι ἀποκτεῖναι ὅτι οὐ μόνον ἔλυε τὸ σάββατον ἀλλὰ καὶ πατέρα **ἴδιον** ἔλεγε τὸν θεόν, ἴσον **ἑαυτὸν** ποιῶν τῷ θεῷ.

For this reason	διὰ τοῦτο οὖν
the Jews **were seeking** all the more	μᾶλλον **ἐζήτουν** . . . οἱ Ἰουδαῖοι
to kill him	αὐτὸν . . . ἀποκτεῖναι
because he was not only breaking	ὅτι οὐ μόνον ἔλυε
the sabbath	τὸ σάββατον
but was also calling God	ἀλλὰ καὶ . . . ἔλεγε τὸν θεόν
his **own** Father	πατέρα **ἴδιον**
thereby making **himself**	**ἑαυτὸν** ποιῶν
equal to God	ἴσον . . . τῷ θεῷ

As Jesus **was about to (Μέλλων)** go up to Jerusalem, He took the twelve **disciples (μαθητὰς)** aside by **themselves (ἰδίαν)**, and on the way He said to them, . . . (NASB)

μέλλω	to be about to, intend	110x
mellō		S3195

    μαθητής ➤ DAY 59   **ἴδιος** ➤ DAY 151

Μέλλων δὲ ἀναβαίνειν Ἰησοῦς εἰς Ἰεροσόλυμα παρέλαβεν τοὺς δώδεκα [**μαθητὰς**] κατ᾽ **ἰδίαν**, καὶ ἐν τῇ ὁδῷ εἶπεν αὐτοῖς

As Jesus **was about to**	**Μέλλων** δὲ . . . Ἰησοῦς
go up	ἀναβαίνειν
to Jerusalem	εἰς Ἰεροσόλυμα
He took . . . aside	παρέλαβεν
the twelve **disciples**	τοὺς δώδεκα [**μαθητὰς**]
by **themselves**	κατ᾽ **ἰδίαν**
and on the way	καὶ ἐν τῇ ὁδῷ
He said to them	εἶπεν αὐτοῖς

But I tell you that Elijah has already come and they did not recognize him, but have done to him **as (ὅσα) they pleased (ἠθέλησαν)**. In a similar way the Son of Man **is about to (μέλλει)** suffer at their hands. (MLB)

ὅσος	as great as, how great	109x
hosos		S3745

θέλω ➤ DAY 78   **μέλλω** ➤ DAY 152

λέγω δὲ ὑμῖν ὅτι Ἡλείας ἤδη ἦλθεν, καὶ οὐκ ἐπέγνωσαν αὐτὸν ἀλλὰ ἐποίησαν ἐν αὐτῷ **ὅσα ἠθέλησαν·** οὕτως καὶ ὁ υἱὸς τοῦ ἀνθρώπου **μέλλει** πάσχειν ὑπ᾽ αὐτῶν.

But I tell you that	λέγω δὲ ὑμῖν ὅτι
Elijah has already come	Ἡλείας ἤδη ἦλθεν
and they did not recognize him	καὶ οὐκ ἐπέγνωσαν αὐτὸν
but have done to him	ἀλλὰ ἐποίησαν ἐν αὐτῷ
as they pleased	**ὅσα ἠθέλησαν**
In a similar way	οὕτως καὶ
the Son of Man **is about to**	ὁ υἱὸς τοῦ ἀνθρώπου **μέλλει**
suffer	πάσχειν
at their hands	ὑπ᾽ αὐτῶν

But when **He (ἐκεῖνος)**, the Spirit of **truth (ἀληθείας)**, comes,
He will guide you into all the **truth (ἀλήθειαν)**; for He will not
speak on His own initiative, but **whatever (ὅσα)** He hears, He will
speak; and He will disclose to you what is to come. (NASB)

| **ἀλήθεια** | truth | 108x |
| *alētheia* | | S225 |

| **ἐκεῖνος** ➤ DAY 64 | **ὅσος** ➤ DAY 153 |

ὅταν δὲ ἔλθῃ **ἐκεῖνος**, τὸ πνεῦμα τῆς **ἀληθείας**, ὁδηγήσει ὑμᾶς
εἰς τὴν **ἀλήθειαν** πᾶσαν, οὐ γὰρ λαλήσει ἀφ᾽ ἑαυτοῦ, ἀλλ᾽ **ὅσα**
ἀκούει λαλήσει, καὶ τὰ ἐρχόμενα ἀναγγελεῖ ὑμῖν.

But when **He** . . . comes	ὅταν δὲ ἔλθῃ **ἐκεῖνος**
the Spirit of **truth**	τὸ πνεῦμα τῆς **ἀληθείας**
He will guide you	ὁδηγήσει ὑμᾶς
into all the **truth**	εἰς τὴν **ἀλήθειαν** πᾶσαν
for He will not speak	οὐ γὰρ λαλήσει
on His own initiative	ἀφ᾽ ἑαυτοῦ
but **whatever** He hears	ἀλλ᾽ **ὅσα** ἀκούει
He will speak	λαλήσει
and He will disclose to you	καὶ . . . ἀναγγελεῖ ὑμῖν
what is to come	τὰ ἐρχόμενα

The Lord said to him, "**Arise (Ἀνάστα)** and go into the street called Straight and **inquire (ζήτησον)** at the **home (οἰκίᾳ)** of Judas for one called Saul of Tarsus; for he is there praying." (MLB)

| ἀνίστημι | to rise, raise | 108x |
| *anistēmi* | | S450 |

οἶκος ➤ DAY 147   **ζητέω** ➤ DAY 150

ὁ δὲ κύριος πρὸς αὐτόν **Ἀνάστα** πορεύθητι ἐπὶ τὴν ῥύμην τὴν καλουμένην Εὐθεῖαν καὶ **ζήτησον** ἐν **οἰκίᾳ** Ἰούδα Σαῦλον ὀνόματι Ταρσέα, ἰδοὺ γὰρ προσεύχεται,

The Lord said to him	ὁ δὲ κύριος πρὸς αὐτόν
Arise	**Ἀνάστα**
and go into the street	πορεύθητι ἐπὶ τὴν ῥύμην
called Straight	τὴν καλουμένην Εὐθεῖαν
and **inquire** . . . for	καὶ **ζήτησον**
at the **home** of Judas	ἐν **οἰκίᾳ** Ἰούδα
one called Saul of Tarsus	Σαῦλον ὀνόματι Ταρσέα
for he is there praying	ἰδοὺ γὰρ προσεύχεται

One of them named Agabus **stood up (ἀναστὰς)** and predicted by the Spirit that **there would (μέλλειν)** be a severe famine over **all (ὅλην)** the world; and this took place during the reign of Claudius. (NRSV)

ὅλος	whole, all	108x
holos		S3650

μέλλω ➤ DAY 152   **ἀνίστημι** ➤ DAY 155

ἀναστὰς δὲ εἷς ἐξ αὐτῶν ὀνόματι Ἄγαβος ἐσήμαινεν διὰ τοῦ πνεύματος λιμὸν μεγάλην **μέλλειν** ἔσεσθαι ἐφ᾽ **ὅλην** τὴν οἰκουμένην· ἥτις ἐγένετο ἐπὶ Κλαυδίου.

One of them . . . **stood up**	**ἀναστὰς** δὲ εἷς ἐξ αὐτῶν
named Agabus	ὀνόματι Ἄγαβος
and predicted . . . that	ἐσήμαινεν
by the Spirit	διὰ τοῦ πνεύματος
there would be	**μέλλειν** ἔσεσθαι
a severe famine	λιμὸν μεγάλην
over **all** the world	ἐφ᾽ **ὅλην** τὴν οἰκουμένην
and this took place	ἥτις ἐγένετο
during the reign of Claudius	ἐπὶ Κλαυδίου

For that indeed is what you are doing to all the **brothers
(ἀδελφοὺς)** throughout [lit., in **all (ὅλῃ)** of] Macedonia. But **we
urge (Παρακαλοῦμεν)** you, **brothers (ἀδελφοί)**, to do this more
and more. (ESV)

παρακαλέω	to ask, beseech, exhort, comfort	107x
parakaleō		S3870

ἀδελφός ➤ DAY 51   **ὅλος** ➤ DAY 156

καὶ γὰρ ποιεῖτε αὐτὸ εἰς πάντας τοὺς **ἀδελφοὺς** [τοὺς] ἐν **ὅλῃ**
τῇ Μακεδονίᾳ. **Παρακαλοῦμεν** δὲ ὑμᾶς, **ἀδελφοί**, περισσεύειν
μᾶλλον,

For that indeed is what you are doing	καὶ γὰρ ποιεῖτε αὐτὸ
to all the **brothers**	εἰς πάντας τοὺς **ἀδελφοὺς**
throughout [lit., in **all** of] Macedonia	[τοὺς] ἐν **ὅλῃ** τῇ Μακεδονίᾳ
But **we urge** you	**Παρακαλοῦμεν** δὲ ὑμᾶς
brothers	**ἀδελφοί**
to do this more and more	περισσεύειν μᾶλλον

Now a large herd of pigs was feeding **there (ἐκεῖ)** on the hillside, and **they begged (παρεκάλεσαν)** him to let them **enter (εἰσελθεῖν)** these. So he gave them permission. (ESV)

ἐκεῖ	there, yonder	105x
ekei		S1563

εἰσέρχομαι ➤ DAY 82   **παρακαλέω** ➤ DAY 157

Ἦν δὲ **ἐκεῖ** ἀγέλη χοίρων ἱκανῶν βοσκομένη ἐν τῷ ὄρει· καὶ **παρεκάλεσαν** αὐτὸν ἵνα ἐπιτρέψῃ αὐτοῖς εἰς ἐκείνους **εἰσελθεῖν**· καὶ ἐπέτρεψεν αὐτοῖς.

Now a large herd of pigs was	Ἦν δὲ . . . ἀγέλη χοίρων ἱκανῶν
feeding **there**	**ἐκεῖ** . . . βοσκομένη
on the hillside	ἐν τῷ ὄρει
and **they begged** him	καὶ **παρεκάλεσαν** αὐτὸν
to let them	ἵνα ἐπιτρέψῃ αὐτοῖς
enter these	εἰς ἐκείνους **εἰσελθεῖν**
So he gave them permission	καὶ ἐπέτρεψεν αὐτοῖς

Jacob's well was **there (ἐκεῖ)**; so Jesus, wearied as he was from his journey, was sitting [lit., was **thus (οὕτως)** sitting] beside the well. It was about the sixth **hour (ὥρα)**. (ESV)

ὥρα	hour, time	105x
hōra		S5610

οὕτως ➤ DAY 77   **ἐκεῖ** ➤ DAY 158

ἦν δὲ **ἐκεῖ** πηγὴ τοῦ Ἰακώβ. ὁ οὖν Ἰησοῦς κεκοπιακὼς ἐκ τῆς ὁδοιπορίας ἐκαθέζετο **οὕτως** ἐπὶ τῇ πηγῇ· **ὥρα** ἦν ὡς ἕκτη.

Jacob's well	πηγὴ τοῦ Ἰακώβ
was **there**	ἦν δὲ **ἐκεῖ**
so Jesus	ὁ οὖν Ἰησοῦς
wearied as he was	κεκοπιακὼς
from his journey	ἐκ τῆς ὁδοιπορίας
was sitting [lit., was **thus** sitting]	ἐκαθέζετο **οὕτως**
beside the well	ἐπὶ τῇ πηγῇ
It was about	ἦν ὡς
the sixth **hour**	**ὥρα** . . . ἕκτη

Jesus, turning and seeing her, said, "Cheer up, daughter, your faith
has healed (σέσωκέν) you." And the **woman (γυνὴ) was well
(ἐσώθη)** from that **hour (ὥρας).** (MLB)

σῴζω	to save, rescue	104x
sōzō		S4982

γυνή	➤ DAY 74	ὥρα	➤ DAY 159

ὁ δὲ Ἰησοῦς στραφεὶς καὶ ἰδὼν αὐτὴν εἶπεν Θάρσει, θύγατερ· ἡ
πίστις σου **σέσωκέν** σε. καὶ **ἐσώθη** ἡ **γυνὴ** ἀπὸ τῆς **ὥρας** ἐκείνης.

Jesus	ὁ δὲ Ἰησοῦς
turning	στραφεὶς
and seeing her	καὶ ἰδὼν αὐτὴν
said	εἶπεν
Cheer up	Θάρσει
daughter	θύγατερ
your faith	ἡ πίστις σου
has healed you	**σέσωκέν** σε
And the **woman was well**	καὶ **ἐσώθη** ἡ **γυνὴ**
from that **hour**	ἀπὸ τῆς **ὥρας** ἐκείνης

And when he led them out he said, "**Sirs (Κύριοι)**, what must I do [lit., what **is necessary (δεῖ)** for me to do] to **be saved (σωθῶ)**?"
(MLB)

δεῖ	to be necessary	102x
dei		S1163

κύριος ➤ DAY 22   σῴζω ➤ DAY 160

καὶ προαγαγὼν αὐτοὺς ἔξω ἔφη **Κύριοι**, τί με **δεῖ** ποιεῖν ἵνα **σωθῶ**;

And when he led them out	καὶ προαγαγὼν αὐτοὺς ἔξω
he said	ἔφη
Sirs	**Κύριοι**
what must I do [lit., what **is necessary** for me to do]	τί με **δεῖ** ποιεῖν
to **be saved?**	ἵνα **σωθῶ**;

When I was daily in the temple with you, you never put out a hand against Me. But **this (αὕτη)** is your **hour (ὥρα)** and the **power (ἐξουσία)** of darkness. (MLB)

ἐξουσία	power, authority	102x
exousia		S1849

οὗτος, αὕτη, τοῦτο ➤ DAY 13   ὥρα ➤ DAY 159

καθ᾽ ἡμέραν ὄντος μου μεθ᾽ ὑμῶν ἐν τῷ ἱερῷ οὐκ ἐξετείνατε τὰς χεῖρας ἐπ᾽ ἐμέ· ἀλλ᾽ **αὕτη** ἐστὶν ὑμῶν ἡ **ὥρα** καὶ ἡ **ἐξουσία** τοῦ σκότους.

When I was	ὄντος μου
daily	καθ᾽ ἡμέραν
in the temple	ἐν τῷ ἱερῷ
with you	μεθ᾽ ὑμῶν
you never put out a hand	οὐκ ἐξετείνατε τὰς χεῖρας
against Me	ἐπ᾽ ἐμέ
But **this** is	ἀλλ᾽ **αὕτη** ἐστὶν
your **hour**	ὑμῶν ἡ **ὥρα**
and the **power**	καὶ ἡ **ἐξουσία**
of darkness	τοῦ σκότους

Let every **person (ψυχὴ)** be subject to the governing **authorities (ἐξουσίαις)**. For there is no **authority (ἐξουσία)** except **from (ὑπὸ)** God, and those that exist have been instituted **by (ὑπὸ)** God. (ESV)

ψυχή	life, soul, self, breath, desire	102x
psuchē		S5590

ὑπό ➤ DAY 72   **ἐξουσία** ➤ DAY 162

Πᾶσα **ψυχὴ ἐξουσίαις** ὑπερεχούσαις ὑποτασσέσθω, οὐ γὰρ ἔστιν **ἐξουσία** εἰ μὴ **ὑπὸ** θεοῦ, αἱ δὲ οὖσαι **ὑπὸ** θεοῦ τεταγμέναι εἰσίν·

Let every **person** be subject	Πᾶσα **ψυχὴ** . . . ὑποτασσέσθω
to the governing **authorities**	**ἐξουσίαις** ὑπερεχούσαις
For there is no **authority**	οὐ γὰρ ἔστιν **ἐξουσία**
except	εἰ μὴ
from God	**ὑπὸ** θεοῦ
and those that exist	αἱ δὲ οὖσαι
have been instituted	τεταγμέναι εἰσίν
by God	**ὑπὸ** θεοῦ

And I will say to my **soul (ψυχῇ)**, "Soul **(Ψυχή)**, you have ample **goods (ἀγαθὰ)** laid up **for (εἰς)** many years; relax, eat, drink, be merry." (NRSV)

ἀγαθός	good	101x
agathos		S18

    εἰς ➤ DAY 10   **ψυχή** ➤ DAY 163

καὶ ἐρῶ τῇ **ψυχῇ** μου **Ψυχή**, ἔχεις πολλὰ **ἀγαθὰ** [κείμενα **εἰς** ἔτη πολλά· ἀναπαύου, φάγε, πίε], εὐφραίνου.

And I will say	καὶ ἐρῶ
to my **soul**	τῇ **ψυχῇ** μου
Soul	**Ψυχή**
you have ample **goods**	ἔχεις πολλὰ **ἀγαθὰ**
laid up	κείμενα
for many years	**εἰς** ἔτη πολλά
relax	ἀναπαύου
eat	φάγε
drink	πίε
be merry	εὐφραίνου

But the seed in the **good (καλῇ)** soil, these are **the ones who
(οἵτινες)** have heard the word in an **honest (καλῇ)** and **good
(ἀγαθῇ)** heart, and hold it fast, and bear fruit with perseverance.
(NASB)

καλός	good, noble, worthy, honorable, beautiful	101x
kalos		S2570

ὅστις, ἥτις, ὅ τι ➤ DAY 127   **ἀγαθός** ➤ DAY 164

τὸ δὲ ἐν τῇ **καλῇ** γῇ, οὗτοί εἰσιν **οἵτινες** ἐν καρδίᾳ **καλῇ** καὶ
ἀγαθῇ ἀκούσαντες τὸν λόγον κατέχουσιν καὶ καρποφοροῦσιν ἐν
ὑπομονῇ.

But the seed	τὸ δὲ
in the **good** soil	ἐν τῇ **καλῇ** γῇ
these are **the ones who**	οὗτοί εἰσιν **οἵτινες**
have heard the word	ἀκούσαντες τὸν λόγον
in an **honest** and **good** heart	ἐν καρδίᾳ **καλῇ** καὶ **ἀγαθῇ**
and hold it fast	κατέχουσιν
and bear fruit	καὶ καρποφοροῦσιν
with perseverance	ἐν ὑπομονῇ

And as he was setting out on his **journey (ὁδὸν)**, a man ran up and knelt before him and asked him, "**Good (ἀγαθέ)** Teacher, what must I do to inherit eternal **life (ζωὴν)**?" (ESV)

ὁδός	road, journey, way	101x
hodos		S3598

ζωή ▷ DAY 125   ἀγαθός ▷ DAY 164

Καὶ ἐκπορευομένου αὐτοῦ εἰς **ὁδὸν** προσδραμὼν εἷς καὶ γονυπετήσας αὐτὸν ἐπηρώτα αὐτόν Διδάσκαλε **ἀγαθέ**, τί ποιήσω ἵνα **ζωὴν** αἰώνιον κληρονομήσω;

And as he was setting out	Καὶ ἐκπορευομένου αὐτοῦ
on his **journey**	εἰς **ὁδὸν**
a man ran up	προσδραμὼν εἷς
and knelt before him	καὶ γονυπετήσας αὐτὸν
and asked him	ἐπηρώτα αὐτόν
Good Teacher	Διδάσκαλε **ἀγαθέ**
what must I do	τί ποιήσω
to inherit	ἵνα . . . κληρονομήσω;
eternal **life**?	**ζωὴν** αἰώνιον

When (ὅτε) they came up out of the water, the Spirit of the Lord suddenly took Philip away, and the eunuch did not see him again, but **went (ἐπορεύετο)** on his **way (ὁδὸν)** rejoicing. (NIV)

ὅτε	when	101x
hote		S3753

πορεύομαι ➤ DAY 105　　　　**ὁδός** ➤ DAY 166

ὅτε δὲ ἀνέβησαν ἐκ τοῦ ὕδατος, πνεῦμα Κυρίου ἥρπασεν τὸν Φίλιππον, καὶ οὐκ εἶδεν αὐτὸν οὐκέτι ὁ εὐνοῦχος, **ἐπορεύετο** γὰρ τὴν **ὁδὸν** αὐτοῦ χαίρων.

When they came up	**ὅτε** δὲ ἀνέβησαν
out of the water	ἐκ τοῦ ὕδατος
the Spirit of the Lord	πνεῦμα Κυρίου
suddenly took Philip away	ἥρπασεν τὸν Φίλιππον
and the eunuch	καὶ . . . ὁ εὐνοῦχος
did not see him again	οὐκ εἶδεν αὐτὸν οὐκέτι
but **went** on his **way**	**ἐπορεύετο** γὰρ τὴν **ὁδὸν** αὐτοῦ
rejoicing	χαίρων

But they kept silent, for **on (ἐν)** the **way (ὁδῷ)** they had argued with **one another (ἀλλήλους)** about who was the greatest. (ESV)

ἀλλήλων	one another	100x
allēlōn		S240

ἐν ➤ DAY 6   ὁδός ➤ DAY 166

οἱ δὲ ἐσιώπων, πρὸς **ἀλλήλους** γὰρ διελέχθησαν **ἐν** τῇ **ὁδῷ** τίς μείζων.

But they kept silent	οἱ δὲ ἐσιώπων
for **on** the **way**	γὰρ . . . **ἐν** τῇ **ὁδῷ**
they had argued with **one another** about	πρὸς **ἀλλήλους** . . . διελέχθησαν
who was the greatest	τίς μείζων

Don't I have the right to do what **I want (θέλω)** with my own money? Or are you envious [lit., is your **eye (ὀφθαλμός)** evil] because I am **generous (ἀγαθός)**? (NIV)

ὀφθαλμός	eye	100x
ophthalmos		S3788

θέλω ➤ DAY 78   **ἀγαθός** ➤ DAY 164

οὐκ ἔξεστίν μοι ὃ **θέλω** ποιῆσαι ἐν τοῖς ἐμοῖς; ἢ ὁ **ὀφθαλμός** σου πονηρός ἐστιν ὅτι ἐγὼ **ἀγαθός** εἰμι;

Don't I have the right	οὐκ ἔξεστίν μοι
to do what **I want**	ὃ **θέλω** ποιῆσαι
with my own money?	ἐν τοῖς ἐμοῖς;
Or are you envious [lit., is your **eye** evil]	ἢ ὁ **ὀφθαλμός** σου πονηρός ἐστιν
because I am **generous**?	ὅτι ἐγὼ **ἀγαθός** εἰμι;

Then again **He laid (ἔθηκεν)** His **hands (χεῖρας)** on his **eyes (ὀφθαλμοὺς)**; and he looked intently and was restored, and began to see everything clearly. (NASB)

τίθημι	to put, place, set forth	99x
tithēmi		S5087

χείρ ➤ DAY 88   ὀφθαλμός ➤ DAY 169

εἶτα πάλιν **ἔθηκεν** τὰς **χεῖρας** ἐπὶ τοὺς **ὀφθαλμοὺς** αὐτοῦ, καὶ διέβλεψεν, καὶ ἀπεκατέστη, καὶ ἐνέβλεπεν τηλαυγῶς ἅπαντα.

Then again	εἶτα πάλιν
He laid His **hands**	**ἔθηκεν** τὰς **χεῖρας**
on his **eyes**	ἐπὶ τοὺς **ὀφθαλμοὺς** αὐτοῦ
and he looked intently	καὶ διέβλεψεν
and was restored	καὶ ἀπεκατέστη
and began to see	καὶ ἐνέβλεπεν
everything	ἅπαντα
clearly	τηλαυγῶς

Owe no one anything except that you love **one another**
(**ἀλλήλους**), for the person who loves his **neighbor** (**ἕτερον**) has
fulfilled the **Law** (**νόμον**). (MLB)

ἕτερος	other, another, different	98x
*he*teros		S2087

νόμος ➤ DAY 80   **ἀλλήλων** ➤ DAY 168

Μηδενὶ μηδὲν ὀφείλετε, εἰ μὴ τὸ **ἀλλήλους** ἀγαπᾶν· ὁ γὰρ
ἀγαπῶν τὸν **ἕτερον νόμον** πεπλήρωκεν.

Owe no one	Μηδενὶ . . . ὀφείλετε
anything	μηδὲν
except	εἰ μὴ
that you love **one another**	τὸ **ἀλλήλους** ἀγαπᾶν
for the person who loves	ὁ γὰρ ἀγαπῶν
his **neighbor**	τὸν **ἕτερον**
has fulfilled the **Law**	**νόμον** πεπλήρωκεν

When our days there were ended, we left and proceeded on our
journey; and all of them, with wives and **children (τέκνοις)**,
escorted us outside the **city (πόλεως)**. There we knelt down [lit.,
and **placing (θέντες)** the knees] on the beach and prayed. (NRSV)

τέκνον	child	98x
teknon		S5043

πόλις ➤ DAY 96   **τίθημι** ➤ DAY 170

ὅτε δὲ ἐγένετο ἐξαρτίσαι ἡμᾶς τὰς ἡμέρας, ἐξελθόντες
ἐπορευόμεθα προπεμπόντων ἡμᾶς πάντων σὺν γυναιξὶ καὶ
τέκνοις ἕως ἔξω τῆς **πόλεως**, καὶ **θέντες** τὰ γόνατα ἐπὶ τὸν
αἰγιαλὸν προσευξάμενοι

When our days there were ended	ὅτε δὲ ἐγένετο ἐξαρτίσαι ἡμᾶς τὰς ἡμέρας
we left	ἐξελθόντες
and proceeded on our journey	ἐπορευόμεθα
and all of them, with wives and **children**	πάντων σὺν γυναιξὶ καὶ **τέκνοις**
escorted us	προπεμπόντων ἡμᾶς
outside the **city**	ἕως ἔξω τῆς **πόλεως**
There we knelt down [lit., and **placing** the knees]	καὶ **θέντες** τὰ γόνατα
on the beach	ἐπὶ τὸν αἰγιαλὸν
and prayed	προσευξάμενοι

So **they took away (ἦραν)** the stone. And Jesus **lifted (ἦρεν)** up his **eyes (ὀφθαλμοὺς)** and said, "Father, I thank you that **you have heard (ἤκουσάς)** me." (ESV)

αἴρω	to raise, lift up, remove, take away	97x
airō		S142

ἀκούω ➤ DAY 42   **ὀφθαλμός** ➤ DAY 169

ἦραν οὖν τὸν λίθον. ὁ δὲ Ἰησοῦς ἦρεν τοὺς ὀφθαλμοὺς ἄνω καὶ εἶπεν Πάτερ, εὐχαριστῶ σοι ὅτι ἤκουσάς μου,

So **they took away**	ἦραν οὖν
the stone	τὸν λίθον
And Jesus **lifted** up	ὁ δὲ Ἰησοῦς ἦρεν . . . ἄνω
his **eyes**	τοὺς ὀφθαλμοὺς
and said	καὶ εἶπεν
Father	Πάτερ
I thank you	εὐχαριστῶ σοι
that **you have heard** me	ὅτι ἤκουσάς μου

He charged them **to take (αἴρωσιν)** nothing for their **journey (ὁδὸν)** except a staff—no **bread (ἄρτον)**, no bag, no money in their belts. (ESV)

ἄρτος	bread, loaf	97x
artos		S740

ὁδός ▷ DAY 166   αἴρω ▷ DAY 173

καὶ παρήγγειλεν αὐτοῖς ἵνα μηδὲν **αἴρωσιν** εἰς **ὁδὸν** εἰ μὴ ῥάβδον μόνον, μὴ **ἄρτον**, μὴ πήραν, μὴ εἰς τὴν ζώνην χαλκόν,

He charged them	καὶ παρήγγειλεν αὐτοῖς
to take nothing	ἵνα μηδὲν **αἴρωσιν**
for their **journey**	εἰς **ὁδὸν**
except a staff	εἰ μὴ ῥάβδον μόνον
no **bread**	μὴ **ἄρτον**
no bag	μὴ πήραν
no money	μὴ . . . χαλκόν
in their belts	εἰς τὴν ζώνην

I appeal to you **for (περὶ)** my **child (τέκνου)** Onesimus, whom **I have begotten (ἐγέννησα)** in my imprisonment. (NASB)

γεννάω	to beget, bring forth	97x
gennaō		S1080

περί ➢ DAY 53   **τέκνον** ➢ DAY 172

παρακαλῶ σε **περὶ** τοῦ ἐμοῦ **τέκνου**, ὅν **ἐγέννησα** ἐν τοῖς δεσμοῖς Ὀνήσιμον,

I appeal to you	παρακαλῶ σε
for my **child**	**περὶ** τοῦ ἐμοῦ **τέκνου**
Onesimus	Ὀνήσιμον
whom **I have begotten**	ὅν **ἐγέννησα**
in my imprisonment	ἐν τοῖς δεσμοῖς

Two (δύο) men went up to the temple to pray, one a **Pharisee (Φαρισαῖος)** and the **other (ἕτερος)** a tax collector. (NIV)

Φαρισαῖος	Pharisee	97x
Pharisaios		S5330

    δύο ➤ DAY 124   **ἕτερος** ➤ DAY 171

Ἄνθρωποι **δύο** ἀνέβησαν εἰς τὸ ἱερὸν προσεύξασθαι, εἷς **Φαρισαῖος** καὶ ὁ **ἕτερος** τελώνης.

Two men	Ἄνθρωποι **δύο**
went up	ἀνέβησαν
to the temple	εἰς τὸ ἱερὸν
to pray	προσεύξασθαι
one a **Pharisee**	εἷς **Φαρισαῖος**
and the **other**	καὶ ὁ **ἕτερος**
a tax collector	τελώνης

One (μιᾷ) of those days He was **teaching (διδάσκων)**, and **Pharisees (Φαρισαῖοι)** and teachers of the law, who had come from every village of Galilee and from Judea and Jerusalem, were sitting there, and the power of the Lord was present so that He healed people. (MLB)

διδάσκω	to teach	96x
didaskō		S1321

εἷς, μία, ἕν ➤ DAY 49   **Φαρισαῖος** ➤ DAY 176

Καὶ ἐγένετο ἐν **μιᾷ** τῶν ἡμερῶν καὶ αὐτὸς ἦν **διδάσκων**, καὶ ἦσαν καθήμενοι **Φαρισαῖοι** καὶ νομοδιδάσκαλοι οἳ ἦσαν ἐληλυθότες ἐκ πάσης κώμης τῆς Γαλιλαίας καὶ Ἰουδαίας καὶ Ἰερουσαλήμ· καὶ δύναμις Κυρίου ἦν εἰς τὸ ἰᾶσθαι αὐτόν.

One of those days	Καὶ ἐγένετο ἐν **μιᾷ** τῶν ἡμερῶν
He was **teaching**	καὶ αὐτὸς ἦν **διδάσκων**
and **Pharisees** and teachers of the law . . . were sitting there	καὶ ἦσαν καθήμενοι **Φαρισαῖοι** καὶ νομοδιδάσκαλοι
who had come from every village of Galilee and from Judea and Jerusalem	οἳ ἦσαν ἐληλυθότες ἐκ πάσης κώμης τῆς Γαλιλαίας καὶ Ἰουδαίας καὶ Ἰερουσαλήμ
and the power of the Lord was present	καὶ δύναμις Κυρίου ἦν
so that He healed people	εἰς τὸ ἰᾶσθαι αὐτόν

The one on the housetop must not go down **to take (ἆραι)** what is in the [lit., **of/from (ἐκ)** his] **house (οἰκίας)**. (NRSV)

οἰκία	house, household, property, belongings	94x
oikia		S3614

ἐκ ➤ DAY 19   **αἴρω** ➤ DAY 173

ὁ ἐπὶ τοῦ δώματος μὴ καταβάτω **ἆραι** τὰ **ἐκ** τῆς **οἰκίας** αὐτοῦ,

The one on the housetop	ὁ ἐπὶ τοῦ δώματος
must not go down	μὴ καταβάτω
to take	**ἆραι**
what is in the [lit., **of/from** his] **house**	τὰ **ἐκ** τῆς **οἰκίας** αὐτοῦ

And they have been told about you, that **you are teaching (διδάσκεις)** all the Jews who are among the Gentiles to forsake Moses, telling them not to circumcise their **children (τέκνα)** nor **to walk (περιπατεῖν)** according to the customs. (NASB)

| περιπατέω | to walk, live | 94x |
| *peripateō* | | S4043 |

τέκνον ➤ DAY 172   **διδάσκω** ➤ DAY 177

κατηχήθησαν δὲ περὶ σοῦ ὅτι ἀποστασίαν **διδάσκεις** ἀπὸ Μωυσέως τοὺς κατὰ τὰ ἔθνη πάντας Ἰουδαίους, λέγων μὴ περιτέμνειν αὐτοὺς τὰ **τέκνα** μηδὲ τοῖς ἔθεσιν **περιπατεῖν**.

And they have been told	κατηχήθησαν δὲ
about you	περὶ σοῦ
that **you are teaching**	ὅτι . . . **διδάσκεις**
all the Jews	τοὺς . . . πάντας Ἰουδαίους
who are among the Gentiles	κατὰ τὰ ἔθνη
to forsake Moses	ἀποστασίαν . . . ἀπὸ Μωυσέως
telling them not to circumcise their **children**	λέγων μὴ περιτέμνειν αὐτοὺς τὰ **τέκνα**
nor **to walk**	μηδὲ . . . **περιπατεῖν**
according to the customs	τοῖς ἔθεσιν

In My Father's **house (οἰκίᾳ)** are many dwelling places. If
this were not so, I would have told you. For **I am going away**
(πορεύομαι) to prepare a **place (τόπον)** for you. (MLB)

τόπος	place, opportunity	94x
topos		S5117

πορεύομαι ➤ DAY 105   **οἰκία** ➤ DAY 178

ἐν τῇ **οἰκίᾳ** τοῦ πατρός μου μοναὶ πολλαί εἰσιν· εἰ δὲ μή, εἶπον ἂν
ὑμῖν, ὅτι **πορεύομαι** ἑτοιμάσαι **τόπον** ὑμῖν·

In My Father's **house**	ἐν τῇ **οἰκίᾳ** τοῦ πατρός μου
are many dwelling places	μοναὶ πολλαί εἰσιν
If this were not so	εἰ δὲ μή
I would have told you	εἶπον ἂν ὑμῖν
For **I am going away**	ὅτι **πορεύομαι**
to prepare a **place** for you	ἑτοιμάσαι **τόπον** ὑμῖν

The Lord said to him, "Untie the sandals from your **feet (ποδῶν)**, for the **place (τόπος)** on which **you are standing (ἕστηκας)** is holy ground." (MLB)

πούς	foot	93x
pous		S4228

ἵστημι ➤ DAY 109   τόπος ➤ DAY 180

εἶπεν δὲ αὐτῷ ὁ κύριος Λῦσον τὸ ὑπόδημα τῶν **ποδῶν** σου, ὁ γὰρ **τόπος** ἐφ᾽ ᾧ **ἕστηκας** γῆ ἁγία ἐστίν.

The Lord said to him	εἶπεν δὲ αὐτῷ ὁ κύριος
Untie the sandals	Λῦσον τὸ ὑπόδημα
from your **feet**	τῶν **ποδῶν** σου
for the **place**	ὁ γὰρ **τόπος**
on which **you are standing**	ἐφ᾽ ᾧ **ἕστηκας**
is holy ground	γῆ ἁγία ἐστίν

But the father told his slaves, "Hurry! Fetch the choicest [lit., **first (πρώτην)**] robe and put it on him; **put (δότε)** a ring on his hand and sandals on his **feet (πόδας)**." (MLB)

| πρῶτος | first | 93x |
| *prōtos* | | S4413 |

δίδωμι ➤ DAY 43   πούς ➤ DAY 181

εἶπεν δὲ ὁ πατὴρ πρὸς τοὺς δούλους αὐτοῦ Ταχὺ ἐξενέγκατε στολὴν τὴν **πρώτην** καὶ ἐνδύσατε αὐτόν, καὶ **δότε** δακτύλιον εἰς τὴν χεῖρα αὐτοῦ καὶ ὑποδήματα εἰς τοὺς **πόδας**,

But the father told his slaves	εἶπεν δὲ ὁ πατὴρ πρὸς τοὺς δούλους αὐτοῦ
Hurry!	Ταχὺ
Fetch	ἐξενέγκατε
the choicest [lit., **first**] robe	στολὴν τὴν **πρώτην**
and put it on him	καὶ ἐνδύσατε αὐτόν
put a ring	καὶ **δότε** δακτύλιον
on his hand	εἰς τὴν χεῖρα αὐτοῦ
and sandals	καὶ ὑποδήματα
on his **feet**	εἰς τοὺς **πόδας**

When I saw Him, I fell at His **feet (πόδας)** like a dead man. He laid His right hand on me and said, "Don't **be afraid (φοβοῦ)**! I am the **First (πρῶτος)** and the Last." (HCSB)

φοβέομαι	to fear, dread, reverence	93x
phobeomai		S5399

πούς ➤ DAY 181   **πρῶτος** ➤ DAY 182

Καὶ ὅτε εἶδον αὐτόν, ἔπεσα πρὸς τοὺς **πόδας** αὐτοῦ ὡς νεκρός· καὶ ἔθηκεν τὴν δεξιὰν αὐτοῦ ἐπ᾽ ἐμὲ λέγων Μὴ **φοβοῦ**· ἐγώ εἰμι ὁ **πρῶτος** καὶ ὁ ἔσχατος,

When I saw Him	Καὶ ὅτε εἶδον αὐτόν
I fell	ἔπεσα
at His **feet**	πρὸς τοὺς **πόδας** αὐτοῦ
like a dead man	ὡς νεκρός
He laid	καὶ ἔθηκεν
His right hand	τὴν δεξιὰν αὐτοῦ
on me	ἐπ᾽ ἐμὲ
and said	λέγων
Don't **be afraid**!	Μὴ **φοβοῦ**
I am	ἐγώ εἰμι
the **First**	ὁ **πρῶτος**
and the Last	καὶ ὁ ἔσχατος

The **first (πρῶτος)** angel sounded his trumpet, and there came hail and fire mixed with **blood (αἵματι)**, and **it was hurled down (ἐβλήθη)** on the earth. (NIV)

αἷμα	blood	92x
haima		S129

     βάλλω ➤ DAY 134   **πρῶτος** ➤ DAY 182

Καὶ ὁ **πρῶτος** ἐσάλπισεν· καὶ ἐγένετο χάλαζα καὶ πῦρ μεμιγμένα ἐν **αἵματι**, καὶ **ἐβλήθη** εἰς τὴν γῆν·

The **first** angel sounded his trumpet	Καὶ ὁ **πρῶτος** ἐσάλπισεν
and there came	καὶ ἐγένετο
hail and fire	χάλαζα καὶ πῦρ
mixed	μεμιγμένα
with **blood**	ἐν **αἵματι**
and **it was hurled down**	καὶ **ἐβλήθη**
on the earth	εἰς τὴν γῆν

Now may the God of **peace (εἰρήνης)**, who brought back from
the **dead (νεκρῶν)** our Lord Jesus, the great shepherd of the
sheep, by the **blood (αἵματι)** of the eternal covenant, . . . (NRSV)

| **εἰρήνη** | peace, welfare | 92x |
| *eirēnē* | | S1515 |

νεκρός ➤ DAY 129   **αἷμα** ➤ DAY 184

Ὁ δὲ θεὸς τῆς **εἰρήνης**, ὁ ἀναγαγὼν ἐκ **νεκρῶν** τὸν ποιμένα τῶν
προβάτων τὸν μέγαν ἐν **αἵματι** διαθήκης αἰωνίου, τὸν κύριον
ἡμῶν Ἰησοῦν,

Now may the God	Ὁ δὲ θεὸς
of **peace**	τῆς **εἰρήνης**
who brought back	ὁ ἀναγαγὼν
from the **dead**	ἐκ **νεκρῶν**
our Lord Jesus	τὸν κύριον ἡμῶν Ἰησοῦν
the great shepherd	τὸν ποιμένα . . . τὸν μέγαν
of the sheep	τῶν προβάτων
by the **blood**	ἐν **αἵματι**
of the eternal covenant	διαθήκης αἰωνίου

And if not, while the other is **yet (ἔτι)** a great way off, **he sends (ἀποστείλας)** a delegation and asks for **terms of peace (εἰρήνην)**.
(ESV)

| ἔτι | still, yet, even, further | 92x |
| *eti* | | S2089 |

ἀποστέλλω ➢ DAY 131   **εἰρήνη** ➢ DAY 185

εἰ δὲ μήγε, **ἔτι** αὐτοῦ πόρρω ὄντος πρεσβείαν **ἀποστείλας** ἐρωτᾷ πρὸς **εἰρήνην**.

And if not	εἰ δὲ μήγε
while the other is **yet**	**ἔτι** αὐτοῦ . . . ὄντος
a great way off	πόρρω
he sends	**ἀποστείλας**
a delegation	πρεσβείαν
and asks	ἐρωτᾷ
for **terms of peace**	πρὸς **εἰρήνην**

Let the evildoer **still (ἔτι)** do evil, and the filthy **still (ἔτι)** be filthy, and the righteous **still (ἔτι)** do **right (δικαιοσύνην)**, and the **holy (ἅγιος) still (ἔτι)** be holy. (NRSV)

δικαιοσύνη	righteousness, justice	91x
dikaiosunē		S1343

ἅγιος ➤ DAY 67   ἔτι ➤ DAY 186

ὁ ἀδικῶν ἀδικησάτω **ἔτι**, καὶ ὁ ῥυπαρὸς ῥυπανθήτω **ἔτι**, καὶ ὁ δίκαιος **δικαιοσύνην** ποιησάτω **ἔτι**, καὶ ὁ **ἅγιος** ἁγιασθήτω **ἔτι**.

Let the evildoer	ὁ ἀδικῶν
still do evil	ἀδικησάτω **ἔτι**
and the filthy	καὶ ὁ ῥυπαρὸς
still be filthy	ῥυπανθήτω **ἔτι**
and the righteous	καὶ ὁ δίκαιος
still do **right**	**δικαιοσύνην** ποιησάτω **ἔτι**
and the **holy**	καὶ ὁ **ἅγιος**
still be holy	ἁγιασθήτω **ἔτι**

Then I saw a new heaven and a new earth; for the **first (πρῶτος)** heaven and the **first (πρώτη)** earth had passed away, and no **longer (ἔτι)** was there any **sea (θάλασσα)**. (MLB)

θάλασσα	sea, lake	91x
thalassa		S2281

πρῶτος ➤ DAY 182   **ἔτι** ➤ DAY 186

Καὶ εἶδον οὐρανὸν καινὸν καὶ γῆν καινήν· ὁ γὰρ **πρῶτος** οὐρανὸς καὶ ἡ **πρώτη** γῆ ἀπῆλθαν, καὶ ἡ **θάλασσα** οὐκ ἔστιν **ἔτι**.

Then I saw	Καὶ εἶδον
a new heaven	οὐρανὸν καινὸν
and a new earth	καὶ γῆν καινήν
for the **first** heaven	ὁ γὰρ **πρῶτος** οὐρανὸς
and the **first** earth	καὶ ἡ **πρώτη** γῆ
had passed away	ἀπῆλθαν
and no **longer** was there any sea	καὶ ἡ **θάλασσα** οὐκ ἔστιν **ἔτι**

That same day Jesus went out of the **house (οἰκίας)** and **sat (ἐκάθητο)** by the **lake (θάλασσαν)**. (NIV)

| **κάθημαι** | to sit, be seated | 91x |
| *kathēmai* | | S2521 |

οἰκία ➤ DAY 178   **θάλασσα** ➤ DAY 188

Ἐν τῇ ἡμέρᾳ ἐκείνῃ ἐξελθὼν ὁ Ἰησοῦς τῆς **οἰκίας ἐκάθητο** παρὰ τὴν **θάλασσαν·**

That same day	Ἐν τῇ ἡμέρᾳ ἐκείνῃ
Jesus went out	ἐξελθὼν ὁ Ἰησοῦς
of the **house**	τῆς **οἰκίας**
and **sat**	**ἐκάθητο**
by the **lake**	παρὰ τὴν **θάλασσαν**

Do not **be afraid (φοβηθῆτε)** of those who kill the body but cannot kill the **soul (ψυχὴν)**; but rather **fear (φοβεῖσθε)** Him who is able **to destroy (ἀπολέσαι)** both **soul (ψυχὴν)** and body in hell. (MLB)

ἀπόλλυμι	to lose, perish, destroy	90x
apollumi		S622

ψυχή ➤ DAY 163   **φοβέομαι** ➤ DAY 183

καὶ μὴ **φοβηθῆτε** ἀπὸ τῶν ἀποκτεινόντων τὸ σῶμα τὴν δὲ **ψυχὴν** μὴ δυναμένων ἀποκτεῖναι· **φοβεῖσθε** δὲ μᾶλλον τὸν δυνάμενον καὶ **ψυχὴν** καὶ σῶμα **ἀπολέσαι** ἐν γεέννῃ.

Do not **be afraid**	καὶ μὴ **φοβηθῆτε**
of those who kill	ἀπὸ τῶν ἀποκτεινόντων
the body	τὸ σῶμα
but cannot kill	δὲ . . . μὴ δυναμένων ἀποκτεῖναι
the **soul**	τὴν . . . **ψυχὴν**
but rather **fear**	**φοβεῖσθε** δὲ μᾶλλον
Him who is able	τὸν δυνάμενον
to destroy	**ἀπολέσαι**
both **soul** and body	καὶ **ψυχὴν** καὶ σῶμα
in hell	ἐν γεέννῃ

And the twenty-four elders and the four living creatures **fell down (ἔπεσαν)** and worshiped God who **is seated (καθημένῳ)** on the throne, saying, "**Amen (Ἀμήν)**. Hallelujah!" (NRSV)

| πίπτω | to fall | 90x |
| *pipt*ō | | S4098 |

ἀμήν ➤ DAY 132   **κάθημαι** ➤ DAY 189

καὶ **ἔπεσαν** οἱ πρεσβύτεροι οἱ εἴκοσι τέσσαρες καὶ τὰ τέσσερα ζῷα, καὶ προσεκύνησαν τῷ θεῷ τῷ **καθημένῳ** ἐπὶ τῷ θρόνῳ λέγοντες Ἀμήν, Ἀλληλουιά.

And . . . **fell down**	καὶ **ἔπεσαν**
the twenty-four elders	οἱ πρεσβύτεροι οἱ εἴκοσι τέσσαρες
and the four living creatures	καὶ τὰ τέσσερα ζῷα
and worshiped God	καὶ προσεκύνησαν τῷ θεῷ
who **is seated**	τῷ **καθημένῳ**
on the throne	ἐπὶ τῷ θρόνῳ
saying	λέγοντες
Amen. Hallelujah!	**Ἀμήν**, Ἀλληλουιά

Another (ἄλλος) angel, a second, **followed (ἠκολούθησεν)**,
saying, "**Fallen (Ἔπεσεν), fallen (ἔπεσεν)** is Babylon the great,
she who made all nations drink the wine of the passion of her
sexual immorality." (ESV)

ἀκολουθέω	to follow, accompany, attend	89x
akolouthéō		S190

ἄλλος ➤ DAY 104   **πίπτω** ➤ DAY 191

Καὶ **ἄλλος** δεύτερος [ἄγγελος] **ἠκολούθησεν** λέγων Ἔπεσεν,
ἔπεσεν Βαβυλὼν ἡ μεγάλη, ἣ ἐκ τοῦ οἴνου τοῦ θυμοῦ τῆς
πορνείας αὐτῆς πεπότικεν πάντα τὰ ἔθνη.

Another angel, a second	Καὶ **ἄλλος** δεύτερος [ἄγγελος]
followed, saying	**ἠκολούθησεν** λέγων
Fallen, fallen	Ἔπεσεν, ἔπεσεν
is Babylon the great	Βαβυλὼν ἡ μεγάλη
she who made all nations drink	ἣ . . . πεπότικεν πάντα τὰ ἔθνη
the wine	ἐκ τοῦ οἴνου
of the passion	τοῦ θυμοῦ
of her sexual immorality	τῆς πορνείας αὐτῆς

Little children (Τεκνία), let no one (μηδεὶς) deceive you.
Whoever practices **righteousness (δικαιοσύνην)** is righteous, as
he is righteous. (ESV)

μηδείς, μηδεμία, μηδέν	no, no one, nothing	89x
mēdeis, mēdemia, mēden		S3367

    τέκνον ➤ DAY 172   **δικαιοσύνη** ➤ DAY 187

Τεκνία, μηδεὶς πλανάτω ὑμᾶς· ὁ ποιῶν τὴν **δικαιοσύνην** δίκαιός
ἐστιν, καθὼς ἐκεῖνος δίκαιός ἐστιν·

Little children	**Τεκνία**
let **no one** deceive you	**μηδεὶς** πλανάτω ὑμᾶς
Whoever practices	ὁ ποιῶν
righteousness	τὴν **δικαιοσύνην**
is righteous	δίκαιός ἐστιν
as he	καθὼς ἐκεῖνος
is righteous	δίκαιός ἐστιν

By **faith (Πίστει)** the walls of Jericho **fell down (ἔπεσαν)** after they had been encircled for **seven (ἑπτὰ)** days. (NASB)

ἑπτά	seven	88x
hepta		S2033

πίστις ➤ DAY 62   **πίπτω** ➤ DAY 191

Πίστει τὰ τείχη Ἰερειχὼ **ἔπεσαν** κυκλωθέντα ἐπὶ **ἑπτὰ** ἡμέρας.

By **faith**	**Πίστει**
the walls of Jericho	τὰ τείχη Ἰερειχὼ
fell down	**ἔπεσαν**
after they had been encircled	κυκλωθέντα
for **seven** days	ἐπὶ **ἑπτὰ** ἡμέρας

Then I saw the **seven (ἑπτὰ)** angels who **were standing
(ἑστήκασιν) before (ἐνώπιον)** God, and they were given **seven
(ἑπτὰ)** trumpets. (MLB)

| **ἐνώπιον** | before, in the presence of, in the eyes of | 87x |
| *enōpion* | | S1799 |

ἵστημι ➤ DAY 109   ἑπτά ➤ DAY 194

καὶ εἶδον τοὺς **ἑπτὰ** ἀγγέλους οἳ **ἐνώπιον** τοῦ θεοῦ **ἑστήκασιν**,
καὶ ἐδόθησαν αὐτοῖς **ἑπτὰ** σάλπιγγες.

Then I saw	καὶ εἶδον
the **seven** angels	τοὺς **ἑπτὰ** ἀγγέλους
who **were standing**	οἳ . . . **ἑστήκασιν**
before God	**ἐνώπιον** τοῦ θεοῦ
and they were given	καὶ ἐδόθησαν αὐτοῖς
seven trumpets	**ἑπτὰ** σάλπιγγες

He will wipe away every tear from their eyes, and death shall be no **more (ἔτι)**, **neither (οὔτε)** shall there be mourning, **nor (οὔτε)** crying, **nor (οὔτε)** pain any**more (ἔτι)**, for the former things **have passed away (ἀπῆλθαν)**. (ESV)

οὔτε	neither, nor	87x
oute		S3777

ἀπέρχομαι ➤ DAY 143   ἔτι ➤ DAY 186

καὶ ἐξαλείψει πᾶν δάκρυον ἐκ τῶν ὀφθαλμῶν αὐτῶν, καὶ ὁ θάνατος οὐκ ἔσται **ἔτι**· **οὔτε** πένθος **οὔτε** κραυγὴ **οὔτε** πόνος οὐκ ἔσται **ἔτι**. τὰ πρῶτα **ἀπῆλθαν**.

He will wipe away	καὶ ἐξαλείψει
every tear	πᾶν δάκρυον
from their eyes	ἐκ τῶν ὀφθαλμῶν αὐτῶν
and death	καὶ ὁ θάνατος
shall be no **more**	οὐκ ἔσται **ἔτι**
neither shall there be mourning, **nor** crying, **nor** pain any**more**	**οὔτε** πένθος **οὔτε** κραυγὴ **οὔτε** πόνος οὐκ ἔσται **ἔτι**
for the former things	τὰ πρῶτα
have passed away	**ἀπῆλθαν**

So the disciples [lit., they] **came (προσελθόντες)** and **woke
him up (ἤγειραν)**, saying, "Lord, save us! **We're going to die
(ἀπολλύμεθα)!**" (CSB)

προσέρχομαι	to come to, come near, approach	87x
proserchomai		S4334

ἐγείρω	➤ DAY 118	ἀπόλλυμι	➤ DAY 190

καὶ **προσελθόντες ἤγειραν** αὐτὸν λέγοντες Κύριε, σῶσον,
ἀπολλύμεθα.

So the disciples [lit., they] **came**	καὶ **προσελθόντες**
and **woke** him **up**	ἤγειραν αὐτὸν
saying	λέγοντες
Lord	Κύριε
save us!	σῶσον
We're going to die!	ἀπολλύμεθα

They had these men stand **before (ἐνώπιον)** the apostles, who **prayed (προσευξάμενοι)** and laid their **hands (χεῖρας)** on them. (NRSV)

| **προσεύχομαι** | to pray | 86x |
| *proseuchomai* | | S4336 |

χείρ ➤ DAY 88   **ἐνώπιον** ➤ DAY 195

οὓς ἔστησαν **ἐνώπιον** τῶν ἀποστόλων, καὶ **προσευξάμενοι** ἐπέθηκαν αὐτοῖς τὰς **χεῖρας**.

They had these men stand	οὓς ἔστησαν
before the apostles	**ἐνώπιον** τῶν ἀποστόλων
who **prayed**	καὶ **προσευξάμενοι**
and laid . . . on them	ἐπέθηκαν αὐτοῖς
their **hands**	τὰς **χεῖρας**

With all prayer and petition **pray (προσευχόμενοι)** at all times [lit., in every **time (καιρῷ)**] in the **Spirit (πνεύματι)**, and with this in view, be on the alert with all perseverance and petition for all the saints. (NASB)

| **καιρός** | occasion, opportunity, (fitting) time, season | 85x |
| *kairos* | | S2540 |

| **πνεῦμα** ➤ DAY 47 | **προσεύχομαι** ➤ DAY 198 |

διὰ πάσης προσευχῆς καὶ δεήσεως, **προσευχόμενοι** ἐν παντὶ **καιρῷ** ἐν **πνεύματι**, καὶ εἰς αὐτὸ ἀγρυπνοῦντες ἐν πάσῃ προσκαρτερήσει καὶ δεήσει περὶ πάντων τῶν ἁγίων,

With all prayer	διὰ πάσης προσευχῆς
and petition	καὶ δεήσεως
pray	**προσευχόμενοι**
at all times [lit., in every **time**]	ἐν παντὶ **καιρῷ**
in the **Spirit**	ἐν **πνεύματι**
and with this in view	καὶ εἰς αὐτὸ
be on the alert	ἀγρυπνοῦντες
with all perseverance	ἐν πάσῃ προσκαρτερήσει
and petition	καὶ δεήσει
for all the saints	περὶ πάντων τῶν ἁγίων

The **time (καιρὸς) is fulfilled (Πεπλήρωται)**, and the **kingdom (βασιλεία)** of God has come near; repent, and believe in the good news. (NRSV)

πληρόω	to fill (up), fulfill, accomplish, carry out	85x
plēroō		S4137

βασιλεία ➤ DAY 97　　　　**καιρός** ➤ DAY 199

Πεπλήρωται ὁ **καιρὸς** καὶ ἤγγικεν ἡ **βασιλεία** τοῦ θεοῦ· μετανοεῖτε καὶ πιστεύετε ἐν τῷ εὐαγγελίῳ.

The **time**	ὁ **καιρὸς**
is fulfilled	**Πεπλήρωται**
and the **kingdom** of God	καὶ . . . ἡ **βασιλεία** τοῦ θεοῦ
has come near	ἤγγικεν
repent	μετανοεῖτε
and believe	καὶ πιστεύετε
in the good news	ἐν τῷ εὐαγγελίῳ

Then **he began (ἤρξατο)** to say **to (πρὸς)** them, "Today this scripture **has been fulfilled (πεπλήρωται)** in your hearing." (NRSV)

| ἄρχω | (middle) to begin; (active) to rule | 84x |
| *archō* | | S756 + S757 |

πρός ➤ DAY 24   **πληρόω** ➤ DAY 200

ἤρξατο δὲ λέγειν **πρὸς** αὐτοὺς ὅτι Σήμερον **πεπλήρωται** ἡ γραφὴ αὕτη ἐν τοῖς ὠσὶν ὑμῶν.

Then **he began**	**ἤρξατο** δὲ
to say	λέγειν
to them	**πρὸς** αὐτοὺς ὅτι
Today	Σήμερον
this scripture	ἡ γραφὴ αὕτη
has been fulfilled	**πεπλήρωται**
in your hearing	ἐν τοῖς ὠσὶν ὑμῶν

But he went out and **began (ἤρξατο)** to proclaim it freely and to spread the news around, **to such an extent that (ὥστε)** Jesus [lit., he] **could (δύνασθαι)** no longer publicly enter a city, but stayed out in unpopulated areas; and they were coming to Him from everywhere. (NASB)

| ὥστε | so that, so as to, consequently, therefore | 83x |
| *hōste* | | S5620 |

δύναμαι ➤ DAY 75   **ἄρχω** ➤ DAY 201

ὁ δὲ ἐξελθὼν **ἤρξατο** κηρύσσειν πολλὰ καὶ διαφημίζειν τὸν λόγον, **ὥστε** μηκέτι αὐτὸν **δύνασθαι** φανερῶς εἰς πόλιν εἰσελθεῖν, ἀλλὰ ἔξω ἐπ᾽ ἐρήμοις τόποις [ἦν]· καὶ ἤρχοντο πρὸς αὐτὸν πάντοθεν.

But he went out	ὁ δὲ ἐξελθὼν
and **began** to proclaim it freely	**ἤρξατο** κηρύσσειν πολλὰ
and to spread the news around	καὶ διαφημίζειν τὸν λόγον
to such an extent that	**ὥστε**
Jesus [lit., he] **could** no longer	μηκέτι αὐτὸν **δύνασθαι**
publicly	φανερῶς
enter a city	εἰς πόλιν εἰσελθεῖν
but stayed out	ἀλλὰ ἔξω . . . [ἦν]
in unpopulated areas	ἐπ᾽ ἐρήμοις τόποις
and they were coming to Him	καὶ ἤρχοντο πρὸς αὐτὸν
from everywhere	πάντοθεν

Therefore (ὥστε) do not pronounce judgment before the **time (καιροῦ)**, before the Lord comes, who will bring to light the things now hidden in darkness and will disclose the purposes of the heart. Then each one will receive commendation [lit., the commendation will be to **each one (ἑκάστῳ)**]] from God. (NRSV)

ἕκαστος	each	82x
*hek*astos		S1538

καιρός ➤ DAY 199   **ὥστε** ➤ DAY 202

ὥστε μὴ πρὸ **καιροῦ** τι κρίνετε, ἕως ἂν ἔλθῃ ὁ κύριος, ὃς καὶ φωτίσει τὰ κρυπτὰ τοῦ σκότους καὶ φανερώσει τὰς βουλὰς τῶν καρδιῶν, καὶ τότε ὁ ἔπαινος γενήσεται **ἑκάστῳ** ἀπὸ τοῦ θεοῦ.

Therefore do not pronounce judgment before the **time**	**ὥστε** μὴ πρὸ **καιροῦ** τι κρίνετε
before the Lord comes	ἕως ἂν ἔλθῃ ὁ κύριος
who will bring to light the things now hidden in darkness	ὃς καὶ φωτίσει τὰ κρυπτὰ τοῦ σκότους
and will disclose the purposes of the heart	καὶ φανερώσει τὰς βουλὰς τῶν καρδιῶν
Then each one will receive commendation [lit., the commendation will be to **each one**] from God	καὶ τότε ὁ ἔπαινος γενήσεται **ἑκάστῳ** ἀπὸ τοῦ θεοῦ

A time **is coming (ἔρχεται)** and in fact **has come (ἐλήλυθεν)** when you will be scattered, **each (ἕκαστος)** to your own home. You will leave me all alone [lit., **And me (κἀμὲ)** you will leave all alone]. Yet I am not alone, for my Father is with me. (NIV)

κἀγώ	and I		82x
kagō			S2504

ἔρχομαι ➤ DAY 30   **ἕκαστος** ➤ DAY 203

ἰδοὺ **ἔρχεται** ὥρα καὶ **ἐλήλυθεν** ἵνα σκορπισθῆτε **ἕκαστος** εἰς τὰ ἴδια **κἀμὲ** μόνον ἀφῆτε· καὶ οὐκ εἰμὶ μόνος, ὅτι ὁ πατὴρ μετ᾽ ἐμοῦ ἐστίν.

A time **is coming**	ἰδοὺ **ἔρχεται** ὥρα
and in fact **has come**	καὶ **ἐλήλυθεν**
when you will be scattered	ἵνα σκορπισθῆτε
each to your own home	**ἕκαστος** εἰς τὰ ἴδια
You will leave me all alone [lit., **And me** you will leave all alone]	**κἀμὲ** μόνον ἀφῆτε
Yet I am not alone	καὶ οὐκ εἰμὶ μόνος
for my Father	ὅτι ὁ πατὴρ
is with me	μετ᾽ ἐμοῦ ἐστίν

The **dead man (νεκρὸς)** sat up and **began (ἤρξατο)** to talk, and Jesus [lit., he] gave him back to his **mother (μητρὶ)**. (NIV)

μήτηρ	mother	82x
mētēr		S3384

νεκρός ➤ DAY 129   ἄρχω ➤ DAY 201

καὶ ἀνεκάθισεν ὁ **νεκρὸς** καὶ **ἤρξατο** λαλεῖν, καὶ ἔδωκεν αὐτὸν τῇ **μητρὶ** αὐτοῦ.

The **dead man**	καὶ . . . ὁ **νεκρὸς**
sat up	ἀνεκάθισεν
and **began**	καὶ **ἤρξατο**
to talk	λαλεῖν
and Jesus [lit., he] gave him back	καὶ ἔδωκεν αὐτὸν
to his **mother**	τῇ **μητρὶ** αὐτοῦ

And after he had dismissed the **crowds (ὄχλους)**, **he went up (ἀνέβη)** the mountain by himself **to pray (προσεύξασθαι)**. When evening came, he was there alone. (NRSV)

ἀναβαίνω	to go up, ascend	81x
anabainō		S305

ὄχλος ➤ DAY 90   **προσεύχομαι** ➤ DAY 198

καὶ ἀπολύσας τοὺς **ὄχλους ἀνέβη** εἰς τὸ ὄρος κατ᾽ ἰδίαν **προσεύξασθαι**. ὀψίας δὲ γενομένης μόνος ἦν ἐκεῖ.

And after he had dismissed	καὶ ἀπολύσας
the **crowds**	τοὺς **ὄχλους**
he went up the mountain	**ἀνέβη** εἰς τὸ ὄρος
by himself	κατ᾽ ἰδίαν
to pray	**προσεύξασθαι**
When evening came	ὀψίας δὲ γενομένης
he was there	ἦν ἐκεῖ
alone	μόνος

And they laughed at him. But he **put** them all **outside (ἐκβαλὼν)** and took the child's **father (πατέρα)** and **mother (μητέρα)** and those who were with him and went in where the child was. (ESV)

| **ἐκβάλλω** | to throw out, cast out, banish, produce | 81x |
| *ekballō* | | S1544 |

πατήρ ➤ DAY 44   **μήτηρ** ➤ DAY 205

καὶ κατεγέλων αὐτοῦ. αὐτὸς δὲ **ἐκβαλὼν** πάντας παραλαμβάνει τὸν **πατέρα** τοῦ παιδίου καὶ τὴν **μητέρα** καὶ τοὺς μετ᾽ αὐτοῦ, καὶ εἰσπορεύεται ὅπου ἦν τὸ παιδίον·

And they laughed at him	καὶ κατεγέλων αὐτοῦ
But he **put** them all **outside**	αὐτὸς δὲ **ἐκβαλὼν** πάντας
and took	παραλαμβάνει
the child's **father**	τὸν **πατέρα** τοῦ παιδίου
and **mother**	καὶ τὴν **μητέρα**
and those who were with him	καὶ τοὺς μετ᾽ αὐτοῦ
and went in	καὶ εἰσπορεύεται
where the child was	ὅπου ἦν τὸ παιδίον

And the scribes who **came down (καταβάντες)** from Jerusalem were saying, "He is possessed by Beelzebul [lit., **He has (ἔχει)** Beelzebul]," and "by the prince of demons **he casts out (ἐκβάλλει)** the demons." (ESV)

| **καταβαίνω** | to go down, come down | 81x |
| *katabainō* | | S2597 |

ἔχω ➤ DAY 23   **ἐκβάλλω** ➤ DAY 207

καὶ οἱ γραμματεῖς οἱ ἀπὸ Ἰεροσολύμων **καταβάντες** ἔλεγον ὅτι Βεεζεβοὺλ **ἔχει**, καὶ ὅτι ἐν τῷ ἄρχοντι τῶν δαιμονίων **ἐκβάλλει** τὰ δαιμόνια.

And the scribes	καὶ οἱ γραμματεῖς
who **came down**	οἱ . . . **καταβάντες**
from Jerusalem	ἀπὸ Ἰεροσολύμων
were saying	ἔλεγον ὅτι
He is possessed by Beelzebul [lit., **He has** Beelzebul]	Βεεζεβοὺλ **ἔχει**
and	καὶ ὅτι
by the prince	ἐν τῷ ἄρχοντι
of demons	τῶν δαιμονίων
he casts out	**ἐκβάλλει**
the demons	τὰ δαιμόνια

Then what **if (ἐὰν)** you were to see the Son of Man **ascending (ἀναβαίνοντα)** to **where (ὅπου)** he was before? (NRSV)

| ὅπου | where | 81x |
| **ho**pou | | S3699 |

ἐάν ➤ DAY 52   ἀναβαίνω ➤ DAY 206

ἐὰν οὖν θεωρῆτε τὸν υἱὸν τοῦ ἀνθρώπου **ἀναβαίνοντα ὅπου** ἦν τὸ πρότερον;

Then	οὖν
what **if**	**ἐὰν**
you were to see	θεωρῆτε
the Son of Man	τὸν υἱὸν τοῦ ἀνθρώπου
ascending	**ἀναβαίνοντα**
to **where**	**ὅπου**
he was	ἦν
before?	τὸ πρότερον;

They laid it at the **apostles' (ἀποστόλων) feet (πόδας)**, and it was distributed to **each (ἑκάστῳ)** as any had need. (NRSV)

ἀπόστολος	messenger, apostle	80x
apostolos		S652

πούς ➤ DAY 181   **ἕκαστος** ➤ DAY 203

καὶ ἐτίθουν παρὰ τοὺς **πόδας** τῶν **ἀποστόλων**· διεδίδετο δὲ **ἑκάστῳ** καθότι ἄν τις χρείαν εἶχεν.

They laid it	καὶ ἐτίθουν
at the **apostles' feet**	παρὰ τοὺς **πόδας** τῶν **ἀποστόλων**
and it was distributed	διεδίδετο δὲ
to **each**	**ἑκάστῳ**
as any	καθότι ἄν τις
had need	χρείαν εἶχεν

Then Peter and the **apostles (ἀπόστολοι) replied (ἀποκριθεὶς)**, "We must obey God **rather (μᾶλλον)** than men." (MLB)

| μᾶλλον | more, rather | 80x |
| *mallon* | | S3123 |

ἀποκρίνομαι ➤ DAY 68   **ἀπόστολος** ➤ DAY 210

ἀποκριθεὶς δὲ Πέτρος καὶ οἱ **ἀπόστολοι** εἶπαν Πειθαρχεῖν δεῖ θεῷ **μᾶλλον** ἢ ἀνθρώποις.

Then Peter and the **apostles**	δὲ Πέτρος καὶ οἱ **ἀπόστολοι**
replied	**ἀποκριθεὶς**. . . εἶπαν
We must obey	Πειθαρχεῖν δεῖ
God	θεῷ
rather than	**μᾶλλον** ἢ
men	ἀνθρώποις

Then he said to them, "These are my words that I spoke to you while I was still with you, that everything **written (γεγραμμένα)** about me in the Law of **Moses (Μωυσέως)** and the Prophets and the Psalms must **be fulfilled (πληρωθῆναι)**." (ESV)

Μωϋσῆς	Moses	80x
Mōusēs		S3475

       γράφω ➤ DAY 84   **πληρόω** ➤ DAY 200

Εἶπεν δὲ πρὸς αὐτούς Οὗτοι οἱ λόγοι μου οὓς ἐλάλησα πρὸς ὑμᾶς ἔτι ὢν σὺν ὑμῖν, ὅτι δεῖ **πληρωθῆναι** πάντα τὰ **γεγραμμένα** ἐν τῷ νόμῳ **Μωυσέως** καὶ τοῖς προφήταις καὶ Ψαλμοῖς περὶ ἐμοῦ.

Then he said to them	Εἶπεν δὲ πρὸς αὐτούς
These are my words	Οὗτοι οἱ λόγοι μου
that I spoke to you	οὓς ἐλάλησα πρὸς ὑμᾶς
while I was still with you	ἔτι ὢν σὺν ὑμῖν
that everything **written** about me	ὅτι . . . πάντα τὰ **γεγραμμένα** . . . περὶ ἐμοῦ
in the Law of **Moses**	ἐν τῷ νόμῳ **Μωυσέως**
and the Prophets	καὶ τοῖς προφήταις
and the Psalms	καὶ Ψαλμοῖς
must **be fulfilled**	δεῖ **πληρωθῆναι**

Truly, truly, I say to you, a **servant (δοῦλος)** is not greater than his master, nor is a **messenger (ἀπόστολος)** greater than the one **who sent (πέμψαντος)** him. (ESV)

πέμπω	to send	79x
*pemp*ō		S3992

δοῦλος ➤ DAY 137   **ἀπόστολος** ➤ DAY 210

ἀμὴν ἀμὴν λέγω ὑμῖν, οὐκ ἔστιν **δοῦλος** μείζων τοῦ κυρίου αὐτοῦ οὐδὲ **ἀπόστολος** μείζων τοῦ **πέμψαντος** αὐτόν.

Truly, truly	ἀμὴν ἀμὴν
I say to you	λέγω ὑμῖν
a **servant** is not greater	οὐκ ἔστιν **δοῦλος** μείζων
than his master	τοῦ κυρίου αὐτοῦ
nor is a **messenger** greater	οὐδὲ **ἀπόστολος** μείζων
than the one **who sent** him	τοῦ **πέμψαντος** αὐτόν

Jesus then said, "I will be with you a little while **longer** (Ἔτι), and then **I am going** (ὑπάγω) to him **who sent** (πέμψαντά) me."
(NRSV)

ὑπάγω	to go away, depart, withdraw	79x
hupagō		S5217

ἔτι ➢ DAY 186   πέμπω ➢ DAY 213

εἶπεν οὖν ὁ Ἰησοῦς Ἔτι χρόνον μικρὸν μεθ᾽ ὑμῶν εἰμὶ καὶ **ὑπάγω** πρὸς τὸν **πέμψαντά** με.

Jesus . . . said	εἶπεν . . . ὁ Ἰησοῦς
then	οὖν
I will be	εἰμὶ
with you	μεθ᾽ ὑμῶν
a little while **longer**	Ἔτι χρόνον μικρὸν
and then **I am going** to	καὶ **ὑπάγω** πρὸς
him **who sent** me	τὸν **πέμψαντά** με

If you then, who are **evil (πονηροὶ)**, know how to give **good (ἀγαθὰ)** gifts to your children, how much **more (μᾶλλον)** will your Father who is in heaven give **good things (ἀγαθὰ)** to those who ask him! (ESV)

πονηρός	evil, wicked, malicious	78x
ponēros		S4190

ἀγαθός ➤ DAY 164   **μᾶλλον** ➤ DAY 211

εἰ οὖν ὑμεῖς **πονηροὶ** ὄντες οἴδατε δόματα **ἀγαθὰ** διδόναι τοῖς τέκνοις ὑμῶν, πόσῳ **μᾶλλον** ὁ πατὴρ ὑμῶν ὁ ἐν τοῖς οὐρανοῖς δώσει **ἀγαθὰ** τοῖς αἰτοῦσιν αὐτόν.

If you then	εἰ οὖν ὑμεῖς
who are **evil**	**πονηροὶ** ὄντες
know how to give	οἴδατε . . . διδόναι
good gifts	δόματα **ἀγαθὰ**
to your children	τοῖς τέκνοις ὑμῶν
how much **more**	πόσῳ **μᾶλλον**
your Father	ὁ πατὴρ ὑμῶν
who is in heaven	ὁ ἐν τοῖς οὐρανοῖς
will . . . give **good things**	δώσει **ἀγαθὰ**
to those who ask him!	τοῖς αἰτοῦσιν αὐτόν

You brood of vipers, how can you speak good, **evil (πονηροὶ)** as you are? **For (γὰρ)** from the overflow of the heart the **mouth (στόμα)** speaks. (MLB)

στόμα	mouth	78x
*sto*ma		S4750

     γάρ ➤ DAY 18   **πονηρός** ➤ DAY 215

γεννήματα ἐχιδνῶν, πῶς δύνασθε ἀγαθὰ λαλεῖν **πονηροὶ** ὄντες; ἐκ **γὰρ** τοῦ περισσεύματος τῆς καρδίας τὸ **στόμα** λαλεῖ.

You brood of vipers	γεννήματα ἐχιδνῶν
how can you	πῶς δύνασθε
speak good	ἀγαθὰ λαλεῖν
evil as you are?	**πονηροὶ** ὄντες;
For from	ἐκ **γὰρ**
the overflow	τοῦ περισσεύματος
of the heart	τῆς καρδίας
the **mouth** speaks	τὸ **στόμα** λαλεῖ

Jesus said to them, "**My (Ἐμὸν)** nourishment is that I do the will of Him **who sent (πέμψαντός)** Me and completely do His **work (ἔργον)**." (MLB)

ἐμός	my, mine	77x
emos		S1699

ἔργον ➢ DAY 92   **πέμπω** ➢ DAY 213

λέγει αὐτοῖς ὁ Ἰησοῦς Ἐμὸν βρῶμά ἐστιν ἵνα ποιήσω τὸ θέλημα τοῦ **πέμψαντός** με καὶ τελειώσω αὐτοῦ τὸ **ἔργον**.

Jesus said to them	λέγει αὐτοῖς ὁ Ἰησοῦς
My nourishment	Ἐμὸν βρῶμά
is	ἐστιν
that I do	ἵνα ποιήσω
the will	τὸ θέλημα
of Him **who sent** Me	τοῦ **πέμψαντός** με
and completely do	καὶ τελειώσω
His **work**	αὐτοῦ τὸ **ἔργον**

And the serpent **poured (ἔβαλεν) water (ὕδωρ)** like a river out of his **mouth (στόματος)** after the woman, so that he might cause her to be swept away with the flood. (NASB)

ὕδωρ	water	77x
hudōr		S5204

βάλλω ➢ DAY 134   **στόμα** ➢ DAY 216

καὶ **ἔβαλεν** ὁ ὄφις ἐκ τοῦ **στόματος** αὐτοῦ ὀπίσω τῆς γυναικὸς **ὕδωρ** ὡς ποταμόν, ἵνα αὐτὴν ποταμοφόρητον ποιήσῃ.

And the serpent	καὶ . . . ὁ ὄφις
poured water	**ἔβαλεν** . . . **ὕδωρ**
like a river	ὡς ποταμόν
out of his **mouth**	ἐκ τοῦ **στόματος** αὐτοῦ
after the woman	ὀπίσω τῆς γυναικὸς
so that he might cause her to be	ἵνα αὐτὴν . . . ποιήσῃ
swept away with the flood	ποταμοφόρητον

I **have baptized (ἐβάπτισα)** you with **water (ὕδατι)**, but He **will baptize (βαπτίσει)** you with the **Holy (ἁγίῳ)** Spirit. (MLB)

βαπτίζω	to baptize	76x
baptizō		S907

ἅγιος ➤ DAY 67   **ὕδωρ** ➤ DAY 218

ἐγὼ **ἐβάπτισα** ὑμᾶς **ὕδατι**, αὐτὸς δὲ **βαπτίσει** ὑμᾶς πνεύματι ἁγίῳ.

I **have baptized** you	ἐγὼ **ἐβάπτισα** ὑμᾶς
with **water**	**ὕδατι**
but He **will baptize** you	αὐτὸς δὲ **βαπτίσει** ὑμᾶς
with the **Holy** Spirit	πνεύματι **ἁγίῳ**

This greeting is in **my own (ἐμῇ)** hand—Paul. This is a **sign (σημεῖον)** in every letter; **this is how (οὕτως)** I write. (HCSB)

σημεῖον	sign, miracle	76x
sēmeion		S4592

οὕτως ➢ DAY 77   **ἐμός** ➢ DAY 217

Ὁ ἀσπασμὸς τῇ **ἐμῇ** χειρὶ Παύλου, ὅ ἐστιν **σημεῖον** ἐν πάσῃ ἐπιστολῇ· **οὕτως** γράφω.

This greeting	Ὁ ἀσπασμὸς
is in **my own** hand	τῇ **ἐμῇ** χειρὶ
Paul	Παύλου
This is a **sign**	ὅ ἐστιν **σημεῖον**
in every letter	ἐν πάσῃ ἐπιστολῇ
this is how	**οὕτως**
I write	γράφω

When all the people **were being baptized (βαπτισθῆναι)**, Jesus too **was baptized (βαπτισθέντος)** and, while **He was praying (προσευχομένου)**, heaven **was opened (ἀνεῳχθῆναι)**. (MLB)

ἀνοίγω	to open	75x
anoigō		S455

προσεύχομαι ➤ DAY 198　　　**βαπτίζω** ➤ DAY 219

Ἐγένετο δὲ ἐν τῷ **βαπτισθῆναι** ἅπαντα τὸν λαὸν καὶ Ἰησοῦ **βαπτισθέντος** καὶ **προσευχομένου ἀνεῳχθῆναι** τὸν οὐρανὸν

When all the people **were being baptized**	Ἐγένετο δὲ ἐν τῷ **βαπτισθῆναι** ἅπαντα τὸν λαὸν
Jesus too **was baptized**	καὶ Ἰησοῦ **βαπτισθέντος**
and, while **He was praying**	καὶ **προσευχομένου**
heaven **was opened**	**ἀνεῳχθῆναι** τὸν οὐρανὸν

And to **them (ἐκείνοις)** he said, "You **go (Ὑπάγετε)** into the vineyard too, and whatever is **right (δίκαιον)** I will give you." (ESV)

δίκαιος	just, righteous	75x
dikaios		S1342

ἐκεῖνος ▷ DAY 64   ὑπάγω ▷ DAY 214

καὶ **ἐκείνοις** εἶπεν Ὑπάγετε καὶ ὑμεῖς εἰς τὸν ἀμπελῶνα, καὶ ὃ ἐὰν ᾖ **δίκαιον** δώσω ὑμῖν·

And to **them** he said	καὶ **ἐκείνοις** εἶπεν
You . . . too	καὶ ὑμεῖς
go	Ὑπάγετε
into the vineyard	εἰς τὸν ἀμπελῶνα
and whatever	καὶ ὃ ἐὰν
is **right**	ᾖ **δίκαιον**
I will give you	δώσω ὑμῖν

And he appointed **twelve (δώδεκα)** (whom he also named **apostles [ἀποστόλους]**) so that **they might be (ὦσιν)** with him and he might send them out to preach. (ESV)

δώδεκα	twelve	75x
dōdeka		S1427

εἰμί ➤ DAY 8　　　　**ἀπόστολος** ➤ DAY 210

καὶ ἐποίησεν **δώδεκα**, οὓς καὶ **ἀποστόλους** ὠνόμασεν, ἵνα **ὦσιν** μετ᾽ αὐτοῦ καὶ ἵνα ἀποστέλλῃ αὐτοὺς κηρύσσειν

And he appointed	καὶ ἐποίησεν
twelve	**δώδεκα**
whom he also named **apostles**	οὓς καὶ **ἀποστόλους** ὠνόμασεν
so that **they might be**	ἵνα **ὦσιν**
with him	μετ᾽ αὐτοῦ
and he might send them out	καὶ ἵνα ἀποστέλλῃ αὐτοὺς
to preach	κηρύσσειν

And a great **sign (σημεῖον)** appeared in heaven: a woman clothed with the sun, with the moon under her feet, and on her **head (κεφαλῆς)** a crown of **twelve (δώδεκα)** stars. (ESV)

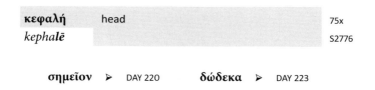

| **κεφαλή** | head | 75x |
| *kephalē* | | S2776 |

σημεῖον ➤ DAY 220 **δώδεκα** ➤ DAY 223

Καὶ **σημεῖον** μέγα ὤφθη ἐν τῷ οὐρανῷ, γυνὴ περιβεβλημένη τὸν ἥλιον, καὶ ἡ σελήνη ὑποκάτω τῶν ποδῶν αὐτῆς, καὶ ἐπὶ τῆς **κεφαλῆς** αὐτῆς στέφανος ἀστέρων **δώδεκα,**

And a great **sign**	Καὶ **σημεῖον** μέγα
appeared	ὤφθη
in heaven	ἐν τῷ οὐρανῷ
a woman clothed	γυνὴ περιβεβλημένη
with the sun	τὸν ἥλιον
with the moon	καὶ ἡ σελήνη
under her feet	ὑποκάτω τῶν ποδῶν αὐτῆς
and on her **head**	καὶ ἐπὶ τῆς **κεφαλῆς** αὐτῆς
a crown	στέφανος
of **twelve** stars	ἀστέρων **δώδεκα**

And John **testified (ἐμαρτύρησεν)**, "I saw the Spirit **descending (καταβαῖνον)** from heaven like a dove, and **it remained (ἔμεινεν)** on him." (NRSV)

| μαρτυρέω | to witness, bear witness, testify | 75x |
| *martureō* | | S3140 |

μένω ➤ DAY 139   **καταβαίνω** ➤ DAY 208

Καὶ **ἐμαρτύρησεν** Ἰωάνης λέγων ὅτι Τεθέαμαι τὸ πνεῦμα **καταβαῖνον** ὡς περιστερὰν ἐξ οὐρανοῦ, καὶ **ἔμεινεν** ἐπ' αὐτόν·

And John **testified**	Καὶ **ἐμαρτύρησεν** Ἰωάνης λέγων ὅτι
I saw	Τεθέαμαι
the Spirit	τὸ πνεῦμα
descending	**καταβαῖνον**
from heaven	ἐξ οὐρανοῦ
like a dove	ὡς περιστερὰν
and **it remained**	καὶ **ἔμεινεν**
on him	ἐπ' αὐτόν

Which of the prophets did your ancestors not persecute? **They killed (ἀπέκτειναν)** those who foretold the coming of the **Righteous One (δικαίου)**, and now you **have become (ἐγένεσθε)** his betrayers and murderers. (NRSV)

ἀποκτείνω	to kill	74x
apokteinō		S615

γίνομαι ➤ DAY 27		**δίκαιος** ➤ DAY 222

τίνα τῶν προφητῶν οὐκ ἐδίωξαν οἱ πατέρες ὑμῶν; καὶ **ἀπέκτειναν** τοὺς προκαταγγείλαντας περὶ τῆς ἐλεύσεως τοῦ **δικαίου** οὗ νῦν ὑμεῖς προδόται καὶ φονεῖς **ἐγένεσθε**,

Which of the prophets	τίνα τῶν προφητῶν
did your ancestors not persecute?	οὐκ ἐδίωξαν οἱ πατέρες ὑμῶν;
They killed	καὶ **ἀπέκτειναν**
those who foretold	τοὺς προκαταγγείλαντας περὶ
the coming	τῆς ἐλεύσεως
of the **Righteous One**	τοῦ **δικαίου**
and now	νῦν
you **have become**	ὑμεῖς . . . **ἐγένεσθε**
his betrayers and murderers	οὗ . . . προδόται καὶ φονεῖς

Simon (Σίμων) Peter said to Him, "Lord, not only my feet but also my **hands (χεῖρας)** and my **head (κεφαλήν)**!" (MLB)

Σίμων	Simon	74x
Simōn		S4613

χείρ ➤ DAY 88   **κεφαλή** ➤ DAY 224

λέγει αὐτῷ **Σίμων** Πέτρος Κύριε, μὴ τοὺς πόδας μου μόνον ἀλλὰ καὶ τὰς **χεῖρας** καὶ τὴν **κεφαλήν**.

Simon Peter	**Σίμων** Πέτρος
said to Him	λέγει αὐτῷ
Lord	Κύριε
not only	μὴ . . . μόνον
my feet	τοὺς πόδας μου
but also	ἀλλὰ καὶ
my **hands**	τὰς **χεῖρας**
and my **head**!	καὶ τὴν **κεφαλήν**

For **I rejoiced (ἐχάρην)** greatly when the brothers came and **testified (μαρτυρούντων)** to your **truth (ἀληθείᾳ)**, as indeed you are walking in the **truth (ἀληθείᾳ)**. (ESV)

χαίρω	to rejoice	74x
chairō		S5463

    ἀλήθεια ➢ DAY 154   **μαρτυρέω** ➢ DAY 225

ἐχάρην γὰρ λίαν ἐρχομένων ἀδελφῶν καὶ **μαρτυρούντων** σου τῇ **ἀληθείᾳ**, καθὼς σὺ ἐν **ἀληθείᾳ** περιπατεῖς.

For **I rejoiced**	**ἐχάρην** γὰρ
greatly	λίαν
when the brothers came	ἐρχομένων ἀδελφῶν
and **testified**	καὶ **μαρτυρούντων**
to your **truth**	σου τῇ **ἀληθείᾳ**
as indeed	καθὼς
you are walking	σὺ . . . περιπατεῖς
in the **truth**	ἐν **ἀληθείᾳ**

Your father **Abraham (Ἀβραάμ)** was overjoyed that **he would see (ἴδῃ)** My day; **he saw (εἶδεν)** it and **rejoiced (ἐχάρη)**. (HCSB)

Ἀβραάμ	Abraham	73x
Abraam		S11

ὁράω ➤ DAY 40　　　χαίρω ➤ DAY 228

Ἀβραὰμ ὁ πατὴρ ὑμῶν ἠγαλλιάσατο ἵνα **ἴδῃ** τὴν ἡμέραν τὴν ἐμήν, καὶ **εἶδεν** καὶ **ἐχάρη**.

Your father	ὁ πατὴρ ὑμῶν
Abraham	Ἀβραὰμ
was overjoyed	ἠγαλλιάσατο
that **he would see**	ἵνα **ἴδῃ**
My day	τὴν ἡμέραν τὴν ἐμήν
he saw it	καὶ **εἶδεν**
and **rejoiced**	καὶ **ἐχάρη**

by the power of signs and wonders, by the power of the Holy Spirit, so that from **Jerusalem (Ἰερουσαλὴμ)** and everywhere as far as Illyricum, I **have fully preached (πεπληρωκέναι)** the **good news (εὐαγγέλιον)** concerning Christ. (MLB)

εὐαγγέλιον	good news, gospel	73x
euangelion		S2098

Ἰερουσαλήμ / Ἰεροσόλυμα ➤ DAY 122   **πληρόω** ➤ DAY 200

ἐν δυνάμει σημείων καὶ τεράτων, ἐν δυνάμει πνεύματος [ἁγίου]· ὥστε με ἀπὸ **Ἰερουσαλὴμ** καὶ κύκλῳ μέχρι τοῦ Ἰλλυρικοῦ **πεπληρωκέναι** τὸ **εὐαγγέλιον** τοῦ χριστοῦ,

by the power	ἐν δυνάμει
of signs and wonders	σημείων καὶ τεράτων
by the power	ἐν δυνάμει
of the Holy Spirit	πνεύματος [ἁγίου]
so that from **Jerusalem**	ὥστε . . . ἀπὸ **Ἰερουσαλὴμ**
and everywhere	καὶ κύκλῳ
as far as Illyricum	μέχρι τοῦ Ἰλλυρικοῦ
I **have fully preached**	με . . . **πεπληρωκέναι**
the **good news**	τὸ **εὐαγγέλιον**
concerning Christ	τοῦ χριστοῦ

But when **you (σὺ)** fast, anoint **your (σου) head (κεφαλὴν)** and wash **your (σου) face (πρόσωπόν).** (MLB)

πρόσωπον	face, presence, appearance	73x
prosōpon		S4383

σύ, (pl) ὑμεῖς ➢ DAY 4　　　　**κεφαλή** ➢ DAY 224

σὺ δὲ νηστεύων ἄλειψαί **σου** τὴν **κεφαλὴν** καὶ τὸ **πρόσωπόν σου** νίψαι,

But when **you** fast	**σὺ** δὲ νηστεύων
anoint	ἄλειψαί
your head	**σου** τὴν **κεφαλὴν**
and wash	καὶ . . . νίψαι
your face	τὸ **πρόσωπόν σου**

There he was transfigured before them. His **face (πρόσωπον)** shone like the sun, and his clothes **became (ἐγένετο)** as white as the **light (φῶς)**. (NIV)

φῶς	light	73x
phōs		S5457

    γίνομαι ➤ DAY 27   **πρόσωπον** ➤ DAY 231

καὶ μετεμορφώθη ἔμπροσθεν αὐτῶν, καὶ ἔλαμψεν τὸ **πρόσωπον** αὐτοῦ ὡς ὁ ἥλιος, τὰ δὲ ἱμάτια αὐτοῦ **ἐγένετο** λευκὰ ὡς τὸ **φῶς**.

There he was transfigured	καὶ μετεμορφώθη
before them	ἔμπροσθεν αὐτῶν
His **face**	καὶ . . . τὸ **πρόσωπον** αὐτοῦ
shone	ἔλαμψεν
like the sun	ὡς ὁ ἥλιος
and his clothes	τὰ δὲ ἱμάτια αὐτοῦ
became	**ἐγένετο**
as white as	λευκὰ ὡς
the **light**	τὸ **φῶς**

A woman from Samaria came to draw **water (ὕδωρ)**. Jesus said to
her, "**Give (Δός)** me a drink [lit., **to drink (πεῖν)**]." (ESV)

πίνω	to drink	72x
pinō		S4095

δίδωμι ➤ DAY 43   **ὕδωρ** ➤ DAY 218

ἔρχεται γυνὴ ἐκ τῆς Σαμαρίας ἀντλῆσαι **ὕδωρ**. λέγει αὐτῇ ὁ
Ἰησοῦς **Δός** μοι **πεῖν**·

A woman from Samaria	γυνὴ ἐκ τῆς Σαμαρίας
came	ἔρχεται
to draw **water**	ἀντλῆσαι **ὕδωρ**
Jesus	ὁ Ἰησοῦς
said to her	λέγει αὐτῇ
Give me	**Δός** μοι
a drink [lit., **to drink**]	**πεῖν**

Jesus answered him, "I have spoken openly to the world; I always taught in synagogues and in the **temple (ἱερῷ)**, **where (ὅπου)** all the **Jews (Ἰουδαῖοι)** come together; and I spoke nothing in secret." (NASB)

ἱερόν	temple	71x
hieron		S2411

Ἰουδαῖος	➤	DAY 83	**ὅπου** ➤	DAY 209

ἀπεκρίθη αὐτῷ Ἰησοῦς Ἐγὼ παρρησίᾳ λελάληκα τῷ κόσμῳ· ἐγὼ πάντοτε ἐδίδαξα ἐν συναγωγῇ καὶ ἐν τῷ **ἱερῷ**, **ὅπου** πάντες οἱ **Ἰουδαῖοι** συνέρχονται, καὶ ἐν κρυπτῷ ἐλάλησα οὐδέν·

Jesus answered him	ἀπεκρίθη αὐτῷ Ἰησοῦς
I have spoken	Ἐγὼ . . . λελάληκα
openly	παρρησίᾳ
to the world	τῷ κόσμῳ
I always taught	ἐγὼ πάντοτε ἐδίδαξα
in synagogues	ἐν συναγωγῇ
and in the **temple**	καὶ ἐν τῷ **ἱερῷ**
where all the **Jews**	**ὅπου** πάντες οἱ **Ἰουδαῖοι**
come together	συνέρχονται
and I spoke nothing	καὶ . . . ἐλάλησα οὐδέν
in secret	ἐν κρυπτῷ

And I saw another mighty angel coming down from heaven, wrapped in a cloud, with a rainbow over his head; his **face** (**πρόσωπον**) was like the sun, and his **legs (πόδες)** like pillars of **fire (πυρός)**. (NRSV)

πῦρ	fire	71x
pur		S4442

    πούς ➤ DAY 181   **πρόσωπον** ➤ DAY 231

Καὶ εἶδον ἄλλον ἄγγελον ἰσχυρὸν καταβαίνοντα ἐκ τοῦ οὐρανοῦ, περιβεβλημένον νεφέλην, καὶ ἡ ἶρις ἐπὶ τὴν κεφαλὴν αὐτοῦ, καὶ τὸ **πρόσωπον** αὐτοῦ ὡς ὁ ἥλιος, καὶ οἱ **πόδες** αὐτοῦ ὡς στῦλοι **πυρός**,

And I saw	Καὶ εἶδον
another mighty angel	ἄλλον ἄγγελον ἰσχυρὸν
coming down	καταβαίνοντα
from heaven	ἐκ τοῦ οὐρανοῦ
wrapped in a cloud	περιβεβλημένον νεφέλην
with a rainbow	καὶ ἡ ἶρις
over his head	ἐπὶ τὴν κεφαλὴν αὐτοῦ
his **face**	καὶ τὸ **πρόσωπον** αὐτοῦ
was like the sun	ὡς ὁ ἥλιος
and his **legs**	καὶ οἱ **πόδες** αὐτοῦ
like pillars of **fire**	ὡς στῦλοι **πυρός**

Then he will say to those on his left, "**Depart (Πορεύεσθε)** from me, you who are cursed, into the **eternal (αἰώνιον) fire (πῦρ)** prepared for the devil and his angels." (NIV)

αἰώνιος	eternal, unending	70x
aiōnios		S166

πορεύομαι ➤ DAY 105   **πῦρ** ➤ DAY 235

τότε ἐρεῖ καὶ τοῖς ἐξ εὐωνύμων **Πορεύεσθε** ἀπ᾽ ἐμοῦ κατηραμένοι εἰς τὸ **πῦρ** τὸ **αἰώνιον** τὸ ἡτοιμασμένον τῷ διαβόλῳ καὶ τοῖς ἀγγέλοις αὐτοῦ·

Then he will say	τότε ἐρεῖ
to those on his left	καὶ τοῖς ἐξ εὐωνύμων
Depart	**Πορεύεσθε**
from me	ἀπ᾽ ἐμοῦ
you who are cursed	κατηραμένοι
into the **eternal fire**	εἰς τὸ **πῦρ** τὸ **αἰώνιον**
prepared	τὸ ἡτοιμασμένον
for the devil	τῷ διαβόλῳ
and his angels	καὶ τοῖς ἀγγέλοις αὐτοῦ

Keep (τηρήσατε) yourselves in the **love (ἀγάπη)** of God, waiting for the mercy of our Lord Jesus Christ that leads to **eternal (αἰώνιον)** life. (ESV)

τηρέω	to watch, observe, guard, keep	70x
tēreō		S5083

ἀγάπη ➤ DAY 145   **αἰώνιος** ➤ DAY 236

ἑαυτοὺς ἐν **ἀγάπη** θεοῦ **τηρήσατε** προσδεχόμενοι τὸ ἔλεος τοῦ κυρίου ἡμῶν Ἰησοῦ Χριστοῦ εἰς ζωὴν **αἰώνιον**.

Keep yourselves	ἑαυτοὺς . . . **τηρήσατε**
in the **love** of God	ἐν **ἀγάπη** θεοῦ
waiting for	προσδεχόμενοι
the mercy	τὸ ἔλεος
of our Lord	τοῦ κυρίου ἡμῶν
Jesus Christ	Ἰησοῦ Χριστοῦ
that leads to **eternal** life	εἰς ζωὴν **αἰώνιον**

And **he led** (Ἤγαγεν) Him to Jerusalem and **had** Him **stand** (ἔστησεν) on the pinnacle of the **temple** (ἱεροῦ), and said to Him, "If You are the Son of God, throw Yourself down from here." (NASB)

| ἄγω | to lead (away), bring | 68x |
| *agō* | | S71 |

| ἵστημι | ➤ DAY 109 | ἱερόν | ➤ DAY 234 |

Ἤγαγεν δὲ αὐτὸν εἰς Ἰερουσαλὴμ καὶ **ἔστησεν** ἐπὶ τὸ πτερύγιον τοῦ **ἱεροῦ**, καὶ εἶπεν [αὐτῷ] Εἰ υἱὸς εἶ τοῦ θεοῦ, βάλε σεαυτὸν ἐντεῦθεν κάτω·

And **he led** Him	Ἤγαγεν δὲ αὐτὸν
to Jerusalem	εἰς Ἰερουσαλὴμ
and **had** Him **stand**	καὶ **ἔστησεν**
on the pinnacle	ἐπὶ τὸ πτερύγιον
of the **temple**	τοῦ **ἱεροῦ**
and said to Him	καὶ εἶπεν [αὐτῷ]
If You are	Εἰ . . . εἶ
the Son of God	υἱὸς . . . τοῦ θεοῦ
throw Yourself down	βάλε σεαυτὸν . . . κάτω
from here	ἐντεῦθεν

Those who conducted Paul **brought (ἤγαγον)** him as far as Athens; and after receiving **instructions (ἐντολὴν)** to have Silas and Timothy join [lit., **come (ἔλθωσιν)** to] him as soon as possible, they left him. (NRSV)

ἐντολή	command, commandment	68x
entolē		S1785

ἔρχομαι ➤ DAY 30 **ἄγω** ➤ DAY 238

οἱ δὲ καθιστάνοντες τὸν Παῦλον **ἤγαγον** ἕως Ἀθηνῶν, καὶ λαβόντες **ἐντολὴν** πρὸς τὸν Σίλαν καὶ τὸν Τιμόθεον ἵνα ὡς τάχιστα **ἔλθωσιν** πρὸς αὐτὸν ἐξῄεσαν.

Those who conducted	οἱ δὲ καθιστάνοντες
Paul	τὸν Παῦλον
brought him	**ἤγαγον**
as far as Athens	ἕως Ἀθηνῶν
and after receiving **instructions**	καὶ λαβόντες **ἐντολὴν**
to have Silas and Timothy join [lit., **come** to] him	πρὸς τὸν Σίλαν καὶ τὸν Τιμόθεον ἵνα ... **ἔλθωσιν** πρὸς αὐτὸν
as soon as possible	ὡς τάχιστα
they left him	ἐξῄεσαν

From the descendants of **this man (τούτου)**, according to promise, God **has brought (ἤγαγεν)** to Israel (**Ἰσραὴλ**) a Savior, Jesus. (NASB)

Ἰσραήλ	Israel	68x
Israēl		S2474

οὗτος, αὕτη, τοῦτο ➢ DAY 13   **ἄγω** ➢ DAY 238

τούτου ὁ θεὸς ἀπὸ τοῦ σπέρματος κατ᾽ ἐπαγγελίαν **ἤγαγεν** τῷ Ἰσραὴλ σωτῆρα Ἰησοῦν,

From the descendants	ἀπὸ τοῦ σπέρματος
of **this man**	**τούτου**
according to promise	κατ᾽ ἐπαγγελίαν
God **has brought**	ὁ θεὸς . . . **ἤγαγεν**
to **Israel**	τῷ **Ἰσραὴλ**
a Savior	σωτῆρα
Jesus	Ἰησοῦν

He stepped into one of the **boats (πλοίων)** which belonged to **Simon (Σίμωνος)**, and asked him to push out a little from the **shore (γῆς)**; then when He had sat down He began to teach the crowd from the **boat (πλοίου)**. (MLB)

πλοῖον	boat, ship	68x
ploion		S4143

γῆ ➤ DAY 61　　　　**Σίμων** ➤ DAY 227

ἐμβὰς δὲ εἰς ἓν τῶν **πλοίων**, ὃ ἦν **Σίμωνος**, ἠρώτησεν αὐτὸν ἀπὸ τῆς **γῆς** ἐπαναγαγεῖν ὀλίγον, καθίσας δὲ ἐκ τοῦ **πλοίου** ἐδίδασκεν τοὺς ὄχλους.

He stepped into	ἐμβὰς δὲ εἰς
one of the **boats**	ἓν τῶν **πλοίων**
which belonged to **Simon**	ὃ ἦν **Σίμωνος**
and asked him	ἠρώτησεν αὐτὸν
to push out a little	ἐπαναγαγεῖν ὀλίγον
from the **shore**	ἀπὸ τῆς **γῆς**
then when He had sat down	καθίσας δὲ
He began to teach the crowd	ἐδίδασκεν τοὺς ὄχλους
from the **boat**	ἐκ τοῦ **πλοίου**

After (Μετὰ) three (τρεῖς) months we put out to sea in a **ship (πλοίῳ)** that had wintered in the island—it was an Alexandrian ship with the figurehead of the twin gods Castor and Pollux [lit., marked with the Dioscuri]. (NIV)

τρεῖς, τρία	three	68x
*treis, **tria***		S5140

    μετά ➤ DAY 41   **πλοῖον** ➤ DAY 241

Μετὰ δὲ **τρεῖς** μῆνας ἀνήχθημεν ἐν **πλοίῳ** παρακεχειμακότι ἐν τῇ νήσῳ Ἀλεξανδρινῷ, παρασήμῳ Διοσκούροις.

After three months	**Μετὰ** δὲ **τρεῖς** μῆνας
we put out to sea	ἀνήχθημεν
in a **ship**	ἐν **πλοίῳ**
that had wintered	παρακεχειμακότι
in the island	ἐν τῇ νήσῳ
it was an Alexandrian ship	Ἀλεξανδρινῷ
with the figurehead of the twin gods Castor and Pollux [lit., marked with the Dioscuri]	παρασήμῳ Διοσκούροις

And whatever **we ask (αἰτῶμεν)** we receive from Him, for **we observe (τηροῦμεν)** His **commands (ἐντολὰς)** and practice what is pleasing in His sight. (MLB)

αἰτέω	to ask, request	67x
aiteō		S154

τηρέω ➤ DAY 237   **ἐντολή** ➤ DAY 239

καὶ ὃ ἂν **αἰτῶμεν** λαμβάνομεν ἀπ᾽ αὐτοῦ, ὅτι τὰς **ἐντολὰς** αὐτοῦ **τηροῦμεν** καὶ τὰ ἀρεστὰ ἐνώπιον αὐτοῦ ποιοῦμεν.

And whatever	καὶ ὃ ἂν
we ask	**αἰτῶμεν**
we receive	λαμβάνομεν
from Him	ἀπ᾽ αὐτοῦ
for **we observe**	ὅτι . . . **τηροῦμεν**
His **commands**	τὰς **ἐντολὰς** αὐτοῦ
and practice	καὶ . . . ποιοῦμεν
what is pleasing	τὰ ἀρεστὰ
in His sight	ἐνώπιον αὐτοῦ

Sirs, I can see that the voyage will be [lit., **is going (μέλλειν)** to be] with danger and much heavy loss, not **only (μόνον)** of the cargo and the **ship (πλοίου)**, but also of our lives. (NRSV)

μόνον	only	67x
*mon*on		S3440

μέλλω	➤	DAY 152	πλοῖον	➤	DAY 241

Ἄνδρες, θεωρῶ ὅτι μετὰ ὕβρεως καὶ πολλῆς ζημίας οὐ **μόνον** τοῦ φορτίου καὶ τοῦ **πλοίου** ἀλλὰ καὶ τῶν ψυχῶν ἡμῶν **μέλλειν** ἔσεσθαι τὸν πλοῦν.

Sirs	Ἄνδρες
I can see that	θεωρῶ ὅτι
the voyage	τὸν πλοῦν
will be [lit., **is going** to be]	**μέλλειν** ἔσεσθαι
with danger	μετὰ ὕβρεως
and much heavy loss	καὶ πολλῆς ζημίας
not **only**	οὐ **μόνον**
of the cargo	τοῦ φορτίου
and the **ship**	καὶ τοῦ **πλοίου**
but also	ἀλλὰ καὶ
of our lives	τῶν ψυχῶν ἡμῶν

So then those who are of **faith (πίστεως)** are blessed with
Abraham (Ἀβραάμ), the **believer (πιστῷ)**. (NASB)

πιστός	faithful, trustworthy, reliable	67x
pistos		S4103

πίστις ➤ DAY 62   **Ἀβραάμ** ➤ DAY 229

ὥστε οἱ ἐκ **πίστεως** εὐλογοῦνται σὺν τῷ **πιστῷ** Ἀβραάμ.

So then	ὥστε
those who are of **faith**	οἱ ἐκ **πίστεως**
are blessed	εὐλογοῦνται
with **Abraham**	σὺν . . . Ἀβραάμ
the **believer**	τῷ **πιστῷ**

And according to Paul's custom, he went [lit., **he entered (εἰσῆλθεν)**] to them, and for **three (τρία) Sabbaths (σάββατα)** reasoned with them from the Scriptures. (NASB)

σάββατον	Sabbath	67x
sabbaton		S4521

εἰσέρχομαι ➤ DAY 82　　　τρεῖς, τρία ➤ DAY 242

κατὰ δὲ τὸ εἰωθὸς τῷ Παύλῳ **εἰσῆλθεν** πρὸς αὐτοὺς καὶ ἐπὶ **σάββατα τρία** διελέξατο αὐτοῖς ἀπὸ τῶν γραφῶν,

And according to Paul's custom	κατὰ δὲ τὸ εἰωθὸς τῷ Παύλῳ
he went [lit., **he entered**]	**εἰσῆλθεν**
to them	πρὸς αὐτοὺς
and for **three Sabbaths**	καὶ ἐπὶ **σάββατα τρία**
reasoned with them	διελέξατο αὐτοῖς
from the Scriptures	ἀπὸ τῶν γραφῶν

Seeing a lone fig tree by the road, He came to it and **found (εὗρεν)** nothing on it except leaves **only (μόνον)**; and He said to it, "No longer shall there ever be any **fruit (καρπὸς)** from you." And at once the fig tree withered. (NASB)

καρπός	fruit	66x
karpos		S2590

εὑρίσκω ➤ DAY 93   **μόνον** ➤ DAY 244

καὶ ἰδὼν συκῆν μίαν ἐπὶ τῆς ὁδοῦ ἦλθεν ἐπ' αὐτήν, καὶ οὐδὲν **εὗρεν** ἐν αὐτῇ εἰ μὴ φύλλα **μόνον**, καὶ λέγει αὐτῇ Οὐ μηκέτι ἐκ σοῦ **καρπὸς** γένηται εἰς τὸν αἰῶνα· καὶ ἐξηράνθη παραχρῆμα ἡ συκῆ.

Seeing a lone fig tree	καὶ ἰδὼν συκῆν μίαν
by the road	ἐπὶ τῆς ὁδοῦ
He came to it	ἦλθεν ἐπ' αὐτήν
and **found** nothing on it	καὶ οὐδὲν **εὗρεν** ἐν αὐτῇ
except leaves **only**	εἰ μὴ φύλλα **μόνον**
and He said to it	καὶ λέγει αὐτῇ
No longer shall there ever be	Οὐ μηκέτι . . . γένηται εἰς τὸν αἰῶνα
any **fruit** from you	ἐκ σοῦ **καρπὸς**
And at once	καὶ . . . παραχρῆμα
the fig tree withered	ἐξηράνθη . . . ἡ συκῆ

The chief priests and the **elders (πρεσβύτεροι)**, however, persuaded the crowds to ask for [lit., so that **they would ask for (αἰτήσωνται)**] Barabbas and to execute [lit., but that **they would execute (ἀπολέσωσιν)**] Jesus. (CSB)

πρεσβύτερος	old, elder, ancestor	66x
*pres**bu**teros*		S4245

ἀπόλλυμι	➤	DAY 190	αἰτέω	➤	DAY 243

Οἱ δὲ ἀρχιερεῖς καὶ οἱ **πρεσβύτεροι** ἔπεισαν τοὺς ὄχλους ἵνα **αἰτήσωνται** τὸν Βαραββᾶν τὸν δὲ Ἰησοῦν **ἀπολέσωσιν**.

The chief priests and the **elders**, however	Οἱ δὲ ἀρχιερεῖς καὶ οἱ **πρεσβύτεροι**
persuaded the crowds	ἔπεισαν τοὺς ὄχλους
to ask for [lit., so that **they would ask for**] Barabbas	ἵνα **αἰτήσωνται** τὸν Βαραββᾶν
and to execute [lit., but that **they would execute**] Jesus	τὸν δὲ Ἰησοῦν **ἀπολέσωσιν**

His master **said (ἔφη)** to him, "Well done, good and **trustworthy (πιστέ) slave (δοῦλε)**; you have been **trustworthy (πιστός)** in a few things, I will put you in charge of many things; enter into the joy of your master." (NRSV)

φημί	to say	66x
phēmi		S5346

    δοῦλος ➤ DAY 137   **πιστός** ➤ DAY 245

ἔφη αὐτῷ ὁ κύριος αὐτοῦ Εὖ, **δοῦλε** ἀγαθὲ καὶ **πιστέ**, ἐπὶ ὀλίγα ἧς **πιστός**, ἐπὶ πολλῶν σε καταστήσω· εἴσελθε εἰς τὴν χαρὰν τοῦ κυρίου σου.

His master	ὁ κύριος αὐτοῦ
said to him	**ἔφη** αὐτῷ
Well done	Εὖ
good and **trustworthy slave**	**δοῦλε** ἀγαθὲ καὶ **πιστέ**
you have been **trustworthy**	ἧς **πιστός**
in a few things	ἐπὶ ὀλίγα
I will put you in charge	σε καταστήσω
of many things	ἐπὶ πολλῶν
enter	εἴσελθε
into the joy	εἰς τὴν χαρὰν
of your master	τοῦ κυρίου σου

So Agrippa **said (ἔφη)** to Festus, "This man **could have (ἐδύνατο) been set free (Ἀπολελύσθαι)**, if he had not appealed to Caesar."

| ἀπολύω | to set free, release, let loose, withdraw | 65x |
| *apoluō* | | S630 |

    δύναμαι   ▷   DAY 75   **φημί**   ▷   DAY 249

Ἀγρίππας δὲ τῷ Φήστῳ **ἔφη Ἀπολελύσθαι ἐδύνατο** ὁ ἄνθρωπος οὗτος εἰ μὴ ἐπεκέκλητο Καίσαρα.

So Agrippa **said**	Ἀγρίππας δὲ . . . **ἔφη**
to Festus	τῷ Φήστῳ
This man	ὁ ἄνθρωπος οὗτος
could have	**ἐδύνατο**
been set free	**Ἀπολελύσθαι**
if he had not appealed to	εἰ μὴ ἐπεκέκλητο
Caesar	Καίσαρα

Only (Μόνον) conduct yourselves in a manner worthy of the gospel of Christ, so that **whether (εἴτε)** I come and see you **or (εἴτε)** remain absent, I will hear of you that you are standing firm in **one (ἑνὶ)** spirit, with **one (μιᾷ)** mind striving together for the faith of the gospel. (NASB)

εἴτε	if, whether	65x
eite		S1535

εἷς, μία, ἕν ➤ DAY 49　　　**μόνον** ➤ DAY 244

Μόνον ἀξίως τοῦ εὐαγγελίου τοῦ χριστοῦ πολιτεύεσθε, ἵνα **εἴτε** ἐλθὼν καὶ ἰδὼν ὑμᾶς **εἴτε** ἀπὼν ἀκούω τὰ περὶ ὑμῶν, ὅτι στήκετε ἐν **ἑνὶ** πνεύματι, **μιᾷ** ψυχῇ συναθλοῦντες τῇ πίστει τοῦ εὐαγγελίου,

Only conduct yourselves	**Μόνον** . . . πολιτεύεσθε
in a manner worthy	ἀξίως
of the gospel of Christ	τοῦ εὐαγγελίου τοῦ χριστοῦ
so that **whether** I come	ἵνα **εἴτε** ἐλθὼν
and see you	καὶ ἰδὼν ὑμᾶς
or remain absent	**εἴτε** ἀπὼν
I will hear of you	ἀκούω τὰ περὶ ὑμῶν
that you are standing firm	ὅτι στήκετε
in **one** spirit	ἐν **ἑνὶ** πνεύματι
with **one** mind	**μιᾷ** ψυχῇ
striving together	συναθλοῦντες
for the faith of the gospel	τῇ πίστει τοῦ εὐαγγελίου

On the first day of the **week (σαββάτων)** at early dawn they went **to (ἐπὶ)** the tomb **taking (φέρουσαι)** the spices they had prepared. (MLB)

φέρω	to bear, carry, bring, lead	64x
pherō		S5342

ἐπί ➤ DAY 21   **σάββατον** ➤ DAY 246

τῇ δὲ μιᾷ τῶν **σαββάτων** ὄρθρου βαθέως **ἐπὶ** τὸ μνῆμα ἦλθαν **φέρουσαι** ἃ ἡτοίμασαν ἀρώματα.

On the first day	τῇ δὲ μιᾷ
of the **week**	τῶν **σαββάτων**
at early dawn	ὄρθρου βαθέως
they went	ἦλθαν
to the tomb	**ἐπὶ** τὸ μνῆμα
taking the spices	**φέρουσαι** . . . ἀρώματα
they had prepared	ἃ ἡτοίμασαν

Once more they entered Jerusalem and, while He **was walking around (περιπατοῦντος)** in the temple, the chief priests and the **scribes (γραμματεῖς)** and the **elders (πρεσβύτεροι)** came to Him.
(MLB)

γραμματεύς	scribe	63x
grammateus		S1122

περιπατέω ➢ DAY 179   **πρεσβύτερος** ➢ DAY 248

Καὶ ἔρχονται πάλιν εἰς Ἱεροσόλυμα. Καὶ ἐν τῷ ἱερῷ **περιπατοῦντος** αὐτοῦ ἔρχονται πρὸς αὐτὸν οἱ ἀρχιερεῖς καὶ οἱ **γραμματεῖς** καὶ οἱ **πρεσβύτεροι**

Once more	Καὶ . . . πάλιν
they entered Jerusalem	ἔρχονται . . . εἰς Ἱεροσόλυμα
and, while He **was walking around**	Καὶ . . . **περιπατοῦντος** αὐτοῦ
in the temple	ἐν τῷ ἱερῷ
the chief priests	οἱ ἀρχιερεῖς
and the **scribes**	καὶ οἱ **γραμματεῖς**
and the **elders**	καὶ οἱ **πρεσβύτεροι**
came to Him	ἔρχονται πρὸς αὐτὸν

The Jews said to him, "Now we know that you have a **demon (δαιμόνιον)**. Abraham **died (ἀπέθανεν)**, and so did the prophets; yet you say, "Whoever **keeps (τηρήσῃ)** my word will never taste death." (NRSV)

δαιμόνιον	demon, evil spirit	63x
daimonion		S1140

ἀποθνήσκω ➤ DAY 148   **τηρέω** ➤ DAY 237

εἶπαν αὐτῷ οἱ Ἰουδαῖοι Νῦν ἐγνώκαμεν ὅτι **δαιμόνιον** ἔχεις. Ἀβραὰμ **ἀπέθανεν** καὶ οἱ προφῆται, καὶ σὺ λέγεις Ἐάν τις τὸν λόγον μου **τηρήσῃ**, οὐ μὴ γεύσηται θανάτου εἰς τὸν αἰῶνα·

The Jews said to him	εἶπαν αὐτῷ οἱ Ἰουδαῖοι
Now we know that	Νῦν ἐγνώκαμεν ὅτι
you have a **demon**	**δαιμόνιον** ἔχεις
Abraham **died**	Ἀβραὰμ **ἀπέθανεν**
and so did the prophets	καὶ οἱ προφῆται
yet you say	καὶ σὺ λέγεις
Whoever **keeps**	Ἐάν τις . . . **τηρήσῃ**
my word	τὸν λόγον μου
will never taste death	οὐ μὴ γεύσηται θανάτου εἰς τὸν αἰῶνα

When they had approached **Jerusalem (Ἰεροσόλυμα)** and had come to Bethphage, at the **Mount (Ὄρος)** of Olives, then Jesus sent **two (δύο)** disciples. (NASB)

ὄρος	hill, mountain	63x
oros		S3735

Ἰερουσαλήμ / Ἰεροσόλυμα ➤ DAY 122   **δύο** ➤ DAY 124

Καὶ ὅτε ἤγγισαν εἰς **Ἰεροσόλυμα** καὶ ἦλθον εἰς Βηθφαγὴ εἰς τὸ **Ὄρος** τῶν Ἐλαιῶν, τότε Ἰησοῦς ἀπέστειλεν **δύο** μαθητὰς

When	Καὶ ὅτε
they had approached	ἤγγισαν εἰς
Jerusalem	**Ἰεροσόλυμα**
and had come	καὶ ἦλθον
to Bethphage	εἰς Βηθφαγὴ
at the **Mount** of Olives	εἰς τὸ **Ὄρος** τῶν Ἐλαιῶν
then	τότε
Jesus sent	Ἰησοῦς ἀπέστειλεν
two disciples	**δύο** μαθητὰς

How **does this seem (δοκεῖ)** to you? If a man has a hundred sheep and one of them strays, **does he** not **leave (ἀφήσει)** the ninety-nine on the **mountains (ὄρη)** to go out in search of the stray one? (MLB)

δοκέω	to seem, think	62x
dokeō		S1380

ἀφίημι ➤ DAY 115   **ὄρος** ➤ DAY 255

τί ὑμῖν **δοκεῖ**; ἐὰν γένηταί τινι ἀνθρώπῳ ἑκατὸν πρόβατα καὶ πλανηθῇ ἓν ἐξ αὐτῶν, οὐχὶ **ἀφήσει** τὰ ἐνενήκοντα ἐννέα ἐπὶ τὰ **ὄρη** καὶ πορευθεὶς ζητεῖ τὸ πλανώμενον;

How **does this seem** to you?	τί ὑμῖν **δοκεῖ**;
If a man has	ἐὰν γένηταί τινι ἀνθρώπῳ
a hundred sheep	ἑκατὸν πρόβατα
and one of them	καὶ . . . ἓν ἐξ αὐτῶν
strays	πλανηθῇ
does he not **leave**	οὐχὶ **ἀφήσει**
the ninety-nine	τὰ ἐνενήκοντα ἐννέα
on the **mountains**	ἐπὶ τὰ **ὄρη**
to go out in search of	καὶ πορευθεὶς ζητεῖ
the stray one?	τὸ πλανώμενον;

Now the woman was Greek, a Syrophoenician by birth, and **she kept asking (ἠρώτα)** Him **to drive (ἐκβάλῃ)** the **demon (δαιμόνιον)** out of her daughter. (HCSB)

ἐρωτάω	to ask, question, request	62x
erōtaō		S2065

ἐκβάλλω ➤ DAY 207   **δαιμόνιον** ➤ DAY 254

ἡ δὲ γυνὴ ἦν Ἑλληνίς, Συροφοινίκισσα τῷ γένει· καὶ **ἠρώτα** αὐτὸν ἵνα τὸ **δαιμόνιον ἐκβάλῃ** ἐκ τῆς θυγατρὸς αὐτῆς.

Now the woman was Greek	ἡ δὲ γυνὴ ἦν Ἑλληνίς
a Syrophoenician	Συροφοινίκισσα
by birth	τῷ γένει
and **she kept asking** Him	καὶ **ἠρώτα** αὐτὸν
to drive the **demon** out	ἵνα τὸ **δαιμόνιον ἐκβάλῃ**
of her daughter	ἐκ τῆς θυγατρὸς αὐτῆς

As he was drawing near—**already (ἤδη)** on the way down the **Mount (Ὄρους)** of Olives—the whole multitude of his disciples began **to rejoice (χαίροντες)** and praise God with a loud voice for all the mighty works that they had seen. (ESV)

ἤδη	already, now	62x
ēdē		S2235

χαίρω ▷ DAY 228   **ὄρος** ▷ DAY 255

ἐγγίζοντος δὲ αὐτοῦ **ἤδη** πρὸς τῇ καταβάσει τοῦ Ὄρους τῶν Ἐλαιῶν ἤρξαντο ἄπαν τὸ πλῆθος τῶν μαθητῶν **χαίροντες** αἰνεῖν τὸν θεὸν φωνῇ μεγάλῃ περὶ πασῶν ὧν εἶδον δυνάμεων,

As he was drawing near	ἐγγίζοντος δὲ αὐτοῦ
already on the way down	**ἤδη** πρὸς τῇ καταβάσει
the **Mount** of Olives	τοῦ Ὄρους τῶν Ἐλαιῶν
the whole multitude of his disciples	ἄπαν τὸ πλῆθος τῶν μαθητῶν
began **to rejoice**	ἤρξαντο . . . **χαίροντες**
and praise God	αἰνεῖν τὸν θεὸν
with a loud voice	φωνῇ μεγάλῃ
for all the mighty works	περὶ πασῶν . . . δυνάμεων
that they had seen	ὧν εἶδον

For through Him all things were created in heaven and on earth, the visible and the invisible, **whether (εἴτε) thrones (θρόνοι) or (εἴτε) lordships or (εἴτε) rulers or (εἴτε) authorities (ἐξουσίαι)**; they are all created through Him and for Him. (MLB)

θρόνος	throne, seat	62x
thronos		S2362

ἐξουσία ➢ DAY 162	**εἴτε** ➢ DAY 251

ὅτι ἐν αὐτῷ ἐκτίσθη τὰ πάντα ἐν τοῖς οὐρανοῖς καὶ ἐπὶ τῆς γῆς, τὰ ὁρατὰ καὶ τὰ ἀόρατα, **εἴτε θρόνοι εἴτε** κυριότητες **εἴτε** ἀρχαὶ **εἴτε ἐξουσίαι**· τὰ πάντα δι᾽ αὐτοῦ καὶ εἰς αὐτὸν ἔκτισται·

For through Him	ὅτι ἐν αὐτῷ
all things were created	ἐκτίσθη τὰ πάντα
in heaven and on earth	ἐν τοῖς οὐρανοῖς καὶ ἐπὶ τῆς γῆς
the visible and the invisible	τὰ ὁρατὰ καὶ τὰ ἀόρατα
whether thrones	**εἴτε θρόνοι**
or lordships	**εἴτε** κυριότητες
or rulers	**εἴτε** ἀρχαὶ
or authorities	**εἴτε ἐξουσίαι**
they are all created	τὰ πάντα . . . ἔκτισται
through Him and for Him	δι᾽ αὐτοῦ καὶ εἰς αὐτὸν

However, they did not understand this **saying (ῥῆμα)**; it was kept hidden from them so that they might not grasp it, and **they were afraid (ἐφοβοῦντο) to question (ἐρωτῆσαι)** Him about this **saying (ῥήματος)**. (MLB)

ῥῆμα	word, utterance, thing, matter	62x
rhēma		S4487

φοβέομαι ➢ DAY 183   **ἐρωτάω** ➢ DAY 257

οἱ δὲ ἠγνόουν τὸ **ῥῆμα** τοῦτο, καὶ ἦν παρακεκαλυμμένον ἀπ᾽ αὐτῶν ἵνα μὴ αἴσθωνται αὐτό, καὶ **ἐφοβοῦντο ἐρωτῆσαι** αὐτὸν περὶ τοῦ **ῥήματος** τούτου.

However, they did not understand	οἱ δὲ ἠγνόουν
this **saying**	τὸ **ῥῆμα** τοῦτο
it was kept hidden	καὶ ἦν παρακεκαλυμμένον
from them	ἀπ᾽ αὐτῶν
so that they might not grasp it	ἵνα μὴ αἴσθωνται αὐτό
and **they were afraid**	καὶ **ἐφοβοῦντο**
to question Him	**ἐρωτῆσαι** αὐτὸν
about this **saying**	περὶ τοῦ **ῥήματος** τούτου

But you, **beloved (ἀγαπητοί)**, ought to remember the **words (ῥημάτων)** that were spoken beforehand by the **apostles (ἀποστόλων)** of our Lord Jesus Christ. (NASB)

| **ἀγαπητός** | beloved | 61x |
| *agapētos* | | S27 |

ἀπόστολος ➤ DAY 210   **ῥῆμα** ➤ DAY 260

Ὑμεῖς δέ, **ἀγαπητοί**, μνήσθητε τῶν **ῥημάτων** τῶν προειρημένων ὑπὸ τῶν **ἀποστόλων** τοῦ κυρίου ἡμῶν Ἰησοῦ Χριστοῦ·

But you	Ὑμεῖς δέ
beloved	**ἀγαπητοί**
ought to remember	μνήσθητε
the **words**	τῶν **ῥημάτων**
that were spoken beforehand	τῶν προειρημένων
by the **apostles**	ὑπὸ τῶν **ἀποστόλων**
of our Lord	τοῦ κυρίου ἡμῶν
Jesus Christ	Ἰησοῦ Χριστοῦ

You yourselves know the **thing (ῥῆμα)** which took place throughout all Judea, starting from **Galilee (Γαλιλαίας)**, after the baptism which **John ('Ιωάνης)** proclaimed. (NASB)

| **Γαλιλαία** | Galilee | | 61x |
| *Galilaia* | | | S1056 |

'Ιωάννης ➤ DAY 126   **ῥῆμα** ➤ DAY 260

ὑμεῖς οἴδατε τὸ γενόμενον **ῥῆμα** καθ᾽ ὅλης τῆς Ἰουδαίας, ἀρξάμενος ἀπὸ τῆς **Γαλιλαίας** μετὰ τὸ βάπτισμα ὃ ἐκήρυξεν **'Ιωάνης,**

You yourselves know	ὑμεῖς οἴδατε
the **thing**	τὸ . . . **ῥῆμα**
which took place	γενόμενον
throughout all Judea	καθ᾽ ὅλης τῆς Ἰουδαίας
starting	ἀρξάμενος
from **Galilee**	ἀπὸ τῆς **Γαλιλαίας**
after the baptism	μετὰ τὸ βάπτισμα
which **John** proclaimed	ὃ ἐκήρυξεν **'Ιωάνης**

So Pilate went **out (ἔξω)** to them and **said (φησιν)**, "What accusation **do you bring (φέρετε)** against this man?" (NRSV)

| ἔξω | outside | | 61x |
| exō | | | S1854 |

φημί ➤ DAY 249   **φέρω** ➤ DAY 252

ἐξῆλθεν οὖν ὁ Πειλᾶτος **ἔξω** πρὸς αὐτοὺς καί **φησιν** Τίνα κατηγορίαν **φέρετε** τοῦ ἀνθρώπου τούτου;

So Pilate	οὖν ὁ Πειλᾶτος
went **out**	ἐξῆλθεν . . . **ἔξω**
to them	πρὸς αὐτοὺς
and **said**	καί **φησιν**
What accusation	Τίνα κατηγορίαν
do you bring	**φέρετε**
against this man?	τοῦ ἀνθρώπου τούτου;

And **at once (εὐθὺς)** his fame spread everywhere throughout **all
(ὅλην)** the surrounding region of **Galilee (Γαλιλαίας)**. (ESV)

εὐθύς	immediately	61x
euthus		S2117

ὅλος ➤ DAY 156   **Γαλιλαία** ➤ DAY 262

Καὶ ἐξῆλθεν ἡ ἀκοὴ αὐτοῦ **εὐθὺς** πανταχοῦ εἰς **ὅλην** τὴν
περίχωρον τῆς **Γαλιλαίας**.

And **at once**	Καὶ . . . **εὐθὺς**
his fame	ἡ ἀκοὴ αὐτοῦ
spread	ἐξῆλθεν
everywhere	πανταχοῦ
throughout **all**	εἰς **ὅλην**
the surrounding region	τὴν περίχωρον
of **Galilee**	τῆς **Γαλιλαίας**

But what does it say? "The **word (ῥῆμά)** is near you, in your **mouth (στόματί)** and in your heart" (that is, the **word [ῥῆμα]** of faith that **we proclaim [κηρύσσομεν]**). (ESV)

κηρύσσω	to proclaim, preach	61x
kērussō		S2784

στόμα ➤ DAY 216   **ῥῆμα** ➤ DAY 260

ἀλλὰ τί λέγει; Ἐγγύς σου τὸ **ῥῆμά** ἐστιν, ἐν τῷ **στόματί** σου καὶ ἐν τῇ καρδίᾳ σου· τοῦτ᾽ ἔστιν τὸ **ῥῆμα** τῆς πίστεως ὃ **κηρύσσομεν**.

But what does it say?	ἀλλὰ τί λέγει;
The **word** is	τὸ **ῥῆμά** ἐστιν
near you	Ἐγγύς σου
in your **mouth**	ἐν τῷ **στόματί** σου
and in your heart	καὶ ἐν τῇ καρδίᾳ σου
that is	τοῦτ᾽ ἔστιν
the **word**	τὸ **ῥῆμα**
of faith	τῆς πίστεως
that **we proclaim**	ὃ **κηρύσσομεν**

For you remember, brothers, our labor and toil: we worked **night (νυκτὸς)** and day, that we might not be a burden to any of you, while **we proclaimed (ἐκηρύξαμεν)** to you the **gospel (εὐαγγέλιον)** of God. (ESV)

νύξ	night	61x
nux		S3571

εὐαγγέλιον ➤ DAY 230　　　**κηρύσσω** ➤ DAY 265

μνημονεύετε γάρ, ἀδελφοί, τὸν κόπον ἡμῶν καὶ τὸν μόχθον· **νυκτὸς** καὶ ἡμέρας ἐργαζόμενοι πρὸς τὸ μὴ ἐπιβαρῆσαί τινα ὑμῶν **ἐκηρύξαμεν** εἰς ὑμᾶς τὸ **εὐαγγέλιον** τοῦ θεοῦ.

For you remember	μνημονεύετε γάρ
brothers	ἀδελφοί
our labor	τὸν κόπον ἡμῶν
and toil	καὶ τὸν μόχθον
we worked	ἐργαζόμενοι
night and day	**νυκτὸς** καὶ ἡμέρας
that we might not be a burden	πρὸς τὸ μὴ ἐπιβαρῆσαί
to any of you	τινα ὑμῶν
while **we proclaimed** to you	**ἐκηρύξαμεν** εἰς ὑμᾶς
the **gospel** of God	τὸ **εὐαγγέλιον** τοῦ θεοῦ

If anyone says to you, "Why are you doing this?" say, "The Lord has need of it and will send it back [lit., **again (πάλιν)**] **here (ὧδε) immediately (εὐθύς)**." (ESV)

ὧδε	here, hither	61x
hōde		S5602

πάλιν ➤ DAY 120　　　**εὐθύς** ➤ DAY 264

καὶ ἐάν τις ὑμῖν εἴπῃ Τί ποιεῖτε τοῦτο; εἴπατε Ὁ κύριος αὐτοῦ χρείαν ἔχει· καὶ **εὐθὺς** αὐτὸν ἀποστέλλει **πάλιν ὧδε**.

If anyone	καὶ ἐάν τις
says to you	ὑμῖν εἴπῃ
Why are you doing this?	Τί ποιεῖτε τοῦτο;
say	εἴπατε
The Lord	Ὁ κύριος
has need of it	αὐτοῦ χρείαν ἔχει
and will send it back [lit., **again**]	καὶ . . . αὐτὸν ἀποστέλλει **πάλιν**
here	ὧδε
immediately	εὐθὺς

Greet (ἀσπάσασθε) Ampliatus, my dear friend (ἀγαπητόν) in the Lord (κυρίῳ). (NIV)

ἀσπάζομαι	to greet, salute	60x
aspazomai		S782

κύριος ➢ DAY 22   **ἀγαπητός** ➢ DAY 261

ἀσπάσασθε Ἀμπλιᾶτον τὸν **ἀγαπητόν** μου ἐν **κυρίῳ.**

Greet	**ἀσπάσασθε**
Ampliatus	Ἀμπλιᾶτον
my **dear friend**	τὸν **ἀγαπητόν** μου
in the **Lord**	ἐν **κυρίῳ**

In the same way, let your **light (φῶς)** shine before others, that
they may see (ἴδωσιν) your good deeds and **glorify (δοξάσωσιν)**
your Father in heaven. (NIV)

δοξάζω	to glorify	60x
doxazō		S1392

ὁράω ➤ DAY 40　　　　**φῶς** ➤ DAY 232

οὕτως λαμψάτω τὸ **φῶς** ὑμῶν ἔμπροσθεν τῶν ἀνθρώπων, ὅπως
ἴδωσιν ὑμῶν τὰ καλὰ ἔργα καὶ **δοξάσωσιν** τὸν πατέρα ὑμῶν τὸν
ἐν τοῖς οὐρανοῖς.

In the same way	οὕτως
let your **light** shine	λαμψάτω τὸ **φῶς** ὑμῶν
before others	ἔμπροσθεν τῶν ἀνθρώπων
that **they may see**	ὅπως **ἴδωσιν**
your good deeds	ὑμῶν τὰ καλὰ ἔργα
and **glorify**	καὶ **δοξάσωσιν**
your Father	τὸν πατέρα ὑμῶν
in heaven	τὸν ἐν τοῖς οὐρανοῖς

All the time, **night (νυκτὸς)** and day, he remained among the tombs and in the **mountains (ὄρεσιν)**, shrieking and cutting himself with **stones (λίθοις)**. (MLB)

λίθος	stone	60x
lithos		S3037

ὄρος ➤ DAY 255   **νύξ** ➤ DAY 266

καὶ διὰ παντὸς **νυκτὸς** καὶ ἡμέρας ἐν τοῖς μνήμασιν καὶ ἐν τοῖς **ὄρεσιν** ἦν κράζων καὶ κατακόπτων ἑαυτὸν **λίθοις**.

All the time	καὶ διὰ παντὸς
night and day	**νυκτὸς** καὶ ἡμέρας
he remained	ἦν
among the tombs	ἐν τοῖς μνήμασιν
and in the **mountains**	καὶ ἐν τοῖς **ὄρεσιν**
shrieking	κράζων
and cutting himself	καὶ κατακόπτων ἑαυτὸν
with **stones**	**λίθοις**

And the twenty-four elders, who **were seated (καθήμενοι)** on their **thrones (θρόνους)** before God, fell on their faces and **worshiped (προσεκύνησαν)** God. (NIV)

προσκυνέω	to worship	60x
proskuneō		S4352

κάθημαι ➤ DAY 189   **θρόνος** ➤ DAY 259

καὶ οἱ εἴκοσι τέσσαρες πρεσβύτεροι [οἱ] ἐνώπιον τοῦ θεοῦ **καθήμενοι** ἐπὶ τοὺς **θρόνους** αὐτῶν ἔπεσαν ἐπὶ τὰ πρόσωπα αὐτῶν καὶ **προσεκύνησαν** τῷ θεῷ,

And the twenty-four elders	καὶ οἱ εἴκοσι τέσσαρες πρεσβύτεροι
who **were seated**	[οἱ] . . . **καθήμενοι**
on their **thrones**	ἐπὶ τοὺς **θρόνους** αὐτῶν
before God	ἐνώπιον τοῦ θεοῦ
fell	ἔπεσαν
on their faces	ἐπὶ τὰ πρόσωπα αὐτῶν
and **worshiped** God	καὶ **προσεκύνησαν** τῷ θεῷ

And Joseph, too, **went up (Ἀνέβη)** from **Galilee (Γαλιλαίας)** out of the city of Nazareth to Judea, to the city of **David (Δαυεὶδ)** called Bethlehem, because he was of the house and family of **David (Δαυείδ)**. (MLB)

Δαυίδ	David	59x
Dauid		S1138

ἀναβαίνω	➢ DAY 206	**Γαλιλαία** ➢ DAY 262

Ἀνέβη δὲ καὶ Ἰωσὴφ ἀπὸ τῆς **Γαλιλαίας** ἐκ πόλεως Ναζαρὲτ εἰς τὴν Ἰουδαίαν εἰς πόλιν **Δαυεὶδ** ἥτις καλεῖται Βηθλεέμ, διὰ τὸ εἶναι αὐτὸν ἐξ οἴκου καὶ πατριᾶς **Δαυείδ**,

And Joseph, too	δὲ καὶ Ἰωσὴφ
went up	**Ἀνέβη**
from **Galilee**	ἀπὸ τῆς **Γαλιλαίας**
out of the city of Nazareth	ἐκ πόλεως Ναζαρὲτ
to Judea	εἰς τὴν Ἰουδαίαν
to the city of **David**	εἰς πόλιν **Δαυεὶδ**
called Bethlehem	ἥτις καλεῖται Βηθλεέμ
because he was	διὰ τὸ εἶναι αὐτὸν
of the house	ἐξ οἴκου
and family of **David**	καὶ πατριᾶς **Δαυείδ**

As he was going out of the **temple (ἱεροῦ)**, one of his disciples said to him, "**Teacher (Διδάσκαλε)**, look! What massive **stones (λίθοι)**! What impressive buildings!" (CSB)

διδάσκαλος	teacher	59x
*di**das**kalos*		S1320

ἱερόν ➤ DAY 234   **λίθος** ➤ DAY 270

Καὶ ἐκπορευομένου αὐτοῦ ἐκ τοῦ **ἱεροῦ** λέγει αὐτῷ εἷς τῶν μαθητῶν αὐτοῦ **Διδάσκαλε**, ἴδε ποταποὶ **λίθοι** καὶ ποταπαὶ οἰκοδομαί.

As he was going out	Καὶ ἐκπορευομένου αὐτοῦ
of the **temple**	ἐκ τοῦ **ἱεροῦ**
one of his disciples	εἷς τῶν μαθητῶν αὐτοῦ
said to him	λέγει αὐτῷ
Teacher	**Διδάσκαλε**
look!	ἴδε
What massive **stones**!	ποταποὶ **λίθοι**
What impressive buildings!	καὶ ποταπαὶ οἰκοδομαί

For in the first place, I hear that as you meet as a **congregation (ἐκκλησία) there are (ὑπάρχειν)** divisions among you, and to some extent **I believe (πιστεύω)** it. (MLB)

ὑπάρχω	to be	59x
huparchō		S5225

        πιστεύω ➤ DAY 66   **ἐκκλησία** ➤ DAY 146

πρῶτον μὲν γὰρ συνερχομένων ὑμῶν ἐν **ἐκκλησίᾳ** ἀκούω σχίσματα ἐν ὑμῖν **ὑπάρχειν**, καὶ μέρος τι **πιστεύω**.

For in the first place	πρῶτον μὲν γὰρ
I hear that	ἀκούω
as you meet	συνερχομένων ὑμῶν
as a **congregation**	ἐν **ἐκκλησίᾳ**
there are divisions	σχίσματα . . . **ὑπάρχειν**
among you	ἐν ὑμῖν
and to some extent	καὶ μέρος τι
I believe it	**πιστεύω**

For you sympathized with the prisoners and accepted with **joy (χαρᾶς)** the confiscation of your **possessions (ὑπαρχόντων)**, **knowing (γινώσκοντες)** that you yourselves have a better and enduring possession. (HCSB)

χαρά	joy, delight	59x
chara		S5479

γινώσκω ➤ DAY 70   **ὑπάρχω** ➤ DAY 274

καὶ γὰρ τοῖς δεσμίοις συνεπαθήσατε, καὶ τὴν ἁρπαγὴν τῶν **ὑπαρχόντων** ὑμῶν μετὰ **χαρᾶς** προσεδέξασθε, **γινώσκοντες** ἔχειν ἑαυτοὺς κρείσσονα ὕπαρξιν καὶ μένουσαν.

For you sympathized	καὶ γὰρ . . . συνεπαθήσατε
with the prisoners	τοῖς δεσμίοις
and accepted	καὶ . . . προσεδέξασθε
with **joy**	μετὰ **χαρᾶς**
the confiscation	τὴν ἁρπαγὴν
of your **possessions**	τῶν **ὑπαρχόντων** ὑμῶν
knowing that	**γινώσκοντες**
you yourselves have	ἔχειν ἑαυτοὺς
a better and enduring	κρείσσονα . . . καὶ μένουσαν
possession	ὕπαρξιν

Then Jesus came [lit., **came out (ἐξῆλθεν)**] **outside (ἔξω)**, wearing the thorny crown and the purple **robe (ἱμάτιον)**. Pilate [lit., he] said to them, "Here is the man!" (MLB)

ἱμάτιον	garment	58x
himation		S2440

    ἐξέρχομαι ➤ DAY 71   **ἔξω** ➤ DAY 263

ἐξῆλθεν οὖν [ὁ] Ἰησοῦς **ἔξω**, φορῶν τὸν ἀκάνθινον στέφανον καὶ τὸ πορφυροῦν **ἱμάτιον**. καὶ λέγει αὐτοῖς Ἰδοὺ ὁ ἄνθρωπος.

Then Jesus	οὖν [ὁ] Ἰησοῦς
came [lit., **came out**] **outside**	**ἐξῆλθεν** . . . **ἔξω**
wearing	φορῶν
the thorny crown	τὸν ἀκάνθινον στέφανον
and the purple **robe**	καὶ τὸ πορφυροῦν **ἱμάτιον**
Pilate [lit., he] said to them	καὶ λέγει αὐτοῖς
Here is	Ἰδοὺ
the man!	ὁ ἄνθρωπος

After **three (τρεῖς)** days they found him in the temple courts, sitting **among (ἐν μέσῳ)** the **teachers (διδασκάλων)**, listening to them and asking them questions. (NIV)

μέσος	middle	58x
mesos		S3319

τρεῖς, τρία ➤ DAY 242   **διδάσκαλος** ➤ DAY 273

καὶ ἐγένετο μετὰ ἡμέρας **τρεῖς** εὗρον αὐτὸν ἐν τῷ ἱερῷ καθεζόμενον ἐν **μέσῳ** τῶν **διδασκάλων** καὶ ἀκούοντα αὐτῶν καὶ ἐπερωτῶντα αὐτούς·

After **three** days	καὶ ἐγένετο μετὰ ἡμέρας **τρεῖς**
they found him	εὗρον αὐτὸν
in the temple courts	ἐν τῷ ἱερῷ
sitting	καθεζόμενον
among the **teachers**	ἐν **μέσῳ** τῶν **διδασκάλων**
listening to them	καὶ ἀκούοντα αὐτῶν
and asking them questions	καὶ ἐπερωτῶντα αὐτούς

For where two or three have **gathered together (συνηγμένοι)** in My name, I am **there (ἐκεῖ)** in their **midst (μέσῳ)**. (NASB)

συνάγω	to gather together, collect, assemble	58x
sunagō		S4863

ἐκεῖ ➤ DAY 158   **μέσος** ➤ DAY 277

οὖ γάρ εἰσιν δύο ἢ τρεῖς **συνηγμένοι** εἰς τὸ ἐμὸν ὄνομα, **ἐκεῖ** εἰμὶ ἐν **μέσῳ** αὐτῶν.

For where	οὖ γάρ
two or three	δύο ἢ τρεῖς
have **gathered together**	εἰσιν . . . **συνηγμένοι**
in My name	εἰς τὸ ἐμὸν ὄνομα
I am **there**	**ἐκεῖ** εἰμὶ
in their **midst**	ἐν **μέσῳ** αὐτῶν

So many people **gathered together (συνήχθησαν) that (ὥστε)** there was no more room, **not even (μηδὲ)** in the doorway, and he was speaking the word to them. (CSB)

μηδέ	nor, not even, but not	57x
mēde		S3366

ὥστε ➤ DAY 202   **συνάγω** ➤ DAY 278

καὶ **συνήχθησαν** πολλοὶ **ὥστε** μηκέτι χωρεῖν **μηδὲ** τὰ πρὸς τὴν θύραν, καὶ ἐλάλει αὐτοῖς τὸν λόγον.

So many people	καὶ . . . πολλοὶ
gathered together	**συνήχθησαν**
that	**ὥστε**
there was no more room	μηκέτι χωρεῖν
not even	**μηδὲ**
in the doorway	τὰ πρὸς τὴν θύραν
and he was speaking	καὶ ἐλάλει
the word	τὸν λόγον
to them	αὐτοῖς

So **we ourselves (ἡμεῖς)** ought to support **such people (τοιούτους)** in order to **be (γινώμεθα)** fellow workers with them in the truth. (MLB)

| τοιοῦτος, τοιαύτη, τοιοῦτον | such (a person), of | 57x |
| *toioutos, toiautē, toiouton* | such a kind | S5108 |

| ἐγώ, (pl) ἡμεῖς | ▷ DAY 7 | γίνομαι | ▷ DAY 27 |

ἡμεῖς οὖν ὀφείλομεν ὑπολαμβάνειν τοὺς **τοιούτους**, ἵνα συνεργοὶ **γινώμεθα** τῇ ἀληθείᾳ.

So **we ourselves**	ἡμεῖς οὖν
ought	ὀφείλομεν
to support	ὑπολαμβάνειν
such people	τοὺς **τοιούτους**
in order to **be**	ἵνα . . . **γινώμεθα**
fellow workers with them	συνεργοὶ
in the truth	τῇ ἀληθείᾳ

For in those days there will be suffering, such as has not been [lit., such that there has not been **such a kind (τοιαύτη)**] from the **beginning (ἀρχῆς)** of the creation that God created until **now (νῦν)**, no, and never will be. (NRSV)

ἀρχή	rule, beginning	56x
archē		S746

νῦν ➤ DAY 108   **τοιοῦτος, τοιαύτη, τοιοῦτον** ➤ DAY 280

ἔσονται γὰρ αἱ ἡμέραι ἐκεῖναι θλίψις οἵα οὐ γέγονεν **τοιαύτη** ἀπ᾽ **ἀρχῆς** κτίσεως ἣν ἔκτισεν ὁ θεὸς ἕως τοῦ **νῦν** καὶ οὐ μὴ γένηται.

For . . . there will be suffering	ἔσονται γὰρ . . . θλίψις
in those days	αἱ ἡμέραι ἐκεῖναι
such as has not been [lit., such that there has not been **such a kind**]	οἵα οὐ γέγονεν **τοιαύτη**
from the **beginning**	ἀπ᾽ **ἀρχῆς**
of the creation	κτίσεως
that God created	ἣν ἔκτισεν ὁ θεὸς
until **now**	ἕως τοῦ **νῦν**
no, and never will be	καὶ οὐ μὴ γένηται

When the apostles Barnabas and Paul **heard (ἀκούσαντες)** of it, they tore their **clothes (ἱμάτια)** and rushed out into the crowd, **shouting (κράζοντες)**, . . . (NRSV)

κράζω	to cry out, cry aloud	56x
krazō		S2896

ἀκούω ➤ DAY 42   **ἱμάτιον** ➤ DAY 276

ἀκούσαντες δὲ οἱ ἀπόστολοι Βαρνάβας καὶ Παῦλος, διαρρήξαντες τὰ **ἱμάτια** ἑαυτῶν ἐξεπήδησαν εἰς τὸν ὄχλον, **κράζοντες**

When the apostles . . . **heard** of it	**ἀκούσαντες** δὲ οἱ ἀπόστολοι
Barnabas and Paul	Βαρνάβας καὶ Παῦλος
they tore	διαρρήξαντες
their **clothes**	τὰ **ἱμάτια** ἑαυτῶν
and rushed out	ἐξεπήδησαν
into the crowd	εἰς τὸν ὄχλον
shouting	**κράζοντες**

Let both grow together until the harvest, and at harvest **time (καιρῷ)** I will tell the reapers, "Gather the weeds **first (πρῶτον)** and bind them in bundles to be burned, but **gather (συνάγετε)** the wheat into my barn." (ESV)

| πρῶτον | first, in the first place | 56x |
| *prō*ton | | S4412 |

| **καιρός** ➤ DAY 199 | **συνάγω** ➤ DAY 278 |

ἄφετε συναυξάνεσθαι ἀμφότερα ἕως τοῦ θερισμοῦ· καὶ ἐν **καιρῷ** τοῦ θερισμοῦ ἐρῶ τοῖς θερισταῖς Συλλέξατε **πρῶτον** τὰ ζιζάνια καὶ δήσατε αὐτὰ [εἰς] δέσμας πρὸς τὸ κατακαῦσαι αὐτά, τὸν δὲ σῖτον **συνάγετε** εἰς τὴν ἀποθήκην μου.

Let both	ἄφετε . . . ἀμφότερα
grow together	συναυξάνεσθαι
until the harvest	ἕως τοῦ θερισμοῦ
and at harvest **time**	καὶ ἐν **καιρῷ** τοῦ θερισμοῦ
I will tell the reapers	ἐρῶ τοῖς θερισταῖς
Gather the weeds	Συλλέξατε . . . τὰ ζιζάνια
first	**πρῶτον**
and bind them in bundles	καὶ δήσατε αὐτὰ [εἰς] δέσμας
to be burned	πρὸς τὸ κατακαῦσαι αὐτά
but **gather** the wheat	τὸν δὲ σῖτον **συνάγετε**
into my barn	εἰς τὴν ἀποθήκην μου

When (Ὅταν) they bring you before the **synagogues (συναγωγὰς)**, the **rulers (ἀρχὰς)**, and the authorities, do not worry about how you are to defend yourselves or what you are to say. (NRSV)

| συναγωγή | meeting, assembly, synagogue | 56x |
| *sunagōgē* | | S4864 |

ὅταν ➤ DAY 135   ἀρχή ➤ DAY 281

Ὅταν δὲ εἰσφέρωσιν ὑμᾶς ἐπὶ τὰς **συναγωγὰς** καὶ τὰς **ἀρχὰς** καὶ τὰς ἐξουσίας, μὴ μεριμνήσητε πῶς [ἢ τί] ἀπολογήσησθε ἢ τί εἴπητε·

When	Ὅταν δὲ
they bring you	εἰσφέρωσιν ὑμᾶς
before the **synagogues**	ἐπὶ τὰς **συναγωγὰς**
the **rulers**	καὶ τὰς **ἀρχὰς**
and the authorities	καὶ τὰς ἐξουσίας
do not worry about	μὴ μεριμνήσητε
how you are to defend yourselves	πῶς [ἢ τί] ἀπολογήσησθε
or what you are to say	ἢ τί εἴπητε

And God **has appointed (ἔθετο)** in the church **first (πρῶτον)**
apostles, second prophets, **third (τρίτον)** teachers; then deeds
of power, then gifts of healing, forms of assistance, forms of
leadership, various kinds of tongues. (NRSV)

τρίτος	third	56x
tritos		S5154

τίθημι ➤ DAY 170	**πρῶτον** ➤ DAY 283

Καὶ οὓς μὲν **ἔθετο** ὁ θεὸς ἐν τῇ ἐκκλησίᾳ **πρῶτον** ἀποστόλους,
δεύτερον προφήτας, **τρίτον** διδασκάλους, ἔπειτα δυνάμεις, ἔπειτα
χαρίσματα ἰαμάτων, ἀντιλήμψεις, κυβερνήσεις, γένη γλωσσῶν.

And God **has appointed**	Καὶ οὓς μὲν **ἔθετο** ὁ θεὸς
in the church	ἐν τῇ ἐκκλησίᾳ
first apostles	**πρῶτον** ἀποστόλους
second prophets	δεύτερον προφήτας
third teachers	**τρίτον** διδασκάλους
then deeds of power	ἔπειτα δυνάμεις
then gifts of healing	ἔπειτα χαρίσματα ἰαμάτων
forms of assistance	ἀντιλήμψεις
forms of leadership	κυβερνήσεις
various kinds of tongues	γένη γλωσσῶν

Then the high priest **stood up (ἀναστὰς)** before them [lit., in the **midst (μέσον)**] and **asked (ἐπηρώτησεν)** Jesus, "Are you not going to answer? What is this testimony that these men are bringing against you?" (NIV)

| **ἐπερωτάω** | to ask, question | 55x |
| *eperōtaō* | | S1905 |

ἀνίστημι ➤ DAY 155   **μέσος** ➤ DAY 277

καὶ **ἀναστὰς** ὁ ἀρχιερεὺς εἰς **μέσον ἐπηρώτησεν** τὸν Ἰησοῦν λέγων Οὐκ ἀποκρίνῃ οὐδέν; τί οὗτοί σου καταμαρτυροῦσιν;

Then the high priest	καὶ . . . ὁ ἀρχιερεὺς
stood up	**ἀναστὰς**
before them [lit., in the **midst**]	εἰς **μέσον**
and **asked**	**ἐπηρώτησεν** . . . λέγων
Jesus	τὸν Ἰησοῦν
Are you not going to answer?	Οὐκ ἀποκρίνῃ οὐδέν;
What is this testimony that these men are bringing against you?	τί οὗτοί σου καταμαρτυροῦσιν;

so that I may come to **you (ὑμᾶς)** with **joy (χαρᾷ)**, by God's **will
(θελήματος)**, and in your company be refreshed [lit., that I may
find rest with **you (ὑμῖν)**]. (NIV)

| **θέλημα** | will | 55x |
| *thelēma* | | S2307 |

σύ, (pl) ὑμεῖς ➤ DAY 4   **χαρά** ➤ DAY 275

ἵνα ἐν **χαρᾷ** ἐλθὼν πρὸς **ὑμᾶς** διὰ **θελήματος** θεοῦ
συναναπαύσωμαι **ὑμῖν**.

so that I may come to **you**	ἵνα . . . ἐλθὼν πρὸς **ὑμᾶς**
with **joy**	ἐν **χαρᾷ**
by God's **will**	διὰ **θελήματος** θεοῦ
and in your company be refreshed [lit., that I may find rest with **you**]	συναναπαύσωμαι **ὑμῖν**

so that (ὥστε) my imprisonment in the cause of Christ has become well known throughout the **whole (ὅλῳ)** praetorian guard and to everyone **else (λοιποῖς)**. (NASB)

λοιπός	left, remainder, other	55x
loipos		S3062

ὅλος ➤ DAY 156　　　ὥστε ➤ DAY 202

ὥστε τοὺς δεσμούς μου φανεροὺς ἐν Χριστῷ γενέσθαι ἐν **ὅλῳ** τῷ πραιτωρίῳ καὶ τοῖς **λοιποῖς** πᾶσιν,

so that my imprisonment	**ὥστε** τοὺς δεσμούς μου
in the cause of Christ	ἐν Χριστῷ
has become well known	φανεροὺς . . . γενέσθαι
throughout the **whole** praetorian guard	ἐν **ὅλῳ** τῷ πραιτωρίῳ
and to everyone **else**	καὶ τοῖς **λοιποῖς** πᾶσιν

Pilate (Πειλᾶτος) asked (ἐπηρώτησεν) him, "Are you the **King (βασιλεὺς)** of the Jews?" He answered him, "You say so." (NRSV)

Πιλᾶτος	Pilate	55x
Pilatos		S4091

βασιλεύς ➤ DAY 144   **ἐπερωτάω** ➤ DAY 286

καὶ **ἐπηρώτησεν** αὐτὸν ὁ **Πειλᾶτος** Σὺ εἶ ὁ **βασιλεὺς** τῶν Ἰουδαίων; ὁ δὲ ἀποκριθεὶς αὐτῷ λέγει Σὺ λέγεις.

Pilate	καὶ . . . ὁ **Πειλᾶτος**
asked him	**ἐπηρώτησεν** αὐτὸν
Are you	Σὺ εἶ
the **King**	ὁ **βασιλεὺς**
of the Jews?	τῶν Ἰουδαίων;
He answered him	ὁ δὲ ἀποκριθεὶς αὐτῷ λέγει
You say so	Σὺ λέγεις

So, **acknowledging (γνόντες)** the grace that had been given me, James and Cephas and John, who were **considered (δοκοῦντες)** as pillars, gave me and Barnabas the **right hand (δεξιὰς)** of fellowship that we should serve the Gentiles and they the circumcised. (MLB)

δεξιός	right, right hand	54x
dexios		S1188

γινώσκω ➤ DAY 70   **δοκέω** ➤ DAY 256

καὶ **γνόντες** τὴν χάριν τὴν δοθεῖσάν μοι, Ἰάκωβος καὶ Κηφᾶς καὶ Ἰωάνης, οἱ **δοκοῦντες** στύλοι εἶναι, **δεξιὰς** ἔδωκαν ἐμοὶ καὶ Βαρνάβᾳ κοινωνίας, ἵνα ἡμεῖς εἰς τὰ ἔθνη, αὐτοὶ δὲ εἰς τὴν περιτομήν·

So, **acknowledging** the grace	καὶ **γνόντες** τὴν χάριν
that had been given me	τὴν δοθεῖσάν μοι
James and Cephas	Ἰάκωβος καὶ Κηφᾶς
and John	καὶ Ἰωάνης
who were **considered** as pillars	οἱ **δοκοῦντες** στύλοι εἶναι
gave me and Barnabas	ἔδωκαν ἐμοὶ καὶ Βαρνάβᾳ
the **right hand** of fellowship	**δεξιὰς** . . . κοινωνίας
that we should serve the Gentiles	ἵνα ἡμεῖς εἰς τὰ ἔθνη
and they the circumcised	αὐτοὶ δὲ εἰς τὴν περιτομήν

Now **it was (ἦσαν) Mary (Μαρία)** Magdalene and Joanna and
Mary (Μαρία) the mother of James and the **other women
(λοιπαὶ)** with them who told these things to the apostles. (ESV)

Μαρία / Μαριάμ	Mary	54x
Maria / Mariam		S3137

εἰμί ➢ DAY 8   λοιπός ➢ DAY 288

ἦσαν δὲ ἡ Μαγδαληνὴ **Μαρία** καὶ Ἰωάνα καὶ **Μαρία** ἡ Ἰακώβου·
καὶ αἱ **λοιπαὶ** σὺν αὐταῖς ἔλεγον πρὸς τοὺς ἀποστόλους ταῦτα.

Now **it was**	**ἦσαν** δὲ
Mary Magdalene	ἡ Μαγδαληνὴ **Μαρία**
and Joanna	καὶ Ἰωάνα
and **Mary**	καὶ **Μαρία**
the mother of James	ἡ Ἰακώβου
and the **other women**	καὶ αἱ **λοιπαὶ**
with them	σὺν αὐταῖς
who told these things	ἔλεγον . . . ταῦτα
to the apostles	πρὸς τοὺς ἀποστόλους

For who of you, **wanting (θέλων)** to build a tower, does **not (οὐχὶ) first (πρῶτον)** sit down to figure out the expense, whether he has enough to complete it? (MLB)

οὐχί	no, not (so)	54x
ouchi		S3780

θέλω ➤ DAY 78   **πρῶτον** ➤ DAY 283

τίς γὰρ ἐξ ὑμῶν **θέλων** πύργον οἰκοδομῆσαι **οὐχὶ πρῶτον** καθίσας ψηφίζει τὴν δαπάνην, εἰ ἔχει εἰς ἀπαρτισμόν;

For who	τίς γὰρ
of you	ἐξ ὑμῶν
wanting to build	**θέλων** . . . οἰκοδομῆσαι
a tower	πύργον
does **not** . . . sit down	**οὐχὶ** . . . καθίσας
first	**πρῶτον**
to figure out	ψηφίζει
the expense	τὴν δαπάνην
whether he has	εἰ ἔχει
enough to complete it?	εἰς ἀπαρτισμόν;

so as to live for the rest of the **time (χρόνον)** in the **flesh (σαρκὶ)** no longer for human passions but for the **will (θελήματι)** of God.

(ESV)

χρόνος	time, period of time	54x
chronos		S5550

     σάρξ ➤ DAY 110   **θέλημα** ➤ DAY 287

εἰς τὸ μηκέτι ἀνθρώπων ἐπιθυμίαις ἀλλὰ **θελήματι** θεοῦ τὸν ἐπίλοιπον ἐν **σαρκὶ** βιῶσαι **χρόνον**.

so as to live	εἰς τὸ . . . βιῶσαι
for the rest of the **time**	τὸν ἐπίλοιπον . . . **χρόνον**
in the **flesh**	ἐν **σαρκὶ**
no longer	μηκέτι
for human passions	ἀνθρώπων ἐπιθυμίαις
but	ἀλλὰ
for the **will** of God	**θελήματι** θεοῦ

Aristarchus, my fellow prisoner, sends you greeting; so does Mark, the cousin of Barnabas, about whom you received **instructions (ἐντολάς)**—if **he comes (ἔλθῃ)** to you, **welcome (δέξασθε)** him. (MLB)

δέχομαι	to receive, welcome	53x
dechomai		S1209

ἔρχομαι ➤ DAY 30   **ἐντολή** ➤ DAY 239

Ἀσπάζεται ὑμᾶς Ἀρίσταρχος ὁ συναιχμάλωτός μου, καὶ Μάρκος ὁ ἀνεψιὸς Βαρνάβα, (περὶ οὗ ἐλάβετε **ἐντολάς**, ἐὰν **ἔλθῃ** πρὸς ὑμᾶς **δέξασθε** αὐτόν,)

Aristarchus	Ἀρίσταρχος
my fellow prisoner	ὁ συναιχμάλωτός μου
sends you greeting	Ἀσπάζεται ὑμᾶς
so does Mark	καὶ Μάρκος
the cousin of Barnabas	ὁ ἀνεψιὸς Βαρνάβα
about whom	περὶ οὗ
you received **instructions**	ἐλάβετε **ἐντολάς**
if **he comes**	ἐὰν **ἔλθῃ**
to you	πρὸς ὑμᾶς
welcome him	**δέξασθε** αὐτόν

Therefore (διὸ) put away all filthiness and rampant wickedness and **receive (δέξασθε)** with meekness the implanted word, which is able **to save (σῶσαι)** your souls. (ESV)

διό	therefore, for this reason	53x
dio		S1352

σῴζω ➢ DAY 160	δέχομαι ➢ DAY 294	

διὸ ἀποθέμενοι πᾶσαν ῥυπαρίαν καὶ περισσείαν κακίας ἐν πραΰτητι **δέξασθε** τὸν ἔμφυτον λόγον τὸν δυνάμενον **σῶσαι** τὰς ψυχὰς ὑμῶν.

Therefore	**διὸ**
put away	ἀποθέμενοι
all filthiness	πᾶσαν ῥυπαρίαν
and rampant wickedness	καὶ περισσείαν κακίας
and **receive**	**δέξασθε**
with meekness	ἐν πραΰτητι
the implanted word	τὸν ἔμφυτον λόγον
which is able	τὸν δυνάμενον
to save	**σῶσαι**
your souls	τὰς ψυχὰς ὑμῶν

based on the **hope (ἐλπίδι)** of **eternal (αἰωνίου)** life which God, who does not lie, promised before time began [lit., before **eternal (αἰωνίων)** times **(χρόνων)**]. (MLB)

ἐλπίς	hope	53x
elpis		S1680

    αἰώνιος ➢ DAY 236   **χρόνος** ➢ DAY 293

ἐπ᾽ **ἐλπίδι** ζωῆς **αἰωνίου**, ἣν ἐπηγγείλατο ὁ ἀψευδὴς θεὸς πρὸ **χρόνων αἰωνίων**

based on the **hope**	ἐπ᾽ **ἐλπίδι**
of **eternal** life	ζωῆς **αἰωνίου**
which . . . promised	ἣν ἐπηγγείλατο
God, who does not lie	ὁ ἀψευδὴς θεὸς
before time began [lit., before **eternal times**]	πρὸ **χρόνων αἰωνίων**

"Look," he said, "**I see (θεωρῶ)** the heavens opened and the Son
of Man **standing (ἑστῶτα)** at the **right hand (δεξιῶν)** of God!"
(NRSV)

| θεωρέω | to look at, behold | 53x |
| *theōreō* | | S2334 |

ἵστημι ➤ DAY 109   **δεξιός** ➤ DAY 290

καὶ εἶπεν Ἰδοὺ **θεωρῶ** τοὺς οὐρανοὺς διηνοιγμένους καὶ τὸν υἱὸν
τοῦ ἀνθρώπου ἐκ **δεξιῶν ἑστῶτα** τοῦ θεοῦ.

Look	Ἰδοὺ
he said	καὶ εἶπεν
I see	**θεωρῶ**
the heavens	τοὺς οὐρανοὺς
opened	διηνοιγμένους
and the Son of Man	καὶ τὸν υἱὸν τοῦ ἀνθρώπου
standing	**ἑστῶτα**
at the **right hand** of God!	ἐκ **δεξιῶν** . . . τοῦ θεοῦ

But **I have (ἔχω)** nothing definite to write to His Majesty about him. **Therefore (διὸ)** I have brought him before all of you, and especially before you, King Agrippa, **so that (ὅπως)** as a result of this investigation **I may have (σχῶ)** something to write. (NIV)

| ὅπως | that, in order that | 53x |
| *hopōs* | | S3704 |

| ἔχω | ➤ | DAY 23 | διό | ➤ | DAY 295 |

περὶ οὗ ἀσφαλές τι γράψαι τῷ κυρίῳ οὐκ **ἔχω**· **διὸ** προήγαγον αὐτὸν ἐφ᾽ ὑμῶν καὶ μάλιστα ἐπὶ σοῦ, βασιλεῦ Ἀγρίππα, **ὅπως** τῆς ἀνακρίσεως γενομένης **σχῶ** τί γράψω·

But **I have** nothing definite	ἀσφαλές τι . . . οὐκ **ἔχω**
to write	γράψαι
to His Majesty about him	περὶ οὗ . . . τῷ κυρίῳ
Therefore I have brought him before all of you	**διὸ** προήγαγον αὐτὸν ἐφ᾽ ὑμῶν
and especially before you	καὶ μάλιστα ἐπὶ σοῦ
King Agrippa	βασιλεῦ Ἀγρίππα
so that as a result	**ὅπως** . . . γενομένης
of this investigation	τῆς ἀνακρίσεως
I may have	σχῶ
something to write	τί γράψω

And behold, I am sending the **promise (ἐπαγγελίαν)** of my
Father upon you. But stay in the **city (πόλει)** until you are clothed
with **power (δύναμιν)** from on high. (ESV)

| ἐπαγγελία | promise | 52x |
| *epangelia* | | S1860 |

πόλις ➤ DAY 96   δύναμις ➤ DAY 141

καὶ ἰδοὺ ἐγὼ ἐξαποστέλλω τὴν **ἐπαγγελίαν** τοῦ πατρός μου ἐφ᾽
ὑμᾶς· ὑμεῖς δὲ καθίσατε ἐν τῇ **πόλει** ἕως οὗ ἐνδύσησθε ἐξ ὕψους
δύναμιν.

And behold	καὶ ἰδοὺ
I am sending	ἐγὼ ἐξαποστέλλω
the **promise**	τὴν **ἐπαγγελίαν**
of my Father	τοῦ πατρός μου
upon you	ἐφ᾽ ὑμᾶς
But stay	ὑμεῖς δὲ καθίσατε
in the **city**	ἐν τῇ **πόλει**
until you are clothed	ἕως οὗ ἐνδύσησθε
with **power**	**δύναμιν**
from on high	ἐξ ὕψους

He who eats My flesh and **drinks (πίνων)** My blood has eternal life and I **shall raise** him **up (ἀναστήσω)** on the **last (ἐσχάτῃ)** day. (MLB)

ἔσχατος	last	52x
*es*chatos		S2078

ἀνίστημι　➤　DAY 155　　　　πίνω　➤　DAY 233

ὁ τρώγων μου τὴν σάρκα καὶ **πίνων** μου τὸ αἷμα ἔχει ζωὴν αἰώνιον, κἀγὼ **ἀναστήσω** αὐτὸν τῇ **ἐσχάτῃ** ἡμέρᾳ·

He who eats	ὁ τρώγων
My flesh	μου τὴν σάρκα
and **drinks**	καὶ **πίνων**
My blood	μου τὸ αἷμα
has	ἔχει
eternal life	ζωὴν αἰώνιον
and I **shall raise** him **up**	κἀγὼ **ἀναστήσω** αὐτὸν
on the **last** day	τῇ **ἐσχάτῃ** ἡμέρᾳ

But He told them, "I must **preach the good news**
(εὐαγγελίσασθαί) of the kingdom of God to **other** (ἑτέραις)
towns as well, because for this purpose **I was sent** (ἀπεστάλην)."

(MLB)

εὐαγγελίζω *euangelizō*	to bring good news, preach good tidings	52x S2097

ἀποστέλλω ➤ DAY 131   **ἕτερος** ➤ DAY 171

ὁ δὲ εἶπεν πρὸς αὐτοὺς ὅτι Καὶ ταῖς **ἑτέραις** πόλεσιν
εὐαγγελίσασθαί με δεῖ τὴν βασιλείαν τοῦ θεοῦ, ὅτι ἐπὶ τοῦτο
ἀπεστάλην.

But He told them	ὁ δὲ εἶπεν πρὸς αὐτοὺς ὅτι
I must **preach the good news**	**εὐαγγελίσασθαί** με δεῖ
of the kingdom of God	τὴν βασιλείαν τοῦ θεοῦ
to **other** towns	ταῖς **ἑτέραις** πόλεσιν
as well	Καὶ
because	ὅτι
for this purpose	ἐπὶ τοῦτο
I was sent	**ἀπεστάλην**

Children (Παιδία), it is the **last (ἐσχάτη)** hour! As **(καθὼς)** you have heard that antichrist is coming, so now many antichrists have come. From this we know that it is the **last (ἐσχάτη)** hour. (NRSV)

| **παιδίον** | child, slave | 52x |
| *paidion* | | S3813 |

καθώς ➤ DAY 87   **ἔσχατος** ➤ DAY 300

Παιδία, ἐσχάτη ὥρα ἐστίν, καὶ **καθὼς** ἠκούσατε ὅτι ἀντίχριστος ἔρχεται, καὶ νῦν ἀντίχριστοι πολλοὶ γεγόνασιν· ὅθεν γινώσκομεν ὅτι **ἐσχάτη** ὥρα ἐστίν.

Children	**Παιδία**
it is the **last** hour!	**ἐσχάτη** ὥρα ἐστίν
As you have heard that	καὶ **καθὼς** ἠκούσατε ὅτι
antichrist is coming	ἀντίχριστος ἔρχεται
so now	καὶ νῦν
many antichrists	ἀντίχριστοι πολλοὶ
have come	γεγόνασιν
From this	ὅθεν
we know that	γινώσκομεν ὅτι
it is the **last** hour	**ἐσχάτη** ὥρα ἐστίν

being confident (πεποιθὼς) of this, that he who began a good **work (ἔργον)** in you will carry it on to completion until the **day (ἡμέρας)** of Christ Jesus. (NIV)

πείθω	to convince, persuade	52x
peithō		S3982

ἡμέρα ➤ DAY 46   ἔργον ➤ DAY 92

πεποιθὼς αὐτὸ τοῦτο ὅτι ὁ ἐναρξάμενος ἐν ὑμῖν **ἔργον** ἀγαθὸν ἐπιτελέσει ἄχρι **ἡμέρας** Ἰησοῦ Χριστοῦ·

being confident	πεποιθὼς
of this	αὐτὸ τοῦτο
that he who began	ὅτι ὁ ἐναρξάμενος
a good **work**	**ἔργον** ἀγαθὸν
in you	ἐν ὑμῖν
will carry it on to completion	ἐπιτελέσει
until the **day**	ἄχρι **ἡμέρας**
of Christ Jesus	Ἰησοῦ Χριστοῦ

And the slaves of the householder came and said to him, "Master, **did you not sow (οὐχὶ . . . ἔσπειρας) good (καλὸν)** seed in your field? Where, then, did these weeds come from?" (NRSV)

σπείρω	to sow	52x
speirō		S4687

καλός ➤ DAY 165   **οὐχί** ➤ DAY 292

προσελθόντες δὲ οἱ δοῦλοι τοῦ οἰκοδεσπότου εἶπον αὐτῷ Κύριε, **οὐχὶ καλὸν** σπέρμα **ἔσπειρας** ἐν τῷ σῷ ἀγρῷ; πόθεν οὖν ἔχει ζιζάνια;

And the slaves	δὲ οἱ δοῦλοι
of the householder	τοῦ οἰκοδεσπότου
came	προσελθόντες
and said to him	εἶπον αὐτῷ
Master	Κύριε
did you not sow	**οὐχὶ . . . ἔσπειρας**
good seed	**καλὸν** σπέρμα
in your field?	ἐν τῷ σῷ ἀγρῷ;
Where, then,	πόθεν οὖν
did these weeds come from?	ἔχει ζιζάνια;

And the **child (παιδίον)** grew and became strong, filled with
wisdom (σοφία). And the **favor (χάρις)** of God was upon him.
(ESV)

σοφία	wisdom	51x
sophia		S4678

χάρις ➤ DAY 106   **παιδίον** ➤ DAY 302

Τὸ δὲ **παιδίον** ηὔξανεν καὶ ἐκραταιοῦτο πληρούμενον **σοφίᾳ**, καὶ
χάρις θεοῦ ἦν ἐπ᾽ αὐτό.

And the **child**	Τὸ δὲ **παιδίον**
grew	ηὔξανεν
and became strong	καὶ ἐκραταιοῦτο
filled	πληρούμενον
with **wisdom**	**σοφίᾳ**
And the **favor** of God	καὶ **χάρις** θεοῦ
was	ἦν
upon him	ἐπ᾽ αὐτό

For what does the **scripture (γραφὴ)** say? "Abraham **believed (Ἐπίστευσεν)** God, and it was reckoned to him as **righteousness (δικαιοσύνην)**." (NRSV)

| γραφή | writing, scripture | 50x |
| *graphē* | | S1124 |

πιστεύω ➤ DAY 66   **δικαιοσύνη** ➤ DAY 187

τί γὰρ ἡ **γραφὴ** λέγει; Ἐπίστευσεν δὲ Ἀβραὰμ τῷ θεῷ, καὶ ἐλογίσθη αὐτῷ εἰς **δικαιοσύνην**.

For what	τί γὰρ
does the **scripture** say?	ἡ **γραφὴ** λέγει;
Abraham **believed**	Ἐπίστευσεν δὲ Ἀβραὰμ
God	τῷ θεῷ
and it was reckoned to him	καὶ ἐλογίσθη αὐτῷ
as **righteousness**	εἰς **δικαιοσύνην**

Dear friend (Ἀγαπητέ), do not imitate what is **evil (κακὸν),** but what is **good (ἀγαθόν).** The one who does good is of God; the one who does evil has not seen God. (CSB)

κακός	bad, evil	50x
kakos		S2556

ἀγαθός ➤ DAY 164   **ἀγαπητός** ➤ DAY 261

Ἀγαπητέ, μὴ μιμοῦ τὸ **κακὸν** ἀλλὰ τὸ **ἀγαθόν.** ὁ ἀγαθοποιῶν ἐκ τοῦ θεοῦ ἐστιν· ὁ κακοποιῶν οὐχ ἑώρακεν τὸν θεόν.

Dear friend	Ἀγαπητέ
do not imitate	μὴ μιμοῦ
what is **evil**	τὸ **κακὸν**
but what is **good**	ἀλλὰ τὸ **ἀγαθόν**
The one who does good	ὁ ἀγαθοποιῶν
is of God	ἐκ τοῦ θεοῦ ἐστίν
the one who does evil	ὁ κακοποιῶν
has not seen	οὐχ ἑώρακεν
God	τὸν θεόν

Blessed (Μακάριοι) are the poor in **spirit (πνεύματι)**, for theirs is the **kingdom (βασιλεία)** of heaven. (NIV)

μακάριος	happy, blessed	50x
makarios		S3107

πνεῦμα ➤ DAY 47   βασιλεία ➤ DAY 97

Μακάριοι οἱ πτωχοὶ τῷ **πνεύματι**, ὅτι αὐτῶν ἐστὶν ἡ **βασιλεία** τῶν οὐρανῶν.

Blessed	Μακάριοι
are the poor	οἱ πτωχοὶ
in **spirit**	τῷ **πνεύματι**
for theirs	ὅτι αὐτῶν
is	ἐστὶν
the **kingdom**	ἡ **βασιλεία**
of heaven	τῶν οὐρανῶν

And he told them many things in **parables (παραβολαῖς)**, saying:
"**Listen! (Ἰδοὺ)** A **sower (σπείρων)** went out **to sow (σπείρειν)**."
(NRSV)

παραβολή	parable, similitude, allegory	50x
parabolē		S3850

    ἰδού ➤ DAY 79   **σπείρω** ➤ DAY 304

καὶ ἐλάλησεν αὐτοῖς πολλὰ ἐν **παραβολαῖς** λέγων Ἰδοὺ ἐξῆλθεν ὁ **σπείρων** τοῦ **σπείρειν**.

And he told them	καὶ ἐλάλησεν αὐτοῖς
many things	πολλὰ
in **parables**	ἐν **παραβολαῖς**
saying	λέγων
Listen!	Ἰδοὺ
A **sower**	ὁ **σπείρων**
went out	ἐξῆλθεν
to sow	τοῦ **σπείρειν**

There is **therefore (ἄρα)** now **no (Οὐδὲν)** condemnation for those who are in Christ **Jesus (Ἰησοῦ)**. (ESV)

| ἄρα / ἄρα | then, therefore, perhaps | 49x |
| *ara* | | S686 + S687 |

     Ἰησοῦς ➤ DAY 20   οὐδείς, οὐδεμία, οὐδέν ➤ DAY 65

Οὐδὲν ἄρα νῦν κατάκριμα τοῖς ἐν Χριστῷ **Ἰησοῦ·**

There is . . . **no** condemnation	**Οὐδὲν** . . . κατάκριμα
therefore	ἄρα
now	νῦν
for those who	τοῖς
are in Christ **Jesus**	ἐν Χριστῷ **Ἰησοῦ**

For he must reign **until (ἄχρι)** he has put **all (πάντας)** his enemies under his **feet (πόδας)**. (NIV)

ἄχρι	as far as, up to, until	49x
*ach*ri		S891

πᾶς ➤ DAY 16   πούς ➤ DAY 181

δεῖ γὰρ αὐτὸν βασιλεύειν **ἄχρι** οὗ θῇ **πάντας** τοὺς ἐχθροὺς ὑπὸ τοὺς **πόδας** αὐτοῦ.

For	γὰρ
he must reign	δεῖ . . . αὐτὸν βασιλεύειν
until	**ἄχρι** οὗ
he has put	θῇ
all his enemies	**πάντας** τοὺς ἐχθροὺς
under his **feet**	ὑπὸ τοὺς **πόδας** αὐτοῦ

Then after **three (τρία) years (ἔτη)** I went up to **Jerusalem (Ἰεροσόλυμα)** to get acquainted with Cephas and stayed in his company for fifteen days. (MLB)

ἔτος	year	49x
etos		S2094

Ἰερουσαλήμ / Ἰεροσόλυμα ➤ DAY 122   **τρεῖς, τρία** ➤ DAY 242

Ἔπειτα μετὰ **τρία ἔτη** ἀνῆλθον εἰς Ἰεροσόλυμα ἱστορῆσαι Κηφᾶν, καὶ ἐπέμεινα πρὸς αὐτὸν ἡμέρας δεκαπέντε·

Then	Ἔπειτα
after **three years**	μετὰ **τρία ἔτη**
I went up	ἀνῆλθον
to **Jerusalem**	εἰς Ἰεροσόλυμα
to get acquainted with	ἱστορῆσαι
Cephas	Κηφᾶν
and stayed	καὶ ἐπέμεινα
in his company	πρὸς αὐτὸν
for fifteen days	ἡμέρας δεκαπέντε

He came (ἦλθεν) to what was his **own (ἴδια)**, and his **own people (ἴδιοι) did** not **accept (παρέλαβον)** him. (NRSV)

παραλαμβάνω	to take, receive	49x
paralambanō		S3880

ἔρχομαι ➢ DAY 30   ἴδιος ➢ DAY 151

Εἰς τὰ **ἴδια ἦλθεν**, καὶ οἱ **ἴδιοι** αὐτὸν οὐ **παρέλαβον**.

He came	**ἦλθεν**
to what was his **own**	Εἰς τὰ **ἴδια**
and his **own people**	καὶ οἱ **ἴδιοι**
did not **accept** him	αὐτὸν οὐ **παρέλαβον**

They brought (Ἄγουσιν) to the Pharisees (Φαρισαίους) the man [lit., him] who had formerly been blind (τυφλόν). (ESV)

| τυφλός | blind | 49x |
| *tuphlos* | | S5185 |

Φαρισαῖος ➤ DAY 176   **ἄγω** ➤ DAY 238

Ἄγουσιν αὐτὸν πρὸς τοὺς **Φαρισαίους** τόν ποτε **τυφλόν**.

They brought	Ἄγουσιν
to the **Pharisees**	πρὸς τοὺς **Φαρισαίους**
the man [lit., him]	αὐτὸν
who had formerly been **blind**	τόν ποτε **τυφλόν**

He was foreknown before the foundation of the world but **was made manifest (φανερωθέντος)** in the last times [lit., the **last (ἐσχάτου)** of the **times (χρόνων)**] for the sake of you. (ESV)

φανερόω	to make manifest, reveal	49x
phaneroō		S5319

χρόνος ➤ DAY 293   **ἔσχατος** ➤ DAY 300

προεγνωσμένου μὲν πρὸ καταβολῆς κόσμου, **φανερωθέντος** δὲ ἐπ᾽ **ἐσχάτου** τῶν **χρόνων** δι᾽ ὑμᾶς

He was foreknown	προεγνωσμένου μὲν
before the foundation	πρὸ καταβολῆς
of the world	κόσμου
but **was made manifest**	**φανερωθέντος** δὲ
in the last times [lit., the **last** of the **times**]	ἐπ᾽ **ἐσχάτου** τῶν **χρόνων**
for the sake of you	δι᾽ ὑμᾶς

And the **eye (ὀφθαλμὸς)** cannot say to the hand, "I have no **need (Χρείαν)** of you"; **or (ἤ)** again the head to the feet, "I have no **need (Χρείαν)** of you." (NASB)

χρεία	need		49x
chreia			S5532

     ἤ ➤ DAY 50   **ὀφθαλμός** ➤ DAY 169

οὐ δύναται [δὲ] ὁ **ὀφθαλμὸς** εἰπεῖν τῇ χειρί **Χρείαν** σου οὐκ ἔχω, **ἤ** πάλιν ἡ κεφαλὴ τοῖς ποσίν **Χρείαν** ὑμῶν οὐκ ἔχω·

And the **eye**	[δὲ] ὁ **ὀφθαλμὸς**
cannot	οὐ δύναται
say	εἰπεῖν
to the hand	τῇ χειρί
I have no	οὐκ ἔχω
need of you	**Χρείαν** σου
or again	**ἤ** πάλιν
the head	ἡ κεφαλὴ
to the feet	τοῖς ποσίν
I have no	οὐκ ἔχω
need of you	**Χρείαν** ὑμῶν

He approached **Pilate (Πειλάτῳ)** and **asked (ᾐτήσατο)** for Jesus' body. Then **Pilate (Πειλᾶτος)** ordered **that it be released (ἀποδοθῆναι)**. (HCSB)

ἀποδίδωμι	to give back, return, restore	48x
apodidōmi		S591

αἰτέω   ➤   DAY 243   Πιλᾶτος   ➤   DAY 289

οὗτος προσελθὼν τῷ **Πειλάτῳ ᾐτήσατο** τὸ σῶμα τοῦ Ἰησοῦ. τότε ὁ **Πειλᾶτος** ἐκέλευσεν **ἀποδοθῆναι**.

He approached	οὗτος προσελθὼν
Pilate	τῷ **Πειλάτῳ**
and **asked** for	**ᾐτήσατο**
Jesus' body	τὸ σῶμα τοῦ Ἰησοῦ
Then	τότε
Pilate	ὁ **Πειλᾶτος**
ordered	ἐκέλευσεν
that it be released	**ἀποδοθῆναι**

For one **who speaks (λαλῶν)** in a **tongue (γλώσσῃ) speaks (λαλεῖ)** not to men but to God; for **no one (οὐδεὶς)** understands him, but **he utters (λαλεῖ)** mysteries in the Spirit. (ESV)

| **γλῶσσα** | tongue, language | 48x |
| *glōssa* | | S1100 |

λαλέω ➤ DAY 57   **οὐδείς, οὐδεμία, οὐδέν** ➤ DAY 65

ὁ γὰρ **λαλῶν γλώσσῃ** οὐκ ἀνθρώποις **λαλεῖ** ἀλλὰ θεῷ, **οὐδεὶς** γὰρ ἀκούει, πνεύματι δὲ **λαλεῖ** μυστήρια·

For one **who speaks**	ὁ γὰρ **λαλῶν**
in a **tongue**	**γλώσσῃ**
speaks not to men	οὐκ ἀνθρώποις **λαλεῖ**
but to God	ἀλλὰ θεῷ
for **no one**	**οὐδεὶς** γὰρ
understands him	ἀκούει
but **he utters** mysteries	δὲ **λαλεῖ** μυστήρια
in the Spirit	πνεύματι

And in front of the **throne (θρόνου)** there is something like a sea of glass, like crystal. Around [lit., And in the **middle (μέσῳ)** of] the **throne (θρόνου)**, and on each side of [lit., and around] the **throne (θρόνου)**, are four living creatures, full of eyes **in front (ἔμπροσθεν)** and behind. (NRSV)

ἔμπροσθεν	in front (of), before the face (of)	48x
*em*prosthen		S1715

θρόνος ➤ DAY 259   **μέσος** ➤ DAY 277

καὶ ἐνώπιον τοῦ **θρόνου** ὡς θάλασσα ὑαλίνη ὁμοία κρυστάλλῳ. καὶ ἐν **μέσῳ** τοῦ **θρόνου** καὶ κύκλῳ τοῦ **θρόνου** τέσσερα ζῷα γέμοντα ὀφθαλμῶν **ἔμπροσθεν** καὶ ὄπισθεν·

And in front of the **throne**	καὶ ἐνώπιον τοῦ **θρόνου**
there is something like a sea of glass	ὡς θάλασσα ὑαλίνη
like crystal	ὁμοία κρυστάλλῳ
Around [lit., And in the **middle** of] the **throne**	καὶ ἐν **μέσῳ** τοῦ **θρόνου**
and on each side of [lit., and around] the **throne**	καὶ κύκλῳ τοῦ **θρόνου**
are four living creatures	τέσσερα ζῷα
full of eyes	γέμοντα ὀφθαλμῶν
in front and behind	**ἔμπροσθεν** καὶ ὄπισθεν

And he answered them, "**Do you think (Δοκεῖτε)** that these Galileans **were (ἐγένοντο)** worse **sinners (ἁμαρτωλοὶ)** than all the other Galileans, because they suffered in this way?" (ESV)

ἁμαρτωλός	sinful, sinner	47x
hamartōlos		S268

γίνομαι ➤ DAY 27   **δοκέω** ➤ DAY 256

καὶ ἀποκριθεὶς εἶπεν αὐτοῖς **Δοκεῖτε** ὅτι οἱ Γαλιλαῖοι οὗτοι **ἁμαρτωλοὶ** παρὰ πάντας τοὺς Γαλιλαίους **ἐγένοντο**, ὅτι ταῦτα πεπόνθασιν;

And he answered them	καὶ ἀποκριθεὶς εἶπεν αὐτοῖς
Do you think that	**Δοκεῖτε** ὅτι
these Galileans	οἱ Γαλιλαῖοι οὗτοι
were	**ἐγένοντο**
worse **sinners** than	**ἁμαρτωλοὶ** παρὰ
all the other Galileans	πάντας τοὺς Γαλιλαίους
because they suffered	ὅτι . . . πεπόνθασιν;
in this way?	ταῦτα

So (Ἄρα) then, brethren, stand firm and **hold to (κρατεῖτε)** the traditions which you were taught, **whether (εἴτε)** by word of mouth **or (εἴτε)** by letter from us. (NASB)

| κρατέω | to take hold of, obtain | 47x |
| *krateō* | | S2902 |

εἴτε ➢ DAY 251　　　ἄρα / ἄρα ➢ DAY 310

Ἄρα οὖν, ἀδελφοί, στήκετε, καὶ **κρατεῖτε** τὰς παραδόσεις ἃς ἐδιδάχθητε **εἴτε** διὰ λόγου **εἴτε** δι᾿ ἐπιστολῆς ἡμῶν.

So then	Ἄρα οὖν
brethren	ἀδελφοί
stand firm	στήκετε
and **hold to**	καὶ **κρατεῖτε**
the traditions	τὰς παραδόσεις
which you were taught	ἃς ἐδιδάχθητε
whether by word of mouth	**εἴτε** διὰ λόγου
or by letter from us	**εἴτε** δι᾿ ἐπιστολῆς ἡμῶν

And just as [lit., according to **as much as (ὅσον)**] it is appointed for people **to die (ἀποθανεῖν)** once—and after this, **judgment (κρίσις)** . . . (CSB)

κρίσις	judgment	47x
krisis		S2920

ἀποθνήσκω ➤ DAY 148   **ὅσος** ➤ DAY 153

καὶ καθ᾽ **ὅσον** ἀπόκειται τοῖς ἀνθρώποις ἅπαξ **ἀποθανεῖν**, μετὰ δὲ τοῦτο **κρίσις**,

And just as [lit., according to **as much as**]	καὶ καθ᾽ **ὅσον**
it is appointed for people	ἀπόκειται τοῖς ἀνθρώποις
to die once	ἅπαξ **ἀποθανεῖν**
and after this	μετὰ δὲ τοῦτο
judgment	**κρίσις**

But he answered, "It is written, 'One does not live by bread **alone (μόνῳ)**, but by every **word (ῥήματι)** that comes from the **mouth (στόματος)** of God.'" (NRSV)

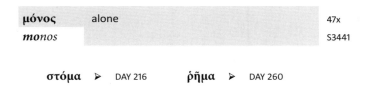

| **μόνος** | alone | 47x |
| *monos* | | S3441 |

στόμα ➤ DAY 216   **ῥῆμα** ➤ DAY 260

ὁ δὲ ἀποκριθεὶς εἶπεν Γέγραπται Οὐκ ἐπ' ἄρτῳ **μόνῳ** ζήσεται ὁ ἄνθρωπος, ἀλλ' ἐπὶ παντὶ **ῥήματι** ἐκπορευομένῳ διὰ **στόματος** θεοῦ.

But he answered	ὁ δὲ ἀποκριθεὶς εἶπεν
It is written	Γέγραπται
One	ὁ ἄνθρωπος
does not live by bread **alone**	Οὐκ ἐπ' ἄρτῳ **μόνῳ** ζήσεται
but by every **word**	ἀλλ' ἐπὶ παντὶ **ῥήματι**
that comes from the **mouth** of God	ἐκπορευομένῳ διὰ **στόματος** θεοῦ

But now that **faith (πίστεως)** has come, **we are (ἐσμεν) no longer (οὐκέτι)** under a guardian. (ESV)

| οὐκέτι | no longer, no more | 47x |
| *ouketi* | | S3765 |

εἰμί ➤ DAY 8   πίστις ➤ DAY 62

ἐλθούσης δὲ τῆς **πίστεως οὐκέτι** ὑπὸ παιδαγωγόν **ἐσμεν**.

But now that **faith** has come	ἐλθούσης δὲ τῆς **πίστεως**
we are	**ἐσμεν**
no longer	**οὐκέτι**
under a guardian	ὑπὸ παιδαγωγόν

And he said **to (πρὸς)** them, "I have eagerly desired **to eat (φαγεῖν)** this Passover with you **before (πρὸ)** I suffer." (NIV)

πρό	before, in front of	47x
pro		S4253

πρός ➤ DAY 24 **ἐσθίω** ➤ DAY 100

καὶ εἶπεν **πρὸς** αὐτούς Ἐπιθυμίᾳ ἐπεθύμησα τοῦτο τὸ πάσχα **φαγεῖν** μεθ᾽ ὑμῶν **πρὸ** τοῦ με παθεῖν·

And he said	καὶ εἶπεν
to them	**πρὸς** αὐτούς
I have eagerly desired	Ἐπιθυμίᾳ ἐπεθύμησα
to eat	**φαγεῖν**
this Passover	τοῦτο τὸ πάσχα
with you	μεθ᾽ ὑμῶν
before I suffer	**πρὸ** τοῦ με παθεῖν

For you have not received a spirit of slavery leading to **fear** (**φόβον**) again, but you have received a spirit of adoption as sons by which **we cry out** (**κράζομεν**), "Abba! **Father** (**πατήρ**)!" (NASB)

φόβος	fear, terror	47x
phobos		S5401

    πατήρ ➤ DAY 44   **κράζω** ➤ DAY 282

οὐ γὰρ ἐλάβετε πνεῦμα δουλείας πάλιν εἰς **φόβον**, ἀλλὰ ἐλάβετε πνεῦμα υἱοθεσίας, ἐν ᾧ **κράζομεν** Ἀββά ὁ **πατήρ**·

For you have not received	οὐ γὰρ ἐλάβετε
a spirit of slavery	πνεῦμα δουλείας
leading to **fear**	εἰς **φόβον**
again	πάλιν
but you have received	ἀλλὰ ἐλάβετε
a spirit of adoption as sons	πνεῦμα υἱοθεσίας
by which	ἐν ᾧ
we cry out	**κράζομεν**
Abba!	Ἀββά
Father!	ὁ **πατήρ**

And **there appeared (ὤφθησαν)** to them tongues as of **fire (πυρός)** distributing themselves, and **they rested (ἐκάθισεν)** on each one of them. (NASB)

καθίζω	to sit, set, make sit	46x
kathizō		S2523

ὁράω ➤ DAY 40   **πῦρ** ➤ DAY 235

καὶ **ὤφθησαν** αὐτοῖς διαμεριζόμεναι γλῶσσαι ὡσεὶ **πυρός**, καὶ **ἐκάθισεν** ἐφ᾽ ἕνα ἕκαστον αὐτῶν,

And **there appeared** to them	καὶ **ὤφθησαν** αὐτοῖς
tongues	γλῶσσαι
as of **fire**	ὡσεὶ **πυρός**
distributing themselves	διαμεριζόμεναι
and **they rested**	καὶ **ἐκάθισεν**
on each one of them	ἐφ᾽ ἕνα ἕκαστον αὐτῶν

And whoever gives [to drink] **even (μόνον)** a cup of cold water to one of these **little ones (μικρῶν)** in the name of a disciple—truly I tell you, none of these will lose their reward [lit., **he will** never **lose (ἀπολέσῃ)** his reward]. (NRSV)

μικρός	small, short		46x
mikros			S3398

ἀπόλλυμι ➤ DAY 190   **μόνον** ➤ DAY 244

καὶ ὃς ἂν ποτίσῃ ἕνα τῶν **μικρῶν** τούτων ποτήριον ψυχροῦ **μόνον** εἰς ὄνομα μαθητοῦ, ἀμὴν λέγω ὑμῖν, οὐ μὴ **ἀπολέσῃ** τὸν μισθὸν αὐτοῦ.

And whoever	καὶ ὃς ἂν
gives [to drink]	ποτίσῃ
even a cup of cold water	ποτήριον ψυχροῦ **μόνον**
to one of these **little ones**	ἕνα τῶν **μικρῶν** τούτων
in the name of a disciple	εἰς ὄνομα μαθητοῦ
truly I tell you	ἀμὴν λέγω ὑμῖν
none of these will lose their reward [lit., **he will** never **lose** his reward]	οὐ μὴ **ἀπολέσῃ** τὸν μισθὸν αὐτοῦ

standing at a distance because of the fear of her torment, saying,
"**Woe (Οὐαί)**, **woe (οὐαί)**, the great **city (πόλις)**, Babylon, the
strong **city (πόλις)**! For in one **hour (ὥρᾳ)** your judgment has
come." (NASB)

οὐαί	woe	46x
ouai		S3759

πόλις ➤ DAY 96   **ὥρα** ➤ DAY 159

ἀπὸ μακρόθεν ἑστηκότες διὰ τὸν φόβον τοῦ βασανισμοῦ αὐτῆς,
λέγοντες **Οὐαί οὐαί**, ἡ **πόλις** ἡ μεγάλη, Βαβυλὼν ἡ **πόλις** ἡ
ἰσχυρά, ὅτι μιᾷ **ὥρᾳ** ἦλθεν ἡ κρίσις σου.

standing at a distance	ἀπὸ μακρόθεν ἑστηκότες
because of the fear	διὰ τὸν φόβον
of her torment	τοῦ βασανισμοῦ αὐτῆς
saying	λέγοντες
Woe, woe	**Οὐαί οὐαί**
the great **city**	ἡ **πόλις** ἡ μεγάλη
Babylon	Βαβυλὼν
the strong **city**!	ἡ **πόλις** ἡ ἰσχυρά
For in one **hour**	ὅτι μιᾷ **ὥρᾳ**
your judgment	ἡ κρίσις σου
has come	ἦλθεν

And **they were bringing (προσέφερον) children (παιδία)** to him that he might touch them, and the **disciples (μαθηταὶ)** rebuked them. (ESV)

προσφέρω	to bring to, offer	46x
prospherō		S4374

μαθητής ➤ DAY 59   **παιδίον** ➤ DAY 302

Καὶ **προσέφερον** αὐτῷ **παιδία** ἵνα αὐτῶν ἅψηται· οἱ δὲ **μαθηταὶ** ἐπετίμησαν αὐτοῖς.

And **they were bringing**	Καὶ **προσέφερον**
children to him	αὐτῷ **παιδία**
that he might touch them	ἵνα αὐτῶν ἅψηται
and the **disciples**	οἱ δὲ **μαθηταὶ**
rebuked them	ἐπετίμησαν αὐτοῖς

And regard the continued patience of our Lord as **salvation
(σωτηρίαν)**, as our **dear (ἀγαπητός)** brother Paul also has written
you, according to the **wisdom (σοφίαν)** that has been granted him.
(MLB)

σωτηρία	salvation, release, deliverance	46x
sōtēria		S4991

ἀγαπητός ➤ DAY 261   **σοφία** ➤ DAY 305

καὶ τὴν τοῦ κυρίου ἡμῶν μακροθυμίαν **σωτηρίαν** ἡγεῖσθε, καθὼς
καὶ ὁ **ἀγαπητὸς** ἡμῶν ἀδελφὸς Παῦλος κατὰ τὴν δοθεῖσαν αὐτῷ
σοφίαν ἔγραψεν ὑμῖν,

And regard	καὶ . . . ἡγεῖσθε
the continued patience	τὴν . . . μακροθυμίαν
of our Lord	τοῦ κυρίου ἡμῶν
as **salvation**	**σωτηρίαν**
as	καθὼς
our **dear** brother Paul also	καὶ ὁ **ἀγαπητὸς** ἡμῶν ἀδελφὸς Παῦλος
has written you	ἔγραψεν ὑμῖν
according to the **wisdom**	κατὰ τὴν . . . **σοφίαν**
that has been granted him	δοθεῖσαν αὐτῷ

Now Herod **had arrested (κρατήσας)** John and bound him and put him in **prison (φυλακῇ)** because of Herodias, his brother Philip's **wife (γυναῖκα)**. (NIV)

φυλακή	prison, guard	46x
phulakē		S5438

γυνή ➤ DAY 74 **κρατέω** ➤ DAY 321

Ὁ γὰρ Ἡρῴδης **κρατήσας** τὸν Ἰωάνην ἔδησεν καὶ ἐν **φυλακῇ** ἀπέθετο διὰ Ἡρῳδιάδα τὴν **γυναῖκα** Φιλίππου τοῦ ἀδελφοῦ αὐτοῦ,

Now Herod	Ὁ γὰρ Ἡρῴδης
had arrested	**κρατήσας**
John	τὸν Ἰωάνην
and bound him	ἔδησεν
and put him	καὶ ... ἀπέθετο
in **prison**	ἐν **φυλακῇ**
because of Herodias	διὰ Ἡρῳδιάδα
his brother Philip's **wife**	τὴν **γυναῖκα** Φιλίππου τοῦ ἀδελφοῦ αὐτοῦ

Pursue (Διώκετε) love (ἀγάπην) and strive for the spiritual gifts, and **especially (μᾶλλον)** that you may prophesy. (NRSV)

| **διώκω** | to pursue, persecute | 45x |
| *diōkō* | | S1377 |

ἀγάπη ➤ DAY 145   **μᾶλλον** ➤ DAY 211

Διώκετε τὴν **ἀγάπην**, ζηλοῦτε δὲ τὰ πνευματικά, **μᾶλλον** δὲ ἵνα προφητεύητε.

Pursue	**Διώκετε**
love	τὴν **ἀγάπην**
and strive for	ζηλοῦτε δὲ
the spiritual gifts	τὰ πνευματικά
and **especially**	**μᾶλλον** δὲ
that you may prophesy	ἵνα προφητεύητε

In those **days (ἡμέραις)** John the Baptist came, **preaching (κηρύσσων)** in the **wilderness (ἐρήμῳ)** of Judea. (NIV)

ἔρημος	desert, wilderness	45x
erēmos		S2048

ἡμέρα ➤ DAY 46   **κηρύσσω** ➤ DAY 265

Ἐν δὲ ταῖς **ἡμέραις** ἐκείναις παραγίνεται Ἰωάνης ὁ βαπτιστὴς **κηρύσσων** ἐν τῇ **ἐρήμῳ** τῆς Ἰουδαίας

In those **days**	Ἐν δὲ ταῖς **ἡμέραις** ἐκείναις
John the Baptist	Ἰωάνης ὁ βαπτιστὴς
came	παραγίνεται
preaching	**κηρύσσων**
in the **wilderness**	ἐν τῇ **ἐρήμῳ**
of Judea	τῆς Ἰουδαίας

And I saw a **beast (θηρίον) rising (ἀναβαῖνον)** out of the sea, having ten horns and seven **heads (κεφαλὰς)**; and on its horns were ten diadems, and on its **heads (κεφαλὰς)** were blasphemous names. (NRSV)

θηρίον	animal, wild beast	45x
*thē**rion***		S2342

ἀναβαίνω ➤ DAY 206   **κεφαλή** ➤ DAY 224

Καὶ εἶδον ἐκ τῆς θαλάσσης **θηρίον ἀναβαῖνον**, ἔχον κέρατα δέκα καὶ **κεφαλὰς** ἑπτά, καὶ ἐπὶ τῶν κεράτων αὐτοῦ δέκα διαδήματα, καὶ ἐπὶ τὰς **κεφαλὰς** αὐτοῦ ὀνόματα βλασφημίας.

And I saw	Καὶ εἶδον
a **beast rising**	**θηρίον ἀναβαῖνον**
out of the sea	ἐκ τῆς θαλάσσης
having	ἔχον
ten horns	κέρατα δέκα
and seven **heads**	καὶ **κεφαλὰς** ἑπτά
and on its horns	καὶ ἐπὶ τῶν κεράτων αὐτοῦ
were ten diadems	δέκα διαδήματα
and on its **heads**	καὶ ἐπὶ τὰς **κεφαλὰς** αὐτοῦ
were blasphemous names	ὀνόματα βλασφημίας

Then I was given a measuring rod like a staff, and I was told [lit., saying], "**Rise (Ἔγειρε)** and measure the **temple (ναὸν)** of God and the altar and those **who worship (προσκυνοῦντας)** there [lit., in it]." (ESV)

| **ναός** | temple, shrine | 45x |
| *naos* | | S3485 |

ἐγείρω ➤ DAY 118   **προσκυνέω** ➤ DAY 271

Καὶ ἐδόθη μοι κάλαμος ὅμοιος ῥάβδῳ, λέγων Ἔγειρε καὶ μέτρησον τὸν **ναὸν** τοῦ θεοῦ καὶ τὸ θυσιαστήριον καὶ τοὺς **προσκυνοῦντας** ἐν αὐτῷ.

Then I was given	Καὶ ἐδόθη μοι
a measuring rod	κάλαμος
like a staff	ὅμοιος ῥάβδῳ
and I was told [lit., saying]	λέγων
Rise	Ἔγειρε
and measure	καὶ μέτρησον
the **temple** of God	τὸν **ναὸν** τοῦ θεοῦ
and the altar	καὶ τὸ θυσιαστήριον
and those **who worship**	καὶ τοὺς **προσκυνοῦντας**
there [lit., in it]	ἐν αὐτῷ

Where (ποῦ) is the wise man? **Where (ποῦ)** is the **scribe (γραμματεύς)?** **Where (ποῦ)** is the debater of this **age (αἰῶνος)?** Has not God made foolish the wisdom of the world? (NASB)

| ποῦ | where? to what place? | 45x |
| *pou* | | S4226 |

αἰών ➤ DAY 136 γραμματεύς ➤ DAY 253

ποῦ σοφός; **ποῦ γραμματεύς**; **ποῦ** συνζητητὴς τοῦ **αἰῶνος** τούτου; οὐχὶ ἐμώρανεν ὁ θεὸς τὴν σοφίαν τοῦ κόσμου;

Where is the wise man?	**ποῦ** σοφός;
Where is the **scribe?**	**ποῦ γραμματεύς**;
Where is the debater	**ποῦ** συνζητητὴς
of this **age?**	τοῦ **αἰῶνος** τούτου;
Has not God made foolish	οὐχὶ ἐμώρανεν ὁ θεὸς
the wisdom	τὴν σοφίαν
of the world?	τοῦ κόσμου;

But **we (ἡμεῖς)** preach Christ **crucified (ἐσταυρωμένον)**: a stumbling block to Jews and foolishness to **Gentiles (ἔθνεσιν)**.
(NIV)

σταυρόω	to crucify	45x
stauroō		S4717

ἐγώ, (pl) **ἡμεῖς** ➢ DAY 7   **ἔθνος** ➢ DAY 98

ἡμεῖς δὲ κηρύσσομεν Χριστὸν **ἐσταυρωμένον**, Ἰουδαίοις μὲν σκάνδαλον **ἔθνεσιν** δὲ μωρίαν,

But **we** preach	**ἡμεῖς** δὲ κηρύσσομεν
Christ **crucified**	Χριστὸν **ἐσταυρωμένον**
a stumbling block	σκάνδαλον
to Jews	Ἰουδαίοις μὲν
and . . . to **Gentiles**	**ἔθνεσιν** δὲ
foolishness	μωρίαν

So then **I ask (αἰτοῦμαι)** you not to be discouraged over my **afflictions (θλίψεσίν)** on your behalf, for they are your **glory (δόξα)**. (CSB)

θλῖψις	distress, affliction, persecution, tribulation	44x
thlipsis		S2347

δόξα ➤ DAY 95   **αἰτέω** ➤ DAY 243

Διὸ **αἰτοῦμαι** μὴ ἐνκακεῖν ἐν ταῖς **θλίψεσίν** μου ὑπὲρ ὑμῶν, ἥτις ἐστὶν **δόξα** ὑμῶν.

So then	Διὸ
I ask you	**αἰτοῦμαι**
not to be discouraged	μὴ ἐνκακεῖν
over my **afflictions**	ἐν ταῖς **θλίψεσίν** μου
on your behalf	ὑπὲρ ὑμῶν
for they are	ἥτις ἐστὶν
your **glory**	**δόξα** ὑμῶν

This, then, was the second **sign (σημεῖον)** Jesus performed when
He came from **Judea (Ἰουδαίας)** into **Galilee (Γαλιλαίαν)**. (MLB)

Ἰουδαία	Judea	44x
Ioudaia		S2449

σημεῖον ➤ DAY 220   **Γαλιλαία** ➤ DAY 262

Τοῦτο [δὲ] πάλιν δεύτερον **σημεῖον** ἐποίησεν ὁ Ἰησοῦς ἐλθὼν ἐκ
τῆς **Ἰουδαίας** εἰς τὴν **Γαλιλαίαν**.

This, then, was the second **sign**	Τοῦτο [δὲ] πάλιν δεύτερον **σημεῖον**
Jesus performed	ἐποίησεν ὁ Ἰησοῦς
when He came	ἐλθὼν
from **Judea**	ἐκ τῆς **Ἰουδαίας**
into **Galilee**	εἰς τὴν **Γαλιλαίαν**

By **faith (Πίστει)** he lived as an alien in the land of **promise (ἐπαγγελίας)**, as in a foreign land, **dwelling (κατοικήσας)** in tents with Isaac and Jacob, fellow heirs of the same **promise (ἐπαγγελίας)**. (NASB)

| **κατοικέω** | to dwell, settle | 44x |
| *katoikeō* | | S2730 |

πίστις ➤ DAY 62   **ἐπαγγελία** ➤ DAY 299

Πίστει παρῴκησεν εἰς γῆν τῆς **ἐπαγγελίας** ὡς ἀλλοτρίαν, ἐν σκηναῖς **κατοικήσας** μετὰ Ἰσαὰκ καὶ Ἰακὼβ τῶν συγκληρονόμων τῆς **ἐπαγγελίας** τῆς αὐτῆς·

By **faith**	**Πίστει**
he lived as an alien	παρῴκησεν
in the land	εἰς γῆν
of **promise**	τῆς **ἐπαγγελίας**
as in a foreign land	ὡς ἀλλοτρίαν
dwelling	**κατοικήσας**
in tents	ἐν σκηναῖς
with Isaac and Jacob	μετὰ Ἰσαὰκ καὶ Ἰακὼβ
fellow heirs	τῶν συγκληρονόμων
of the same **promise**	τῆς **ἐπαγγελίας** τῆς αὐτῆς

Everyone **who remains (μένων)** in him **does** not **sin (ἁμαρτάνει)**; everyone **who sins (ἁμαρτάνων)** has not seen him or **known (ἔγνωκεν)** him. (CSB)

ἁμαρτάνω	to sin, make a mistake, miss the mark	43x
hamartanō		S264

γινώσκω ➢ DAY 70   **μένω** ➢ DAY 139

πᾶς ὁ ἐν αὐτῷ **μένων** οὐχ **ἁμαρτάνει**· πᾶς ὁ **ἁμαρτάνων** οὐχ ἑώρακεν αὐτὸν οὐδὲ **ἔγνωκεν** αὐτόν.

Everyone **who remains**	πᾶς ὁ . . . **μένων**
in him	ἐν αὐτῷ
does not **sin**	οὐχ **ἁμαρτάνει**
everyone **who sins**	πᾶς ὁ **ἁμαρτάνων**
has not seen him	οὐχ ἑώρακεν αὐτὸν
or **known** him	οὐδὲ **ἔγνωκεν** αὐτόν

After **they were released** (Ἀπολυθέντες), they went to their own people and **reported** (ἀπήγγειλαν) everything the **chief priests** (ἀρχιερεῖς) and the elders had said to them. (CSB)

ἀπαγγέλλω	to announce, report	43x
apangellō		S518

ἀρχιερεύς	➤ DAY 133	ἀπολύω	➤ DAY 250

Ἀπολυθέντες δὲ ἦλθον πρὸς τοὺς ἰδίους καὶ ἀπήγγειλαν ὅσα πρὸς αὐτοὺς οἱ ἀρχιερεῖς καὶ οἱ πρεσβύτεροι εἶπαν.

After **they were released**	Ἀπολυθέντες δὲ
they went	ἦλθον
to their own people	πρὸς τοὺς ἰδίους
and **reported** everything	καὶ ἀπήγγειλαν ὅσα
the **chief priests**	οἱ ἀρχιερεῖς
and the elders	καὶ οἱ πρεσβύτεροι
had said	εἶπαν
to them	πρὸς αὐτοὺς

But to **what (Τίνι)** shall I compare this **generation (γενεὰν)**? It is like children **sitting (καθημένοις)** in the market places, who call out to the other children. (NASB)

γενεά	generation	43x
genea		S1074

    τίς, τί ➤ DAY 32   **κάθημαι** ➤ DAY 189

Τίνι δὲ ὁμοιώσω τὴν **γενεὰν** ταύτην; ὁμοία ἐστὶν παιδίοις **καθημένοις** ἐν ταῖς ἀγοραῖς ἃ προσφωνοῦντα τοῖς ἑτέροις

But to **what**	**Τίνι** δὲ
shall I compare	ὁμοιώσω
this **generation?**	τὴν **γενεὰν** ταύτην;
It is like	ὁμοία ἐστὶν
children	παιδίοις
sitting	**καθημένοις**
in the market places	ἐν ταῖς ἀγοραῖς
who call out	ἃ προσφωνοῦντα
to the other children	τοῖς ἑτέροις

Then the **second (δεύτερος)** angel blew his trumpet, and
something like an immense mountain ablaze with **fire (πυρὶ)**
was hurled into the **sea (θάλασσαν)**, so that one-third of the **sea
(θαλάσσης)** turned to blood. (MLB)

δεύτερος	second	43x
deuteros		S1208

θάλασσα ➢ DAY 188   **πῦρ** ➢ DAY 235

Καὶ ὁ **δεύτερος** ἄγγελος ἐσάλπισεν· καὶ ὡς ὄρος μέγα **πυρὶ**
καιόμενον ἐβλήθη εἰς τὴν **θάλασσαν**· καὶ ἐγένετο τὸ τρίτον τῆς
θαλάσσης αἷμα,

Then the **second** angel	Καὶ ὁ **δεύτερος** ἄγγελος
blew his trumpet	ἐσάλπισεν
and something like	καὶ ὡς
an immense mountain	ὄρος μέγα
ablaze with **fire**	**πυρὶ** καιόμενον
was hurled	ἐβλήθη
into the **sea**	εἰς τὴν **θάλασσαν**
so that . . . turned to blood	καὶ ἐγένετο . . . αἷμα
one-third of the **sea**	τὸ τρίτον τῆς **θαλάσσης**

for which I suffer hardship, even to the point of being chained like a criminal. **But (ἀλλὰ)** the **word (λόγος)** of God **is** not **chained (δέδεται)**. (NRSV)

δέω	to bind	43x
deō		S1210

ἀλλά ➤ DAY 29   λόγος ➤ DAY 54

ἐν ᾧ κακοπαθῶ μέχρι δεσμῶν ὡς κακοῦργος. **ἀλλὰ** ὁ **λόγος** τοῦ θεοῦ οὐ **δέδεται·**

for which	ἐν ᾧ
I suffer hardship	κακοπαθῶ
even to the point of	μέχρι
being chained	δεσμῶν
like a criminal	ὡς κακοῦργος
But	**ἀλλὰ**
the **word** of God	ὁ **λόγος** τοῦ θεοῦ
is not **chained**	οὐ **δέδεται**

Then **Herod (Ἡρῴδης) called (καλέσας)** the Magi secretly and found out [lit., found out exactly] from them the exact time [lit., the **time (χρόνον)**] the star had appeared. (NIV)

Ἡρῴδης	Herod	43x
Hērōdēs		S2264

καλέω ➤ DAY 112　　　　**χρόνος** ➤ DAY 293

Τότε **Ἡρῴδης** λάθρᾳ **καλέσας** τοὺς μάγους ἠκρίβωσεν παρ᾽ αὐτῶν τὸν **χρόνον** τοῦ φαινομένου ἀστέρος,

Then **Herod**	Τότε **Ἡρῴδης**
called	**καλέσας**
the Magi	τοὺς μάγους
secretly	λάθρᾳ
and found out [lit., found out exactly]	ἠκρίβωσεν
from them	παρ᾽ αὐτῶν
the exact time [lit., the **time**]	τὸν **χρόνον**
the star had appeared	τοῦ φαινομένου ἀστέρος

Do not **be surprised (θαυμάζετε), brothers (ἀδελφοί)**, if the **world (κόσμος)** hates you. (MLB)

| θαυμάζω | to wonder (at), admire | 43x |
| *thaumazō* | | S2296 |

　　ἀδελφός ➤ DAY 51　　　　**κόσμος** ➤ DAY 85

Μὴ **θαυμάζετε, ἀδελφοί**, εἰ μισεῖ ὑμᾶς ὁ **κόσμος**.

Do not **be surprised**	Μὴ **θαυμάζετε**
brothers	**ἀδελφοί**
if the **world**	εἰ ... ὁ **κόσμος**
hates you	μισεῖ ὑμᾶς

Departing (Ἐξερχόμενοι), they began going throughout the villages, **preaching the gospel** (εὐαγγελιζόμενοι) and **healing** (θεραπεύοντες) everywhere. (NASB)

| θεραπεύω | to heal, care for, treat, serve | 43x |
| *therapeuō* | | S2323 |

ἐξέρχομαι　▷　DAY 71　　　εὐαγγελίζω　▷　DAY 301

Ἐξερχόμενοι δὲ διήρχοντο κατὰ τὰς κώμας **εὐαγγελιζόμενοι** καὶ **θεραπεύοντες** πανταχοῦ.

Departing	Ἐξερχόμενοι δὲ
they began going throughout the villages	διήρχοντο κατὰ τὰς κώμας
preaching the gospel	**εὐαγγελιζόμενοι**
and **healing**	καὶ **θεραπεύοντες**
everywhere	πανταχοῦ

For the whole law **is summed up (πεπλήρωται)** in a single commandment, "**You shall love (Ἀγαπήσεις)** your neighbor as **yourself (σεαυτόν)**." (NRSV)

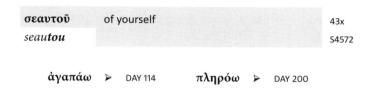

| σεαυτοῦ | of yourself | 43x |
| *seautou* | | S4572 |

ἀγαπάω ➤ DAY 114   πληρόω ➤ DAY 200

ὁ γὰρ πᾶς νόμος ἐν ἑνὶ λόγῳ **πεπλήρωται**, ἐν τῷ Ἀγαπήσεις τὸν πλησίον σου ὡς **σεαυτόν**.

For	γὰρ
the whole law	ὁ . . . πᾶς νόμος
is summed up	πεπλήρωται
in a single commandment	ἐν ἑνὶ λόγῳ . . . ἐν τῷ
You shall love	Ἀγαπήσεις
your neighbor	τὸν πλησίον σου
as **yourself**	ὡς **σεαυτόν**

Blessed be the God and Father of our Lord Jesus Christ, who according to His great mercy has caused us to be born again to a living **hope (ἐλπίδα)** through the **resurrection (ἀναστάσεως)** of Jesus Christ from the **dead (νεκρῶν)**. (NASB)

ἀνάστασις	resurrection	42x
anastasis		S386

   νεκρός ➤ DAY 129   **ἐλπίς** ➤ DAY 296

Εὐλογητὸς ὁ θεὸς καὶ πατὴρ τοῦ κυρίου ἡμῶν Ἰησοῦ Χριστοῦ, ὁ κατὰ τὸ πολὺ αὐτοῦ ἔλεος ἀναγεννήσας ἡμᾶς εἰς **ἐλπίδα** ζῶσαν δι' **ἀναστάσεως** Ἰησοῦ Χριστοῦ ἐκ **νεκρῶν**,

Blessed be	Εὐλογητὸς
the God and Father	ὁ θεὸς καὶ πατὴρ
of our Lord Jesus Christ	τοῦ κυρίου ἡμῶν Ἰησοῦ Χριστοῦ
who according to	ὁ κατὰ
His great mercy	τὸ πολὺ αὐτοῦ ἔλεος
has caused us to be born again	ἀναγεννήσας ἡμᾶς
to a living **hope**	εἰς **ἐλπίδα** ζῶσαν
through the **resurrection**	δι' **ἀναστάσεως**
of Jesus Christ	Ἰησοῦ Χριστοῦ
from the **dead**	ἐκ **νεκρῶν**

Repent, **for (γὰρ)** the kingdom of **heaven (οὐρανῶν) has come near (ἤγγικεν)**! (MLB)

| ἐγγίζω | to approach, come near | 42x |
| engizō | | S1448 |

γάρ ➤ DAY 18   οὐρανός ➤ DAY 58

Μετανοεῖτε, **ἤγγικεν γὰρ** ἡ βασιλεία τῶν **οὐρανῶν**.

Repent	Μετανοεῖτε
for	γὰρ
the kingdom	ἡ βασιλεία
of **heaven**	τῶν **οὐρανῶν**
has come near!	ἤγγικεν

When he came out, he could not **speak (λαλῆσαι)** to them. **They realized (ἐπέγνωσαν)** he had seen a vision in the **temple (ναῷ)**, for he kept making signs to them but remained unable to speak. (NIV)

| **ἐπιγινώσκω** | to recognize, perceive, discern, find out | 42x |
| *epiginōskō* | | S1921 |

λαλέω ➤ DAY 57   **ναός** ➤ DAY 336

ἐξελθὼν δὲ οὐκ ἐδύνατο **λαλῆσαι** αὐτοῖς, καὶ **ἐπέγνωσαν** ὅτι ὀπτασίαν ἑώρακεν ἐν τῷ **ναῷ·** καὶ αὐτὸς ἦν διανεύων αὐτοῖς, καὶ διέμενεν κωφός.

When he came out	ἐξελθὼν δὲ
he could not	οὐκ ἐδύνατο
speak to them	**λαλῆσαι** αὐτοῖς
They realized	καὶ **ἐπέγνωσαν** ὅτι
he had seen a vision	ὀπτασίαν ἑώρακεν
in the **temple**	ἐν τῷ **ναῷ**
for he kept making signs to them	καὶ αὐτὸς ἦν διανεύων αὐτοῖς
but remained	καὶ διέμενεν
unable to speak	κωφός

Bless (εὐλογεῖτε) those who persecute (διώκοντας) you; bless (εὐλογεῖτε) and do not (μὴ) curse them. (NRSV)

εὐλογέω	to bless, speak well of	42x
eulogeō		S2127

μή ➤ DAY 17   **διώκω** ➤ DAY 333

εὐλογεῖτε τοὺς διώκοντας, εὐλογεῖτε καὶ μὴ καταρᾶσθε.

Bless	**εὐλογεῖτε**
those **who persecute** you	τοὺς **διώκοντας**
bless	**εὐλογεῖτε**
and do **not** curse them	καὶ **μὴ** καταρᾶσθε

James (Ἰάκωβος), a servant of God and of the Lord Jesus Christ, To the **twelve (δώδεκα)** tribes in the Dispersion: **Greetings (χαίρειν)**. (ESV)

Ἰάκωβος	James	42x
Iakōbos		S2385

δώδεκα ➤ DAY 223   **χαίρω** ➤ DAY 228

Ἰάκωβος θεοῦ καὶ κυρίου Ἰησοῦ Χριστοῦ δοῦλος ταῖς **δώδεκα** φυλαῖς ταῖς ἐν τῇ διασπορᾷ **χαίρειν**.

James	Ἰάκωβος
a servant of God	θεοῦ . . . δοῦλος
and of the Lord	καὶ κυρίου
Jesus Christ	Ἰησοῦ Χριστοῦ
To the **twelve** tribes	ταῖς **δώδεκα** φυλαῖς
in the Dispersion	ταῖς ἐν τῇ διασπορᾷ
Greetings	**χαίρειν**

Go into the village in front of you, and immediately **you will find**
(**εὑρήσετε**) a donkey **tied** (**δεδεμένην**), and a colt with her. **Untie**
(**λύσαντες**) them and bring them to me. (ESV)

λύω	to loose, release, untie, break, destroy, annul	42x
luō		S3089

εὑρίσκω ➤ DAY 93   **δέω** ➤ DAY 346

Πορεύεσθε εἰς τὴν κώμην τὴν κατέναντι ὑμῶν, καὶ εὐθὺς
εὑρήσετε ὄνον **δεδεμένην** καὶ πῶλον μετ᾽ αὐτῆς· **λύσαντες**
ἀγάγετέ μοι.

Go	Πορεύεσθε
into the village	εἰς τὴν κώμην
in front of you	τὴν κατέναντι ὑμῶν
and immediately	καὶ εὐθὺς
you will find	**εὑρήσετε**
a donkey **tied**	ὄνον **δεδεμένην**
and a colt	καὶ πῶλον
with her	μετ᾽ αὐτῆς
Untie them	**λύσαντες**
and bring them to me	ἀγάγετέ μοι

For **we know (γινώσκομεν) in (ἐκ) part (μέρους)** and we prophesy **in (ἐκ) part (μέρους)**. (NIV)

| μέρος | part, portion | 42x |
| *meros* | | S3313 |

    ἐκ   ➤   DAY 19   γινώσκω   ➤   DAY 70

ἐκ μέρους γὰρ **γινώσκομεν** καὶ **ἐκ μέρους** προφητεύομεν·

For	γὰρ
we know	**γινώσκομεν**
in part	**ἐκ μέρους**
and we prophesy	καὶ . . . προφητεύομεν
in part	**ἐκ μέρους**

And if you are Christ's, **then (ἄρα)** you are Abraham's **offspring (σπέρμα)**, heirs according to **promise (ἐπαγγελίαν)**. (ESV)

σπέρμα	seed, offspring, descendants	42x
sperma		S4690

ἐπαγγελία ➤ DAY 299   **ἄρα / ἄρα** ➤ DAY 310

εἰ δὲ ὑμεῖς Χριστοῦ, **ἄρα** τοῦ Ἀβραὰμ **σπέρμα** ἐστέ, κατ᾽ **ἐπαγγελίαν** κληρονόμοι.

And if you	εἰ δὲ ὑμεῖς
are Christ's	Χριστοῦ
then you are	**ἄρα** . . . ἐστέ
Abraham's **offspring**	τοῦ Ἀβραὰμ **σπέρμα**
heirs	κληρονόμοι
according to **promise**	κατ᾽ **ἐπαγγελίαν**

Worthy (Ἄξιόν) is the Lamb who was slain, **to receive (λαβεῖν)** power and wealth and **wisdom (σοφίαν)** and might and honor and glory and blessing! (ESV)

ἄξιος	worthy, deserving		41x
axios			S514

    λαμβάνω ➤ DAY 60   **σοφία** ➤ DAY 305

Ἄξιόν ἐστιν τὸ ἀρνίον τὸ ἐσφαγμένον **λαβεῖν** τὴν δύναμιν καὶ πλοῦτον καὶ **σοφίαν** καὶ ἰσχὺν καὶ τιμὴν καὶ δόξαν καὶ εὐλογίαν.

Worthy is	Ἄξιόν ἐστιν
the Lamb	τὸ ἀρνίον
who was slain	τὸ ἐσφαγμένον
to receive power	**λαβεῖν** τὴν δύναμιν
and wealth	καὶ πλοῦτον
and **wisdom**	καὶ **σοφίαν**
and might	καὶ ἰσχὺν
and honor	καὶ τιμὴν
and glory	καὶ δόξαν
and blessing!	καὶ εὐλογίαν

The woman said to him, "Sir, **give (δός)** me this **water (ὕδωρ)**, so that I may never be thirsty or **have to keep coming (διέρχωμαι)** here to draw water." (NRSV)

διέρχομαι	to go through, itinerate	41x
dierchomai		S1330

δίδωμι ➤ DAY 43   **ὕδωρ** ➤ DAY 218

λέγει πρὸς αὐτὸν ἡ γυνή Κύριε, **δός** μοι τοῦτο τὸ **ὕδωρ**, ἵνα μὴ διψῶ μηδὲ **διέρχωμαι** ἐνθάδε ἀντλεῖν.

The woman said	λέγει . . . ἡ γυνή
to him	πρὸς αὐτὸν
Sir	Κύριε
give me	**δός** μοι
this **water**	τοῦτο τὸ **ὕδωρ**
so that	ἵνα
I may never be thirsty	μὴ διψῶ
or **have to keep coming**	μηδὲ **διέρχωμαι**
here	ἐνθάδε
to draw water	ἀντλεῖν

For the anger of **man (ἀνδρὸς) does** not **produce (ἐργάζεται)** the **righteousness (δικαιοσύνην)** of God. (ESV)

ἐργάζομαι	to work, be at work, produce	41x
ergazomai		S2038

ἀνήρ ➤ DAY 73   δικαιοσύνη ➤ DAY 187

ὀργὴ γὰρ **ἀνδρὸς δικαιοσύνην** θεοῦ οὐκ **ἐργάζεται**.

For	γὰρ
the anger of **man**	ὀργὴ . . . **ἀνδρὸς**
does not **produce**	οὐκ **ἐργάζεται**
the **righteousness** of God	**δικαιοσύνην** θεοῦ

And the one **who was seated (καθήμενος)** on the **throne (θρόνῳ)** said, "See, I am making all things **new (καινὰ)**." Also he said, "Write this, for these words are trustworthy and true." (NRSV)

καινός	new	41x
kainos		S2537

κάθημαι ➤ DAY 189   **θρόνος** ➤ DAY 259

καὶ εἶπεν ὁ **καθήμενος** ἐπὶ τῷ **θρόνῳ** Ἰδοὺ **καινὰ** ποιῶ πάντα. καὶ λέγει Γράψον, ὅτι οὗτοι οἱ λόγοι πιστοὶ καὶ ἀληθινοί εἰσιν.

And the one **who was seated**	καὶ . . . ὁ **καθήμενος**
on the **throne**	ἐπὶ τῷ **θρόνῳ**
said	εἶπεν
See	Ἰδοὺ
I am making all things	ποιῶ πάντα
new	**καινὰ**
Also he said	καὶ λέγει
Write this	Γράψον
for these words	ὅτι οὗτοι οἱ λόγοι
are trustworthy	πιστοὶ . . . εἰσιν
and true	καὶ ἀληθινοί

When morning [lit., **day (ἡμέρας)**] came, there was no **small (ὀλίγος)** commotion among the soldiers over what had become of **Peter (Πέτρος)**. (NRSV)

ὀλίγος	few, little, small, short	41x
oligos		S3641

ἡμέρα　➤　DAY 46　　　　Πέτρος　➤　DAY 103

Γενομένης δὲ **ἡμέρας** ἦν τάραχος οὐκ **ὀλίγος** ἐν τοῖς στρατιώταις, τί ἄρα ὁ **Πέτρος** ἐγένετο.

When morning [lit., **day**] came	Γενομένης δὲ **ἡμέρας**
there was	ἦν
no **small** commotion	τάραχος οὐκ **ὀλίγος**
among the soldiers	ἐν τοῖς στρατιώταις
over what had become of **Peter**	τί ἄρα ὁ **Πέτρος** ἐγένετο

Again (Πάλιν), the kingdom of heaven is **like (ὁμοία)** a merchant **looking for (ζητοῦντι)** beautiful pearls. (MLB)

ὅμοιος	like	41x
homoios		S3664

πάλιν ➢ DAY 120　　　　**ζητέω** ➢ DAY 150

Πάλιν ὁμοία ἐστὶν ἡ βασιλεία τῶν οὐρανῶν ἐμπόρῳ ζητοῦντι καλοὺς μαργαρίτας·

Again	Πάλιν
the kingdom	ἡ βασιλεία
of heaven	τῶν οὐρανῶν
is **like**	**ὁμοία** ἐστὶν
a merchant	ἐμπόρῳ
looking for	**ζητοῦντι**
beautiful pearls	καλοὺς μαργαρίτας

But the Lord **stood by (παρέστη)** me and strengthened me, so
that through me the message might be fully proclaimed and all
the **Gentiles (ἔθνη)** might hear it. So I was rescued from the lion's
mouth (στόματος). (ESV)

παρίστημι	to bring, present, offer, cause to stand beside	41x
paristēmi		S3936

ἔθνος ➤ DAY 98   **στόμα** ➤ DAY 216

ὁ δὲ κύριός μοι **παρέστη** καὶ ἐνεδυνάμωσέν με, ἵνα δι᾿ ἐμοῦ
τὸ κήρυγμα πληροφορηθῇ καὶ ἀκούσωσιν πάντα τὰ **ἔθνη**, καὶ
ἐρύσθην ἐκ **στόματος** λέοντος.

But the Lord	ὁ δὲ κύριός
stood by me	μοι **παρέστη**
and strengthened me	καὶ ἐνεδυνάμωσέν με
so that through me	ἵνα δι᾿ ἐμοῦ
the message	τὸ κήρυγμα
might be fully proclaimed	πληροφορηθῇ
and all the **Gentiles**	καὶ . . . πάντα τὰ **ἔθνη**
might hear it	ἀκούσωσιν
So I was rescued	καὶ ἐρύσθην
from the lion's **mouth**	ἐκ **στόματος** λέοντος

Index of Scripture References